Money First, Freedom Next

Money First, Freedom Next

A Gen Z Guide to Earning, Saving, and Investing Before You're Even 20

Riley K. Morgan

Mindful Pages

Published in 2025

ISBN: 9789371772426 (PB)
ISBN: 9789371777582 (eBook)

Published by

Mindful Pages
Imprint of Alpha Editions LLC
312 W. 2nd St #1834
Casper, WY 82601, USA

This book was developed using advanced writing tools to support the drafting and ideation process. All content has been thoughtfully curated, refined, and reviewed to ensure quality and relevance.

Content

Introduction The Teenage Wallet Is a Battleground viii

Chapter 1 Why Nobody Taught You This 1

Chapter 2 The Psychology of Your Wallet.................................24

Chapter 3 The Real Cost of Being a Teen....................................44

Chapter 4 How to Earn Before 20..64

Chapter 5 How to Spend Without Screwing Yourself.............84

Chapter 6 Saving Without Feeling Deprived 103

Chapter 7 Investing 101—Without the B.S. 122

Chapter 8 Digital Money Traps 141

Chapter 9 Your First Bank (and What They Won't Tell You) 161

Chapter 10 Money and Your People.. 181

Chapter 11 Building Wealth on Your Own Terms.................. 199

Chapter 12 Your Future Money Self... 220

About the Author 240

Introduction
The Teenage Wallet Is a Battleground

There is no such thing as "just money" anymore.

To understand money today is to understand the world itself: rapid, digital, emotionally charged, and profoundly unequal. For Gen Z—the first generation raised entirely within the glow of smartphones, global crises, and infinite scrolling—money is no longer merely a medium of exchange. It is identity. It is access. It is both visibility and shame, autonomy and dependence. It is coded into algorithms, shaped by social norms, reshaped by influencers, and complicated by advice that was written for a world that no longer exists.

Here lies the problem: almost everything you've been told about money assumes a world that vanished long before you were born. Schools teach you how to find the area of a triangle, not how to avoid overdraft fees. Parents might insist you "just focus on your studies," as if grades alone can secure rent, groceries, or the occasional meal delivery. Even the internet—overflowing with "finance hacks" and viral investing tips—is a minefield of contradictions, swinging between toxic scarcity mantras and relentless hustle culture. For a generation contending with climate instability, rising costs, and the erosion of traditional career paths, these old narratives ring hollow. You deserve better. And better begins with a new kind of financial literacy—one that actually makes sense before you need it.

This book is not a lecture. It is a decoding manual.

Money First, Freedom Next was not written to help you build a retirement fund by 65. It was written to help you stop merely surviving and begin designing your financial life before your twenties are even half over. That doesn't mean handing you a checklist of "adult" milestones—pension schemes, mortgage comparisons, or investment portfolios. It means equipping you with mental clarity, emotional intelligence, and practical tools so that when you look at the world around you, you can say: I understand how this works. And I know what I want to do about it.

Money is reframed here not as an abstract goal or status symbol, but as a tool for freedom: the freedom to choose where you live, what you work on, who you answer to, and the risks you're willing to take. That freedom doesn't come from wealth alone; it comes from being prepared, informed, and intentional.

Before you can earn with purpose, spend with confidence, or save without dread, you must see the battlefield clearly.

What are you really up against?

You live in a world where money flows invisibly—embedded in games, subscriptions, and every swipe or click. You can spend hundreds without ever touching a note. You can earn, invest, and lose—all through apps designed to keep you addicted rather than informed. Meanwhile, the culture around you pressures you to "grind" like a millionaire entrepreneur, "save like a minimalist," and "invest like a crypto bro," often in the same breath. There is no single narrative, no clear path. Just a tangle of signals, shortcuts, scams, and shame.

Traditional financial literacy pretends this complexity doesn't exist. It assumes a steady job, a savings account that earns interest, a predictable rent cycle, and parents who taught you about taxes. It imagines envelopes and budgets, not Venmo splits and emotional splurges after a bad day. Most of all, it speaks to you as if you were 40 with a mortgage, not a teenager navigating a gig-driven, digital-first, psychologically intense economy.

This book begins by acknowledging the truth: money is emotional, social, political, and digital. And every one of those dimensions touches your wallet, your mental health, and your future.

It matters that your school never explained credit scores. It matters that the real cost of a night out often only becomes clear when it lands on your bank statement. It matters that you are expected to invest early without guidance on earning your first $100 ethically. It matters that independence is preached without even the basic maps to navigate it.

Money First, Freedom Next exists to change that. This is your map.

Let's be clear: this is not a self-help book about "manifesting abundance." It won't advise cutting coffee to save for a house, or romanticise struggle and hustle. What it does offer is practical insight grounded in how the economy actually operates for young people today. We'll discuss side hustles—but also scams. We'll break down investing—but without the hype. We'll examine how social comparison distorts spending, and how peer pressure quietly empties wallets.

More importantly, we will build something deeper than strategies: a philosophy.

Every financial choice rests on values, fears, stories, and pressures. Without understanding these, no budget app or spreadsheet will save you. Every time you tap your card, check your balance, or feel envy at someone else's possessions, you engage with a system far bigger than yourself. That system is not neutral. Yet it can be understood, navigated, and even bent toward your own objectives.

What are those objectives? That is up to you. But first, myths must be cleared. You must grasp what is happening with your money—not just its quantity, but its meaning, its flow, who benefits, and where the traps lie. You must understand why saving can feel like losing, why some purchases soothe like therapy, and why your first bank account might hide dozens of small fees.

You'll examine the emotional triggers behind spending, the hidden costs of friendship, and the invisible ways digital tools manipulate your choices. You'll learn how to earn in a world with few stable jobs, but many platforms eager to monetise your time and creativity—if you let them.

Above all, you'll cultivate a mindset that is flexible, realistic, and free from shame. Mistakes will happen. You'll overspend. Undercharge. Fall for deals that seemed too good to be true. That's not failure—it is training. The difference lies in how quickly you recover, adjust, and move forward with more clarity than before.

Why now? Because your financial life is not waiting for age 30—you already have one. Every day, your decisions affect your future: what you buy, what you save, what you say yes or no to. You might be contributing to family income, covering your own expenses, or wondering how to turn a hobby into more. Or you may be just starting, unsure where to begin, but aware that stakes are rising. The time to act is now—not for perfection, but for awareness.

Financial literacy is not about spreadsheets or market trends. It is about understanding enough to make decisions you won't regret later. It is about building a life where money supports your values, rather than forcing compromises. It is about creating freedom—not just from financial stress, but from the need to prove worth through possessions or income.

The promise of this book is simple: clarity, not complexity.

By the end of *Money First, Freedom Next*, you will not know everything—but you will understand how money interacts with your psychology, choices, digital life, and future. You will have tools to use today, not five years from now. You will see the game being played—and learn to play it on your terms.

This is not about playing it safe. It's about playing it smart.

If you have ever felt intimidated, confused, or bored by traditional advice, you are not alone. This book is different. It is written for you: curious, capable, and tired of being underestimated. The world will not make it easy—but you need not make it harder by going in blind.

Read closely. Question boldly. Remember: money is not the goal. Freedom is. And freedom comes first to those who understand what money can truly do.

Let's begin.

Chapter 1
Why Nobody Taught You This

There is a peculiar hush around money in most young people's upbringing. It isn't absent from conversation—it lurks everywhere, threaded through subtle dinner-table tensions, casual remarks about careers, or sidelong glances when a bill arrives—but it is rarely explained. For many teenagers, money seeps into consciousness not through formal instruction or frank discussion, but via a patchwork of half-truths, inherited anxieties, and cultural cues absorbed unconsciously, much like learning which seat at the kitchen table is "yours."

The paradox is stark: we expect young people eventually to handle rent, credit, taxes, insurance, loans, and investments, yet we provide none of the scaffolding—conceptual or practical—to navigate them. They enter one of the most complex systems of adult life armed with myths, metaphors, and misplaced confidence. Many only discover the flaws in these assumptions after costly mistakes. The result is a generation caught between two forces: the pressure to be financially independent and the confusion over how to achieve it.

What makes this confusion particularly insidious is its invisibility. Without instruction, financial struggles are easily internalised as personal failings—a failure to budget, to earn, to plan. Yet the truth is structural. Society has constructed an economic initiation ritual that relies on trial by fire. And when young people burn their fingers—through impulsive online purchases, predatory credit schemes, or simply not understanding a direct debit—they are exhorted to "be more responsible," without ever being shown what that responsibility entails.

To grasp this fully, one must begin not with bank accounts or spreadsheets, but with stories. Long before your first paycheque or app-based account, you absorb narratives about what money means: who deserves it, what it signals about worth, how it should be used, and when discussion is—or is not—appropriate. These stories are far from random. They are cultural scripts, passed through families, reinforced by media, and shaped by socioeconomic conditions. Some carry kernels of caution, others unexamined fear. Most are outdated; many are actively harmful.

Consider the old admonition that "money is evil." At first glance, it appears a moral principle—a warning against greed. But for a young person internalising this, the consequences are profound: desiring money feels suspect, earning it feels morally fraught, discussing it feels taboo. The result is not prudent savers or mindful spenders, but avoiders—individuals paralysed by guilt or shame whenever financial strain arises.

Or take the advice to "just focus on school" and let money matters sort themselves out later. While education remains vital, the assumption that academic achievement alone ensures financial stability is dangerously obsolete. Jobs are fragmented, degrees no longer guarantee employment, and crucial income-generating skills—creativity, entrepreneurship, digital fluency—are often absent from curricula. Delaying financial awareness does not shield young people from stress; it denies them the tools to navigate a world in which they already live.

Perhaps most misleading is the notion that "real income starts at 25." This myth is insidious. It suggests that meaningful financial agency belongs only to the distant future, discouraging early efforts to earn, experiment, and learn. In reality, the first pound earned matters less for its size than for the lessons it imparts—about value, exchange, effort, and autonomy.

These inherited myths shape baseline assumptions, erecting invisible walls around choices before young people even recognise them. Compounding the problem, institutions designed to educate and prepare them—particularly schools—have largely abdicated this responsibility.

The failure is measurable. Surveys across the UK repeatedly reveal that financial education, where it exists, is superficial, inconsistent, and poorly prioritised. A handful of lessons on budgeting or mock stock-market exercises do little to prepare students for the nuanced, emotionally charged, and technology-driven reality of modern money. What's required is not rote instruction, but a curriculum attuned to contemporary financial life.

Today's teenagers are far more likely to earn through digital platforms—reselling trainers, freelancing in design, monetising content, tutoring online—than through traditional part-time jobs. Yet formal finance education rarely covers self-employment, variable income, platform fees, or intellectual property rights. Nor does it prepare students to navigate buy-now-pay-later schemes, identify predatory influencers, or manage subscription fatigue from dozens of microtransactions.

The gap between what is taught and what is needed continues to widen. Students calculate compound interest on paper but remain unaware of payday loans' mechanics, or the ease with which overdrafts can spiral into debt. They are primed for exams, not banks; essays, not earnings. The consequence is dual alienation: unprepared for adulthood and blamed for their ignorance.

This failure is philosophical as well as pedagogical. It reflects a reluctance to regard teenagers as financial actors, even as the economy treats them as such—marketing to them, extracting value, profiling them algorithmically. Consumers before earners, they are rendered vulnerable.

The remedy begins with understanding money as it exists today. Gone are the days of single income streams, predictable careers, and neatly packaged financial products. The new rules are digital, fragmented, and fast. Income may arrive from multiple sources, spending may traverse several apps, and one's financial footprint—what is owed, owned, or risked—is often shaped by interface design as much as by conscious choice.

This fluidity offers opportunity—creativity, access, autonomy—but it demands a new literacy. One capable of navigating microtransactions and impulse algorithms. One able to distinguish financial advice from influencer marketing. One that separates volatility from genuine risk, pleasure from signalling.

It also requires context. Gen Z is the most digitally connected yet economically precarious generation. They have observed parents struggle through recessions, watched student debt balloon, and seen living costs outpace wages. They confront the tension between expectation and reality—the pressure to thrive against the awareness that the system may be stacked against them.

This has created a distinctive psychological landscape: part hustle culture, part economic nihilism. Some respond by monetising constantly, turning every skill or hour into cash. Others withdraw, paralysed by complexity and contradiction. Many oscillate between extremes. Anxiety, not laziness or entitlement, is the common denominator—born of shifting rules and static guidance.

Financial guidance that ignores these emotional realities—fear, shame, confusion—is incomplete, even harmful. Engaging Gen Z requires frameworks as well as tools, strategies as well as narratives that can be rewritten.

This chapter undertakes precisely that task. It traces inherited myths—not to chastise, but to equip. It exposes the failings of traditional financial education and proposes realistic alternatives. It maps the modern financial landscape: its speed, risks, and potential. And it explores the generational mindset shaping teenagers' relationships with money—not as a distant concern, but as a daily force affecting autonomy, identity, and ambition.

By the end, you will not only understand why no one taught you this—you will recognise why it matters that you learn it now. Not because you are behind, but because you are early. And with insight, that timing becomes your greatest asset.

Money Myths You Inherited Without Knowing It

Before most teenagers ever earn their first pound, they've already inherited a portfolio of beliefs about money—none of which appear on a balance sheet. These beliefs aren't the result of personal failure, poor maths skills, or lack of interest; they are culturally transmitted ideas, absorbed over time and rarely questioned. The trouble is, while these myths might feel like common sense, they often work like blindfolds—restricting agency, stunting confidence, and distorting a young person's capacity to make clear-eyed financial decisions. Myths do not have to be false to be dangerous. They only need to be incomplete, misapplied, or accepted without interrogation.

Children learn about money long before they understand it. Not in the form of ledgers or lectures, but in glances exchanged between adults when finances are tight, in offhand remarks like "we can't afford that" or "money doesn't grow on trees," in television shows where wealth is either glorified or vilified. These messages form the early scaffolding of a money mindset—not taught, but caught. And by the time a teenager begins managing their own spending or earning, the internal operating system is already primed with scripts they didn't write. To build financial agency, one must first become fluent in the cultural code one has inherited.

One of the most enduring and corrosive of these inherited ideas is the notion that *money is inherently corrupting*. Versions of this myth are everywhere: "money is the root of all evil," "rich people are selfish," "you can either be happy or rich, not both." These statements masquerade as moral wisdom but often breed quiet self-sabotage. For a teenager raised on stories where financial success is linked to greed, there is little incentive to pursue wealth ethically or enthusiastically. Worse, they may feel guilt when they do want more—interpreting ambition as betrayal of their values. The psychological cost is subtle but profound: money becomes a source of inner conflict, rather than a lever of freedom.

There is, of course, historical context behind this moral suspicion of money. In post-war Britain, in working-class communities, and in many religious traditions, wealth was often viewed as something earned at moral cost or inherited through unjust systems. That scepticism was not unfounded. But when inherited uncritically, such narratives can turn principled critique into paralysing aversion. The modern economy does not reward those who wait for permission to engage. It rewards those who understand how the system works and are willing to play consciously within it.

A parallel myth, more subtle but equally limiting, is the belief that *money is something adults deal with*. Teenagers are often told to "just focus on school," as though their financial reality begins the moment they get a degree or their first full-time job. This is a convenient fiction. Many teenagers are already managing irregular income from side gigs, negotiating spending decisions within their families, or subsidising their own expenses. By implying that financial literacy is premature, adults delay essential knowledge. The result is a generation that arrives at adulthood burdened by credit card debt, student loans, and financial anxiety—armed only with outdated clichés.

This framing also reveals a persistent cultural discomfort with seeing young people as economic actors. We are comfortable marketing to them, extracting value from their attention and consumer behaviour, but hesitant to equip them with the tools to navigate those systems critically. Consider how few school curriculums offer practical lessons on budgeting, self-employment, or digital income. Meanwhile, young people are already engaging with microtransactions in video games, buy-now-pay-later schemes in fashion apps, and advertising masquerading as advice on social media. The asymmetry is startling: economic exposure without economic literacy.

A related myth is that *talking about money is impolite or dangerous.* In many households, money is treated with the same hush as religion or politics—acceptable in abstract, never discussed directly. This silence breeds ignorance, and ignorance breeds shame. If you don't know how your parents manage finances, or what a typical salary looks like, or how much a mobile plan *should* cost, you're likely to make guesses. And when those guesses turn out to be wrong, the embarrassment is not just financial—it's personal. You believe you should have known better. But how could you?

This culture of secrecy is compounded by a media environment saturated with polarised depictions of wealth. On one end, influencers flaunt designer clothing, rented cars, and exotic holidays, often funded by debt or deception. On the other, there's an undercurrent of financial nihilism—memes that romanticise being broke, slogans that celebrate "treating yourself" into overdraft, and jokes that make poverty seem like a personality. In both cases, the message is the same: money is either performative or pointless. Neither invites real literacy.

Perhaps the most quietly damaging myth is that *some people are just "bad with money"*, as though financial competence is a personality trait rather than a learnable skill. This belief often becomes self-fulfilling. A teenager who struggles with saving or overspends on impulse may internalise that behaviour as a character flaw rather than a solvable problem. The myth implies permanence—once you're "bad with money," you're always at risk. But the truth is that financial behaviour is shaped far more by environment, stress levels, and access to information than by fixed traits.

Contrary to the "bad with money" narrative, most poor financial decisions stem from emotional blind spots, not intellectual deficits. Spending habits are shaped by identity, self-worth, and psychological coping mechanisms. Buying something you can't afford is rarely about stupidity; it's often about relief, belonging, or compensation. Yet our cultural discourse treats overspending as laziness, debt as irresponsibility, and frugality as virtue, without examining the emotional infrastructure beneath those behaviours.

Then there's the myth of *linear financial progression*. The traditional script—study hard, get a degree, find a stable job, buy a house—still exerts enormous influence, even as it crumbles under scrutiny. Many of today's teens will enter a workforce with less job security, more freelance structures, and rising housing costs. But if you believe there is only one path to financial legitimacy, and your life doesn't fit that mould, it's easy to feel like you've failed before you've begun.

This belief also skews risk perception. Young people who deviate from the norm—starting a business, freelancing, investing early—are often viewed as reckless or naive. Yet, ironically, those willing to explore alternative paths are often better equipped to adapt to the realities of modern finance. They develop resilience, learn to navigate uncertainty, and build diverse income streams. The myth of linearity teaches conformity at the expense of adaptability.

Finally, many teenagers absorb the myth that *wealth equals freedom*. While this appears to align with the ethos of this book, it is a misreading. Wealth, in and of itself, does not guarantee autonomy. Plenty of high-earning individuals are financially fragile—trapped by inflated lifestyles, debt cycles, or golden handcuffs. True freedom comes from understanding how money works, aligning spending with values, and maintaining flexibility. It is about *agency*, not accumulation.

When these myths combine, they create a cognitive framework that is hard to escape. You might hesitate to negotiate for a freelance gig because you think it's greedy. You might avoid looking at your bank account because you assume you'll never be good at managing it. You might feel embarrassed for caring about money, or guilty for wanting more of it. And you might defer important financial decisions because you've been told that real financial life hasn't started yet.

But the truth is: it has. If you're earning, spending, or thinking about money, your financial life is already in motion. The question is not whether you will engage with it—it's whether you'll do so consciously or blindly.

Disentangling yourself from inherited myths doesn't mean rejecting your family, culture, or community. It means updating your beliefs in light of present reality. It means asking better questions: not "Am I good with money?" but "What have I been taught about money, and is it serving me?" It means recognising that literacy is not about knowing all the answers but about *knowing where to look and what to ask.*

Every generation inherits myths. What defines progress is not the myths themselves, but the willingness to examine them. The power to change your financial future begins with the courage to scrutinise the past—not just the economic past of a country or system, but the personal and cultural past that lives in your own mind.

Myths lose their power the moment you see them clearly. And once that happens, what remains is possibility—uncluttered, informed, and entirely yours to define.

Why Schools Are Failing at Finance

It is possible today for a teenager to sit through more than a decade of formal education without once being taught how to interpret a payslip, negotiate a contract, read a bank statement, or detect a scam. And yet that same teenager may already have a debit card, a student loan offer, an online shopping account, and an income stream from a side hustle. The dissonance is not subtle. It is structural. The formal education system continues to operate as though financial life begins at thirty—steady job, pension plan, fixed mortgage—when in fact it now begins, for many, before their sixteenth birthday and on entirely different terms. The gap between what schools teach and what young people actually need to navigate the financial world is not just wide—it is growing.

This failure is not a simple oversight. It is the result of a deeper confusion: an inability to reconcile the changing nature of money with the outdated assumptions of institutional education. Schools continue to offer financial education as a static subject—brief, compartmentalised, and often delivered through abstract principles—while money itself has become dynamic, digital, and deeply entangled in everyday decisions. This mismatch leaves students unprepared not just practically, but philosophically. They don't merely lack tools; they lack a frame of reference.

Take the current approach to personal finance within the British curriculum. Where it exists, it is often bundled into Citizenship or PSHE (Personal, Social, Health and Economic) education, taught irregularly by teachers with little subject expertise. A typical lesson might cover budgeting, savings accounts, or the idea of compound interest. But such topics, while technically important, bear little resemblance to the lived financial challenges of most teenagers. How does one apply a theoretical knowledge of interest rates when the immediate concern is covering data top-ups, avoiding overdraft charges, or figuring out how to monetise a YouTube channel without being exploited? These are not marginal problems. They are foundational. And they are ignored.

Meanwhile, the actual financial ecosystem young people are immersed in is both more accessible and more dangerous than ever. Buy-now-pay-later schemes like Klarna or Clearpay have normalised delayed liability for online purchases. Subscription fatigue drains accounts through invisible auto-renewals. Teen-targeted investment platforms offer "beginner-friendly" crypto tools without disclosing volatility risk. Influencers package financial advice in 30-second reels, often with no accountability, nuance, or regulatory constraint. All of this constitutes an environment that demands a new kind of literacy—one rooted not in formulas, but in discernment.

Schools are structurally unequipped to meet this need. Their curriculums still reflect a world of fixed incomes, linear career paths, and paper statements. Yet today's teenagers are more likely to experience irregular income, multiple revenue sources, and financial tools driven by algorithmic design. The median age of first-time digital entrepreneurship is falling. A 15-year-old might earn money editing videos on Fiverr, flipping trainers online, or growing a niche TikTok page. These activities involve contracts, taxes, and pricing strategy—topics conspicuously absent from any school finance module. The omission is not benign. It reinforces the fiction that money only becomes "real" when it flows through traditional channels.

Critics of more expansive financial education often point to an overcrowded curriculum, or the risk of promoting commercial thinking too early. But this is a false dichotomy. Teaching students how to protect their digital financial identity, how to evaluate the trustworthiness of financial information online, or how to understand their first payslip is not commercial—it is civic. In a world where financial decisions are increasingly entwined with identity, security, and mental health, literacy is not optional. It is protective.

There is also a deeper cultural issue: the myth of delayed relevance. Schools are built on the assumption that young people are preparing for the future, not participating in the present. But Gen Z is not waiting for adulthood to engage economically. They are already earning, spending, borrowing, and sometimes lending. The idea that financial knowledge should be delayed until it becomes immediately applicable is both paternalistic and self-defeating. No one suggests that we should only teach biology when a student becomes ill, or only teach civics when they turn eighteen. Yet we treat money as a life stage, not a life skill.

Even when financial education is introduced, it is too often delivered in reductive or moralistic tones. Lessons may revolve around telling students to "save more" or "avoid debt," without unpacking why saving is psychologically difficult or how debt structures are often predatory by design. This framing not only lacks nuance—it fails to generate trust. Teenagers are quick to detect when adults are lecturing rather than listening, simplifying rather than clarifying. To be credible, financial education must respect the complexity of the environment students are navigating and offer tools that acknowledge emotional, social, and systemic factors—not just individual choices.

The failure of schools to teach finance is also a failure of adaptability. Curriculums are slow to respond to social change. Bureaucracy and risk-aversion make innovation difficult. Meanwhile, financial technologies evolve at a rapid pace. When a student learns about budgeting on paper, but does their real-world spending through Apple Pay, their ability to translate that lesson is compromised. When lessons cover how to write cheques—still a feature in some syllabi—but not how to use digital wallets or understand in-app purchases, they lose relevance. And when a teacher unfamiliar with freelance work explains income, the message is muddled before it's even delivered.

There are examples of progress. A handful of independent initiatives—such as MyBnk in the UK or Next Gen Personal Finance in the US—have attempted to fill the gap, offering practical, youth-centred financial education. But these efforts, while admirable, remain piecemeal. They depend on school interest, charitable funding, or motivated educators willing to go beyond mandated content. Systemic reform remains elusive, and the result is a postcode lottery of competence: some students receive meaningful guidance, while others graduate without understanding how interest accrues on a credit card.

The failure to equip students with meaningful financial tools also has long-term socioeconomic consequences. Financial illiteracy compounds inequality. Students from wealthier households may learn informally through parental guidance, exposure, or resources. Those from low-income backgrounds, who arguably stand to benefit most from early financial knowledge, are the least likely to receive it. Schools, which should be equalising institutions, instead reinforce disparities—not through malice, but through neglect.

To move forward, financial education must be reimagined not as a static subject, but as a fluid framework integrated across disciplines. Economics teachers should explain inflation not just as theory but in terms of how it affects the cost of groceries. English teachers can explore how media portrays wealth and scarcity. Maths teachers can embed lessons on interest, budgeting, and risk. Most importantly, schools must partner with outside organisations, financial experts, and digital platforms to ensure that the knowledge being shared is not only current, but credible.

But curriculum change alone is not enough. What's needed is a cultural shift: a recognition that teenagers are not passive subjects to be prepared for the economy, but active participants already embedded within it. They are not too young to understand risk, too naïve to discuss income, or too distracted to care. They are, in many cases, more financially engaged than their parents were at the same age—just less supported.

The real scandal is not that schools don't have time to teach finance. It's that they don't treat it as urgent. That they assume ignorance is harmless. That they act as though learning through mistakes—overdrafts, scams, unsustainable spending—is inevitable. But it isn't. Ignorance isn't a rite of passage. It's a policy choice.

Every generation enters adulthood with a few blind spots. But to systematically deprive young people of the knowledge they need to navigate the most pervasive system in their lives—money—is a failure of imagination and duty. The question is not whether students can handle real-world financial content. It's whether the institutions around them are willing to admit how much they've fallen behind. And until they do, teenagers will continue to learn finance not in classrooms, but in crisis.

The New Rules of the Game

Most people assume money operates under fixed principles—save more than you spend, invest early, avoid debt, plan for retirement. These aren't wrong, exactly. But they belong to a different gameboard—one where salaries were predictable, inflation was relatively stable, and financial products were tangible and regulated. For today's teenager, that version of the game is all but obsolete. The new rules are faster, messier, and encoded in code, not cash. Money no longer lives solely in wallets or statements. It lives in apps, subscriptions, tokens, and algorithms. The platforms have changed. The players have multiplied. And the logic of the system has become fluid enough to demand a whole new literacy—one that's not just about managing resources, but decoding the system that moves them.

The most critical feature of modern financial life is *speed*. Transactions occur in seconds, decision cycles are compressed, and outcomes—positive or catastrophic—can materialise without warning. A teenager can sign up for Klarna and accumulate deferred debt with three taps. They can invest in cryptocurrency before they understand what volatility means. A single viral video can trigger a revenue stream—or a fine. There's no buffer between choice and consequence. Where older models of finance allowed for deliberation—walking into a bank, speaking to a human advisor, reading through paper terms—digital finance is deliberately frictionless. The default state of the system is urgency.

This acceleration has shifted the nature of risk. In the analogue world, financial risk was usually slow-moving and transparent. You had time to recover from a bad decision, or at least to understand it. Now, risk is *ambient*—baked into every interface. It's in the auto-renew checkbox you didn't see, the targeted ad for a "free trial" that leads to recurring charges, the persuasive design of apps nudging you to spend, donate, or invest. Financial harm has become granular, decentralised, and—most importantly—*psychologically invisible*. You don't need to make one big mistake to find yourself in trouble. You just need to make lots of small ones in environments designed to reward convenience over clarity.

But speed alone doesn't explain the difficulty of navigating this new terrain. What complicates it further is *fragmentation*. In previous generations, money flowed through a few trusted institutions: banks, employers, and government programmes. Now, it flows through dozens—sometimes hundreds—of micro-platforms. A young person might earn money from a Patreon account, resell limited-edition trainers on Depop, invest via Revolut, split bills with friends using Monzo, and lose money to in-game purchases on Steam. These are not edge cases. They are the financial architecture of the present.

This fragmentation comes with both empowerment and risk. On one hand, it allows teenagers to experiment with earning in ways previously unimaginable. You don't need a job offer to build an income. You need an idea, an account, and often an audience. But on the other hand, it diffuses accountability. When something goes wrong—when a payment is withheld, when a subscription auto-renews without consent, when a transfer fails—there is often no clear recourse. No manager to speak to. No institutional structure designed to protect you. The platforms may be slick and responsive, but their incentives are commercial, not fiduciary. And the more you use them, the more scattered your financial awareness becomes.

This leads to a paradoxical reality: teenagers are more financially active than ever, but less financially centralised. Their money is not just in one place, doing one thing. It is flowing—across platforms, currencies, obligations, and interfaces—often without a complete picture of what it's doing at any given time. The spreadsheet model of budgeting, with fixed categories and predictable cycles, begins to look quaint in the face of this liquidity. A more relevant model would be that of *attention economics*: what you track shapes what you control. But if you can't see the flows—because they're too small, too dispersed, or too automated—you can't make informed choices.

And this brings us to perhaps the most defining feature of the new game: *the psychological complexity of decision-making*. Modern finance is not just a mathematical exercise; it's a behavioural minefield. You are constantly bombarded with signals—some overt, some covert—about what to do with your money. Social media doesn't just display content; it constructs aspirational lifestyles. The visibility of wealth, curated and filtered, distorts expectations. You don't just want a pair of trainers. You want the ones worn by someone whose follower count signals success. Spending becomes identity work. Earning becomes performance. Saving becomes restraint in the face of an algorithm engineered to trigger dopamine.

This isn't an accident. It is by design. Digital financial tools are optimised for engagement, not clarity. Banks now gamify savings with badges. Trading apps celebrate risk-taking with confetti animations. Shopping apps blur the line between browsing and buying. Even your bank balance may be visually framed in ways that affect your emotional state—green if healthy, red if low. These design choices shape behaviour in subtle but powerful ways. And without awareness of these dynamics, users are not participants. They are products.

One might argue that these changes simply reflect technological evolution, and that young people are well-equipped to navigate them. After all, Gen Z is digitally native. They understand apps, algorithms, and social cues intuitively. But this fluency is not the same as mastery. Knowing *how* to use a tool does not mean understanding its economic logic. A teenager may be fluent in the mechanics of Instagram, but unaware of how targeted advertising drives spending behaviour. They may understand how to accept a brand partnership, but not what tax implications come with it. They may be accustomed to managing multiple income sources, but unable to calculate their effective hourly rate—or whether their labour is being exploited.

Mastery begins with visibility. And visibility requires a new conceptual toolkit. The old language of income, expenses, assets, and liabilities is necessary, but insufficient. We need to add terms like *liquidity friction*, *platform lock-in*, *algorithmic persuasion*, and *time-value asymmetry*. We need to teach not just what an interest rate is, but how interfaces influence attention and how digital ecosystems shape incentives. Understanding money today requires understanding the *systems* that scaffold it—the behavioural architectures, the terms of service, the data models.

It also requires recognising that financial life is now inseparable from digital identity. Your financial behaviour is tracked, profiled, and often monetised—not just by banks, but by third-party apps, advertising networks, and platforms that offer financial services as part of a larger data-harvesting strategy. Your purchases reveal your habits. Your subscriptions reveal your values. Your browsing history can influence your credit offers. This is not financial surveillance in the dystopian sense. It is simply the operational logic of the system. But if you do not understand it, you cannot resist its more manipulative tendencies.

Yet, despite these challenges, there is also opportunity. The decentralisation of finance—its fragmentation and digitisation—opens doors that once required gatekeepers. A teenager in Manchester can design graphics for a client in New York. A student can publish a zine and sell it globally through Shopify. Micro-investing platforms allow anyone with £5 to gain exposure to equity markets. None of this was imaginable a generation ago. But it demands a new kind of responsibility: *contextual awareness*. It's no longer enough to ask, "What does this tool do?" You must also ask, "Who designed it? What incentives does it embed? What behaviours does it reward or punish?"

The financial game has not become harder in a linear sense. It has become *more complex*. And complexity is not the enemy—ignorance is. The most powerful thing a young person can do is to see the game for what it is: not rigged, but asymmetrical. The rules favour those who can see multiple levels at once—those who understand not just money, but systems. Those who can hold in mind the interface and the infrastructure, the immediate and the long-term, the personal and the structural.

Learning the new rules does not mean memorising a new set of tactics. It means developing *systems fluency*: the ability to think critically about design, incentive, trade-off, and consequence. It means cultivating *delayed intuition*—pausing before clicking, questioning before committing, seeking clarity before consent. It means understanding that in a world of ambient risk and fragmented responsibility, the most valuable skill is not caution or ambition, but discernment.

You cannot play the new game well if you're still following old instructions. And no one will stop to explain that to you. But if you can see how the rules have changed—if you can decode the speed, the fragmentation, and the psychological design—you won't just survive the system. You'll learn to shape it. And that is the beginning of financial agency.

How Gen Z Thinks About Money Differently

It would be a mistake to assume that Gen Z is financially illiterate. In truth, they are *hyper-aware*—but that awareness is rarely linear, and almost never calm. This generation was born into a financial atmosphere laced with contradiction: raised by adults who told them to save, in economies where saving seemed futile; taught that hard work would lead to security, while watching entire industries destabilised by automation and austerity; urged to avoid debt, yet encouraged—almost expected—to take on loans for education, often before they've earned a penny of their own. In such an environment, financial thinking becomes less about logic and more about survival. Less a question of strategy, more a question of identity.

The traditional advice—budget wisely, save early, avoid debt—has not lost its technical merit. But its emotional relevance has eroded. For Gen Z, finance is not a distant adult concern but a present, daily negotiation. A 2022 Deloitte study found that over 45% of Gen Z respondents felt anxious about their financial futures *on a weekly basis*. This anxiety is not born of ignorance. It is born of exposure. They are the first generation raised entirely in the shadow of the 2008 financial crisis, the gig economy, and the pervasive reach of algorithmic platforms. Their instincts have been shaped not by textbooks, but by volatility.

That volatility has bred a unique mindset: a blend of *cynicism*, *urgency*, and *ambition without a roadmap*. Many Gen Z teens distrust traditional financial institutions. According to a 2021 survey by Morning Consult, fewer than 36% trust banks to prioritise their best interests. Yet these same teens are increasingly drawn to decentralised financial tools like cryptocurrency or digital wallets—often without fully grasping the risks involved. The contradiction here is telling. On one hand, there is suspicion: the belief that conventional systems are rigged, extractive, or irrelevant. On the other, there is hunger—for autonomy, for early success, for systems that offer access without bureaucracy.

This mindset is perhaps best exemplified in the popularity of hustle culture among Gen Z. Unlike previous generations, who largely accepted a clear divide between youth and work, Gen Z has internalised the notion that *you should already be building something*. The internet is saturated with 17-year-olds running dropshipping stores, freelancing in design, or documenting their "rise and grind" routines. Work is no longer a phase that begins after school; it is woven into adolescence itself. While this might appear enterprising, the emotional cost is considerable. Burnout, imposter syndrome, and toxic productivity are frequently reported among teenagers attempting to "make it" before they've even had a chance to define what *it* is.

The paradox is this: for a generation raised on the promise of limitless possibility, many feel boxed in. Economic uncertainty and social comparison produce a kind of *ambitious paralysis*—a psychological state where the desire to take control clashes with the fear of getting it wrong. One study by the Financial

Industry Regulatory Authority (FINRA) found that young adults often delay critical financial decisions not because of apathy, but because of information overload. They are drowning in content—TikToks about investing, YouTube tutorials on passive income, Instagram influencers offering "financial freedom" blueprints—and yet they're paralysed by choice. The sheer abundance of advice becomes a barrier to action.

In this environment, impulsiveness often disguises itself as decisiveness. It is easier to act quickly than to sit with uncertainty. A teenager might, after seeing a viral post about cryptocurrency gains, decide to invest their savings in a volatile token they barely understand. Or they might sign up for a buy-now-pay-later scheme, lured by a fashion ad optimised for conversion. These are not stupid decisions. They are *informed by environment*. When every app is optimised for speed, and every peer appears to be winning, restraint becomes countercultural.

And yet, beneath the surface of impulsiveness lies a much deeper emotional terrain. Gen Z's relationship with money is fundamentally *emotive*, not merely transactional. Money is tied to self-worth, belonging, independence, and even justice. In surveys, many report a desire not simply to earn or save, but to align their financial behaviour with personal ethics. This shows up in preferences for sustainable brands, boycotts of unethical companies, and investment interest in ESG (Environmental, Social, and Governance) funds. Unlike earlier generations who may have viewed finance as value-neutral, Gen Z sees money as *a moral force*. This ethical awareness is admirable—but it also complicates decision-making. When every purchase feels like a political act, spending becomes fraught with overanalysis or guilt.

Social context compounds this complexity. In a digital world, financial behaviours are not private—they are performative. A new phone, a designer item, a trip abroad: these are not merely expenses; they are signals. They say something about your status, your taste, your "success trajectory." Conversely, financial struggle is often hidden, or filtered into self-deprecating humour online. There's a double bind here. Teens are encouraged to live authentically and manage their finances responsibly, but the culture around them rewards aesthetic excess and conspicuous consumption. The result is a tension between *internal values* and *external validation*.

This tension plays out in emotional symptoms. Anxiety is not the only by-product of this climate—*numbness* is another. For every Gen Z teen meticulously tracking their budget, there is another who avoids checking their balance altogether. For every teen studying investment strategies, there is one who can't bring themselves to cancel a draining subscription, out of inertia or discomfort. This avoidance is not laziness. It is a trauma response, a natural consequence of being overwhelmed. When financial systems feel both important and incomprehensible, avoidance becomes a coping strategy.

What's striking is how much of this behaviour mirrors adult patterns, but with fewer resources and support systems. Adults too experience financial stress, impulsive spending, and social comparison—but they often have years of practice, buffers like credit histories or emergency savings, and in many cases, access to professional advice. Teenagers have none of these. They are navigating similar terrain with less visibility and more noise.

And yet, the picture is not bleak. The very qualities that complicate Gen Z's financial life also hold promise. Their scepticism guards them against blind trust. Their digital fluency gives them early exposure to financial tools. Their moral seriousness motivates them to ask not just "how do I earn?" but "why do I earn?" and "what matters more than money?" These are not trivial questions. They are the foundation of financial agency.

The key is not to pathologise Gen Z's financial mindset, but to understand it *on its own terms*. It is shaped by context—global instability, digital saturation, and the erosion of conventional milestones. It is fuelled by a desire for autonomy and tempered by a fear of misstep. It is sometimes chaotic, often improvised, but rarely indifferent. What it lacks is not motivation, but *translation*—a way to bridge their values and anxieties with practical, grounded frameworks for action.

Understanding how Gen Z thinks about money differently requires that we abandon outdated narratives. This is not a generation in need of generic advice or finger-wagging prescriptions. It is a generation asking thoughtful, difficult, sometimes contradictory questions. Our task is not to silence those contradictions, but to help them navigate them—slowly, wisely, and with tools that actually fit the shape of their lives. Only then can their financial thinking evolve from reactive to reflective, from survival to strategy. And only then can they begin to define wealth on their own terms.

Chapter 2
The Psychology of Your Wallet

Money has never been solely about arithmetic, but in today's world, its human dimensions have never been more central. For teenagers, in particular, decisions about earning, spending, or saving are rarely made with a ledger in mind. They are made with a phone in hand, an emotion in motion, and an identity in flux. Purchases, paycheques, and savings are not merely reflections of financial skill—they are expressions of self-image, social standing, and mood. To grasp money in this context, one must look beyond balances and budgets, to the impulses and beliefs guiding the hand that spends.

Teens are rarely taught money in theory; they encounter it daily, viscerally. They earn to feel capable, spend to feel included, and check accounts to feel secure. Traditional financial advice assumes a rational, neutral actor, but that model is obsolete. Beneath every swipe is an emotion. Beneath every plan is a story about worth, progress, and identity. The stakes are personal long before they are monetary.

The link between money and identity has intensified in the age of social media. Once visible, money becomes symbolic, a metric of independence, maturity, and even moral standing. A young person earning online may not be financially secure by conventional standards, yet the act of earning carries profound psychological significance. It signals agency: "I am moving forward, I am building myself, I am not being left behind."

Modern work amplifies this. For Gen Z, early income often comes through freelance, creative, or digital ventures—content creation, tutoring, selling products online—rather than formal employment. Each transaction doubles as a performance, a presentation of self. Success bolsters confidence; failure feels personal. Income and identity entwine. The line between financial and existential stakes blurs.

Understanding this dynamic is crucial. Earning is no longer just a skill; it is a psychological exercise. Why are you chasing income? Out of excitement, necessity, or validation? Are your projects driven by intrinsic value or external optics? Recognising motivation is as important as tracking numbers.

Spending is equally complex. Behavioural economics consistently shows that most financial decisions are affective, not rational. Fatigue, loneliness, or stress can skew choices, while apps and algorithms exploit these impulses. Small decisions accumulate rapidly. Discipline alone is insufficient; awareness is necessary. Pausing to ask, "Am I buying this for joy, avoidance, or validation?" transforms micro-decisions into intentional action.

Patterns matter because money is never neutral. Teenagers' financial behaviour is shaped by peer pressure, identity formation, and constant social visibility. That takeaway lunch may not be about food—it may be about conformity. That hoodie may not be about style—it may signal belonging. Money decisions become intertwined with social signalling, often unconsciously.

Social media intensifies these pressures. Peer lives are broadcast as highlight reels, distorting what is normal and heightening comparison. Savings feel slow, purchases feel inadequate, and financial decisions shift from personal to performative. The result is Financial FOMO: the anxiety that others are advancing while you lag behind, turning money into a metric of existential progress. Impulsive investing, side hustles, and conspicuous spending may follow, sometimes leading to burnout, sometimes to a persistent low-level anxiety.

The danger is internalising failure. Overspending, missed payments, or flopped projects can feel like moral failings: "I'm bad with money; I'm irresponsible." But financial mistakes are data points, not indictments. They signal context, assumptions, and emotional patterns. Learning to interpret these signals without shame fosters resilience. Understanding emotional drivers allows deliberate disruption of unhelpful habits. Separating self-worth from balance is the cornerstone of sustainable financial behaviour.

Clarity, then, is the strategic asset. It is less about accumulating more money and more about understanding one's relationship to it. Mental models—simple, robust frameworks for decision-making—can help. Ask not "Can I afford this?" but "Will I be proud of this purchase tomorrow?" Frame savings as delayed agency, not restriction. Treat budgeting as design, a method of allocating energy as well as funds.

These reframes do not deny emotional complexity; they harness it. Financial competence does not require emotional neutrality; it demands emotional literacy. Recognising the motivations behind spending, earning, and saving is essential. Which actions are energising, which compensatory? What signals identity, and what merely signals to others?

This chapter does not attempt to strip money of its emotional charge—it is inseparable from who we are. Instead, it invites exploration: curiosity, precision, and compassion in understanding how identity, mood, and social context shape financial behaviour. Patterns are not failures but data. With reflection, one can make decisions aligned with values rather than impulses.

Money, in this view, becomes a mirror, a tool, and occasionally a test. Handled with insight and intention, it transforms from stressor to signal, from obligation to agency. This chapter guides that shift—not through rigid rules, but through reflection; not by suppressing emotion, but by tracing its influence through the wallet, and recognising how it shapes the life quietly constructed, swipe by swipe.

Why Earning Isn't Just Math—It's Identity

The moment money is earned, it ceases to be just a number. It becomes a message—about who you are, what you can contribute, and how you are seen by others. Especially in adolescence, and especially today, earning is not experienced merely as a financial event; it is a psychological and social signal. It tells you something about your agency, your autonomy, your place in the world. For Gen Z, who are coming of age in an environment where self-worth is often constructed in public and measured by visibility, income isn't just a means of subsistence. It's a proxy for value.

This isn't a dramatic overstatement. Studies in behavioural economics and developmental psychology consistently show that teenagers interpret early income—whether through part-time jobs, entrepreneurial ventures, or digital side hustles—as a marker of legitimacy. A 2023 survey by Pew Research Centre revealed that over 62% of teens who earn their own money associate it directly with a sense of "growing up" or becoming "more real in the adult world." The income itself may be modest—£20 from selling vintage clothing on Depop, or £50 from tutoring a younger student—but the emotional impact is often disproportionately large. That's because the act of earning engages something deeper than arithmetic. It engages identity.

What makes this link especially potent for Gen Z is the extent to which public perception and self-perception are now intertwined. Social media platforms have not just amplified expression—they have standardised it. A teenager doesn't simply earn money; they may document the process, aestheticise the outcome, or fold it into a personal brand. Even when not explicitly posted, the awareness of visibility affects behaviour. The line between earning as function and earning as performance becomes blurry. And when you perform, you don't just ask, *What does this pay?* You ask, *What does this say about me?*

This question is not trivial. For a generation that has grown up alongside influencers who monetise personality, creativity, and even vulnerability, the idea that earning should reflect identity is almost intuitive. It's not enough to make money; the *how* matters. Is it interesting? Is it ethical? Is it aligned with my values or aesthetic? These considerations are not mere vanity—they are reflections of a broader cultural shift where income is not just an outcome but a narrative.

This narrative can be empowering. It allows teenagers to feel that their work has meaning beyond survival. But it can also become burdensome. When every earning activity is expected to express something personal, the pressure to be constantly *authentic* and *successful* intensifies. A side hustle no longer feels like just a source of pocket money. It becomes a statement of ambition, of competence, of maturity. And if it fails—or underperforms—it doesn't feel like a simple setback. It feels like a threat to identity.

The psychological consequences of this identity-earning nexus are significant. For one, it introduces a subtle but persistent performance anxiety. You are not simply working; you are proving. You are not simply building income; you are building self-image. This dynamic is not limited to influencers or creatives. It is now part of the ambient logic of teenage economics. A teenager working in a café may not post their earnings, but they may compare them—silently, relentlessly—to those of peers who seem to be "doing better." And because income is rarely discussed with transparency, the comparisons are based on surface indicators: clothing, travel, gadgets, experiences. The result is a quiet, corrosive form of self-evaluation: *Am I behind? Am I doing enough?*

And when this anxiety becomes chronic, it shapes behaviour in predictable and problematic ways. Some teens will overextend themselves—taking on too much, monetising too early, or making decisions driven by optics rather than sustainability. Others will withdraw—avoiding income opportunities altogether, paralysed by the fear that they won't "measure up." Both responses stem from the same distorted belief: that earning is a referendum on worth.

This distortion is compounded by educational and familial environments that still tend to separate financial literacy from emotional literacy. Earning is taught as a function of skill and effort—study hard, work hard, earn well. But what's missing from that equation is the inner experience: how it feels to earn, to fail, to compare, to not be chosen. The silence around these feelings does not eliminate them. It intensifies them. Because when income is seen as purely rational, any emotional response to it—shame, pride, envy, anxiety—feels irrational. And when your feelings about money feel like a problem, you're less likely to talk about them. The taboo grows. The isolation deepens.

Yet the truth is simple and universal: *Earning is always emotional.* It is, at its core, an affirmation of exchange. You offer something—time, effort, skill, creativity—and someone else validates that offering by paying you. That validation may be symbolic or literal, but either way, it confirms something essential: you have value in a shared system. And for teenagers, who are still forming their sense of self, this confirmation can be powerfully formative.

But not all validation is equal. One of the more subtle consequences of tying identity to earning is the emergence of *income elitism*—the belief that certain forms of earning are inherently more valuable, more legitimate, or more respectable than others. This belief often shows up in how teens assess each other's financial choices. Selling art online may be seen as more impressive than working retail. Coding an app may confer more status than babysitting. Yet in practice, the skills, resilience, and character built through so-called "low-status" work are often more transferable and more grounding.

The hierarchy of earning is not neutral—it reflects broader societal biases about class, creativity, and labour. And unless challenged early, it can shape a teenager's willingness to try, to fail, and to grow. If your first income source is met with subtle condescension—"That's cute, but is it real work?"—you may internalise that as a message about your legitimacy. And when legitimacy is questioned, motivation suffers. This is not a hypothetical risk. A 2022 report from the UK's Youth Employment Group found that young people who perceived their early income sources as "unserious" were less likely to pursue entrepreneurial or non-traditional paths in the future, even when those paths had higher long-term potential.

So what does it mean to earn without losing yourself? Or more precisely, how can young people engage with money in a way that affirms their identity *without* letting it define them?

The answer lies in reframing. Income is not identity—it is *expression*. It reflects parts of who you are, not the whole. It is influenced by skill, effort, luck, access, and timing. It is never a pure meritocracy. And it is always evolving. A teenager who earns little today may be developing the habits, values, and insights that will lead to meaningful success later. But if they interpret their current income as the sum total of their worth, they may never get the chance to grow into that future.

This reframing also requires cultural change. Schools, parents, and mentors must begin to speak differently about earning. Not just in terms of strategy, but in terms of meaning. Not just what to do, but *how it feels*. Financial literacy cannot be divorced from emotional intelligence. Because the first lesson a teenager needs is not how to calculate gross profit—it's how to hold their self-worth steady when the numbers are low.

Only then can earning become what it should be: a dynamic, evolving practice that supports identity, rather than consumes it. A signal of possibility, not pressure. A tool for agency, not a test of value. When income is allowed to be part of your story—but not the whole story—you regain your power. Not just to earn, but to choose what earning means to you. And that is the beginning of real financial maturity.

Emotions Behind Every Swipe

The average teenager today can spend money without touching it, talking about it, or even consciously deciding to do so. A moment of boredom on a bus becomes an online purchase. A wave of social pressure turns into a food delivery split three ways on a digital wallet. A quick scroll through Instagram ends in an impulsive "add to cart" at 2:00 a.m., justified by stress, habit, or a vague sense of reward. Financial transactions are no longer discrete events—they are ambient behaviours, folded into daily life and often guided more by emotion than by logic. If we want to understand teenage spending, we must stop asking *what they bought* and start asking *why*.

Modern spending isn't irrational—it's emotionally encoded. The logic is there, but it's not financial logic. It's psychological logic. You buy because you're tired and need a treat. You spend to celebrate a win or soothe a loss. You upgrade because your friends have, and you fear falling behind. And you do it not always in a burst of thoughtless indulgence, but often in a quiet act of self-regulation. A purchase becomes a coping mechanism, a social tool, or a performance of identity. Money, in this framework, is not just a means of exchange—it's a medium of emotion.

This isn't new behaviour, but the infrastructure surrounding it has changed dramatically. Shopping is now algorithmic. Payment is frictionless. Visibility is constant. Emotional states that might once have faded before they translated into action are now directly monetised. A moment of low self-esteem can trigger a targeted ad. A late-night scroll can end with a click that costs £80. The platforms are designed not to wait for need, but to *anticipate desire*, especially when that desire is emotionally charged.

One of the most overlooked drivers of teen spending is boredom—not laziness or apathy, but the psychological discomfort that arises when stimulation decreases and agency feels limited. Boredom is not empty time; it's time seeking direction. In the past, that restlessness might have led to creative exploration or social activity. Today, it often leads to the app store. Buying something becomes a shortcut to feeling something. It punctuates the monotony. And because digital commerce offers not just products but anticipation—the pleasure of tracking, unboxing, showing—it satisfies more than just material desire. It creates an event.

The same emotional mechanics apply to stress. A 2022 study published in *Frontiers in Psychology* found that teenagers under academic or social stress were significantly more likely to engage in "compensatory consumption"—spending motivated by the desire to regain a sense of control or comfort. The logic is subtle but powerful: when your external world feels uncertain, internal control becomes paramount. Buying something—choosing, acquiring, possessing—restores agency, if only temporarily. The object is almost incidental. What matters is the feeling of action.

And then there is the force of social belonging—perhaps the most potent and least acknowledged driver of teenage spending. To belong is not just to be included. It is to be *visibly aligned*. Teenagers spend not only to acquire things, but to maintain participation in a shared culture. That culture might be aesthetic (a fashion trend), functional (owning the same headphones as your peers), or experiential (going out instead of staying home). The transactions are rarely about indulgence. They are about participation. Not spending can feel like *opting out*, or worse, *falling behind*.

This creates a delicate tension between autonomy and conformity. A teenager might deeply want to save money for something important, but they may also fear the social cost of abstaining from a group activity. That cost is rarely articulated—it's coded in tone, gesture, invitation. The £15 spent on a group dinner may not be a conscious trade-off against their longer-term goals. It may feel like a survival expense: the price of social cohesion. And unless they've been taught how to weigh those trade-offs explicitly, they will default to emotion over arithmetic. Not because they are undisciplined, but because they are human.

Financial advice that ignores these emotional undercurrents is incomplete. Telling young people to "just stick to a budget" without acknowledging the psychological landscape in which that budget operates is like giving someone a map without telling them there's fog. The map may be accurate, but it doesn't reflect the actual terrain. What's needed is not more instruction, but more awareness—*emotional fluency around money*. The ability to ask, *Why do I want this right now? What am I feeling? What will this purchase do for me emotionally—and will it last?*

Some may argue that teenagers should be taught to suppress these emotional impulses. But suppression is a brittle strategy. It relies on willpower, which is both finite and context-dependent. A more effective approach is *integration*: recognising that emotion will always be part of the equation, and learning to factor it in wisely. This is the foundation of emotional intelligence in financial decision-making—not denying the role of feelings, but decoding them.

Consider how digital payment systems influence this decoding process. When you use physical cash, you feel the transaction. You hand over something tangible, and your wallet becomes lighter. With digital payments—especially contactless or mobile—the loss is abstract. There is no moment of friction, no tactile interruption. Behavioural researchers call this the *pain of paying*, and its absence makes emotional spending easier and more frequent. Without conscious awareness, your brain doesn't register the loss in the same way. The dopamine reward remains, but the cost feels distant.

This is not a flaw in character—it's a feature of design. Payment systems are engineered for ease, not reflection. But ease often disables friction, and friction is what gives us pause. For teenagers, whose prefrontal cortices are still developing (the part of the brain responsible for impulse control and future planning), the absence of friction is especially potent. It's not that they lack discipline. It's that the system is tilted toward immediacy.

To counter this, some behavioural economists recommend *artificial friction*: small delays or questions embedded into the spending process that create a moment of reflection. This could be as simple as a notification that says, "You've spent £120 this week—still want to buy this?" Or a practice of writing down every non-essential purchase in a notebook, by hand. These interventions don't prevent spending; they slow it down. And in that pause, emotion becomes visible.

The deeper task, however, is not just to slow down. It is to understand the *narrative* behind the spending. Every purchase tells a story—about who you are, who you want to be, what you lack, and what you hope for. Sometimes that story is empowering. Sometimes it is compensatory. Either way, it is worth listening to. Not with shame or self-judgement, but with curiosity. Why does this brand make me feel more "me"? Why do I shop more when I'm anxious? Why does saying yes to this dinner feel harder than saying no?

These are not trivial questions. They are diagnostic tools. And over time, they build a kind of internal clarity that no budgeting app can replicate. They help you distinguish between *spending for relief* and *spending for value*, between *buying for display* and *buying for use*. And once those distinctions become habitual, financial autonomy follows—not because you're making fewer emotional decisions, but because you're making *wiser* ones.

In the long term, the most financially resilient young people will not be the ones who suppress emotion, but the ones who *integrate it skilfully*. They will know when their spending is reactive and when it's intentional. They will understand that money is not just about what you *have*—it's about what you're trying to *feel*. And they will develop the ability to pause long enough to ask: *Is this feeling worth the cost?*

This is the psychology of your wallet in action. It's not glamorous, and it won't go viral. But it is deeply transformative. Because once you understand the emotions behind every swipe, you can begin to rewrite the patterns. Not by force, but by insight. Not through control, but through clarity. And in that clarity, you gain something even more valuable than money: the ability to choose what really matters.

Financial FOMO and the Comparison Trap

No generation in history has had so much visibility into the lives—and spending habits—of others. In the past, financial comparison operated through limited and often private channels. You might have known what your neighbours drove or where they holidayed, but those insights were circumstantial, occasional, and anchored in some degree of context. Today, comparison is constant, curated, and global. Through a smartphone screen, a teenager in Birmingham can watch another in Dubai unbox luxury trainers, invest in crypto, or launch a Shopify store. These aren't isolated moments; they are designed to be consumed as narratives of success. And they are driving a profound shift in how young people assess their own financial standing, ambitions, and risks.

Financial FOMO—fear of missing out on financial success—is not a minor side-effect of social media. It is a pervasive psychological current that shapes behaviour, confidence, and identity. It distorts what counts as "normal," compresses timelines, and redefines success as something that must be *visible, early,* and *impressive.* For teenagers still forming their sense of self and agency, this creates an impossible standard: not just to be financially responsible, but to be financially *exceptional, immediately.*

This phenomenon is not merely anecdotal. A 2022 report by the UK's Financial Capability Lab found that young people exposed to aspirational financial content on social media were significantly more likely to express anxiety about their financial future, even when they were objectively doing well for their age. The visibility of others' apparent wins—side hustles, passive income, investment returns—creates a distorted baseline. Success no longer feels relative to your goals or circumstances. It feels like a scoreboard you can never catch up to, because you're not just behind—you're *invisible.*

The mechanisms of this comparison are subtle but potent. One post may show a 19-year-old claiming to earn £10,000 a month through affiliate marketing. Another reveals someone else who turned a TikTok following into a brand deal. These are presented as attainable and replicable. But the context is often omitted: the years of failed attempts, the luck involved, the financial backing from family, or the non-disclosure of actual net profit versus gross revenue. What's left is a mirage of meritocracy—a sense that *you could be there too, if you just worked harder or moved faster.* The pressure is not just to succeed, but to explain *why you haven't.*

This anxiety breeds two common reactions: *paralysis* or *impulsiveness.* Some teenagers, overwhelmed by the scale and speed of others' success, retreat. They convince themselves it's too late to start, or that they lack the skills, resources, or personality to compete. Others respond with urgency—

rushing into high-risk ventures, investing in things they don't understand, or burning out on projects that haven't been tested. In both cases, the decision-making is distorted by *perceived timelines*, not actual ones.

The notion of financial timelines—when you should start earning, how quickly you should scale, how soon you should invest—has always been culturally constructed. But social media has radically accelerated those expectations. What once might have been a 10-year plan is now condensed into a six-month case study, polished into a carousel post. And because teens see only the highlight, not the timeline, they internalise an impossible urgency: *Why am I not already there?*

This is where risk distortion enters the picture. Financial FOMO doesn't just alter your sense of timing—it warps your sense of *risk and reward*. When peers appear to be succeeding through bold moves—crypto investments, dropshipping stores, influencer deals—it's easy to conclude that *risk equals reward*. But what's often missing from these narratives is a sober analysis of *downside*. Losses are rarely documented. Failure is sanitised or reframed as resilience. The result is a culture in which teenagers are encouraged to take entrepreneurial risks without being taught how to evaluate them.

This is not to say that ambition is harmful. Quite the opposite. But ambition without grounding becomes volatility. Young people should absolutely explore early income, digital platforms, and scalable ideas. But they need a framework for understanding *the difference between high effort and high stakes*. They need to know that experimentation is valuable, but not every experiment needs to be a public performance or a personal referendum on success.

The social comparison trap also creates deeper psychological consequences. At its core, comparison distorts not just financial behaviour, but *self-concept*. If you believe your worth is measured by how quickly you monetise your skills or how large your audience is, you're more likely to neglect slower, less visible forms of growth—like learning, resilience, patience, or adaptability. These traits are harder to measure and celebrate online, but they're essential for long-term success. The distortion lies in *visibility bias*: what you see most often feels most real, even if it's not most common.

A teenager quietly learning to code, building savings through part-time work, or developing a service-based skill might feel behind simply because their progress isn't aesthetic or shareable. But that kind of growth—incremental, deliberate, grounded—is often the most sustainable. It's just harder to romanticise. And in a digital culture built on storytelling, anything that doesn't make a good story can feel like a failure.

To resist this pressure, teenagers need more than financial advice—they need *narrative clarity*. The ability to separate someone else's edited reality from their actual goals. The awareness that visibility is not a guarantee of value, and that speed is not a proxy for success. They need to ask better questions: *What do I actually want money to do for me? Whose definition of success am I following? Am I taking a risk because it aligns with my values, or because I feel left behind?*

This internal clarity is not taught in schools, nor is it easily modelled by adults who didn't grow up in a world of monetised identity. But it can be developed through reflective practice—tracking not just spending and saving, but *feelings and beliefs*. Noticing when comparison triggers action, and asking whether that action serves a long-term intention or a short-term relief. Creating distance between emotional urgency and financial behaviour.

It also helps to build a more diverse mental archive of success. To seek out stories of people who took longer paths, who pivoted, who failed, who redefined wealth on their own terms. To recognise that financial well-being is not just about how much you earn, but about how stable, ethical, and meaningful your income is. In short, to make peace with the idea that *your path will not look like anyone else's, and that is not a problem—it is a feature.*

Ultimately, financial FOMO thrives in silence. When young people don't talk honestly about money, struggle, and ambiguity, the only voices that fill the space are the loudest—and often the least honest. The antidote to distorted comparison is not disengagement. It's discernment. The ability to *see without absorbing*, to *witness without imitating*. And to hold space for ambition without letting it collapse into anxiety.

When you reclaim your sense of timing, of value, and of pace, you don't just resist the comparison trap. You build something stronger in its place: a self-defined financial identity, rooted in clarity, not performance. That identity is not built in a single post or transaction—it is built over time. Quietly. Intentionally. And far from the algorithms that are trying to sell you someone else's version of success.

How to Build a Calm Mind Around Money

Most people don't think with money—they *feel* with it. Behind every purchase, every budget skipped, and every late-night swipe of a digital wallet is not merely a calculation, but a reflex—rooted in emotion, shaped by stories, and reinforced by repetition. Money, despite its numeric appearance, is rarely approached rationally. This is especially true for Gen Z, who navigate a financial world defined by instability, hyper-visibility, and constant digital nudges. The question, then, is not simply how to earn, spend, or save more effectively—but how to *think* about money without being hijacked by fear, shame, urgency, or comparison. The pursuit of a calm mind around money is not a soft luxury; it is a foundational strength. And like all forms of strength, it can be trained.

Money anxiety does not begin with insufficient funds. It begins with *incoherence*—the internal dissonance between what we believe we should do, what we feel pressured to do, and what we actually do. A calm financial mind does not eliminate stress altogether; it integrates competing needs into a coherent internal system. This system doesn't emerge automatically. It must be constructed intentionally—through reflection, frameworks, and mental habits that reduce noise and anchor decision-making.

One of the most effective starting points is the mental model of *enough*. The idea that, for any decision, there exists a version of financial sufficiency that aligns with your actual context—not someone else's. Most anxiety around money is not about survival; it is about ambiguity. "Should I be spending less?" "Should I be investing more?" "Should I have more by now?" The lack of clear internal thresholds allows comparison and fear to fill the vacuum. By defining your own version of "enough"—across spending, saving, and earning—you begin to insulate your mind from the volatile expectations of external benchmarks. It's not about being minimalist; it's about being specific. *Enough* is not an abstract ideal. It is a number, a lifestyle boundary, a personal benchmark that lets you stop reacting and start choosing.

Another powerful reframe comes from separating *financial facts* from *financial feelings*. Consider this: two teenagers with the exact same bank balance can experience entirely different emotional realities. One feels secure; the other panics. One sees progress; the other sees failure. The difference is not their account—it's their narrative. When feelings masquerade as facts, they distort judgement. To build clarity, it's essential to externalise the numbers regularly. Create a space—weekly or monthly—where you look at your income, expenses, and savings with full transparency. Don't wait for anxiety to trigger the review. Make it a ritual. This converts money from an emotional ghost into a visible system. You stop imagining where you stand, and start *knowing*.

But emotional calm is not only about spreadsheets. It also depends on how we interpret the financial choices of others. One of the most corrosive forces on a calm financial mind is *comparison distortion*. Social media, peer conversations, and influencer culture constantly present success as both immediate and aesthetic. If you internalise these portrayals uncritically, your own choices will always feel inadequate. The antidote is not cynicism, but calibration. When you see a post about someone earning £5,000 a month online, remind yourself: what's not shown is as important as what is. Was there a parental safety net? Was this a highlight from a much longer timeline? Are the numbers net or gross? A calm financial mind recognises the limits of other people's stories—it admires outcomes without internalising their urgency.

Still, even private goals can generate anxiety if they're not managed well. This is where *timeline realism* becomes essential. Modern culture fetishises acceleration: fast income, rapid scaling, viral success. But sustainable finances rarely move in straight lines. Income fluctuates. Investments underperform. Unexpected expenses arise. Anxiety emerges not from these events themselves, but from the belief that they signal personal failure. A calm financial mind is one that expects volatility without panicking. It holds the long view. One way to build this capacity is by visualising multiple paths to your financial goals—not just one. If Plan A stalls, can Plan B extend the timeline rather than abandon the goal? Flexibility reduces fear. Rigidity breeds panic.

Perhaps the most underappreciated mental model in cultivating calm is *the separation of identity from income*. In a world where teenagers are encouraged to "monetise themselves," it's easy to tie self-worth to earnings. But this entanglement makes every financial setback feel like an existential crisis. To break this, you must deliberately diversify your sources of validation. Who are you outside your bank balance? What skills, values, or relationships affirm your worth regardless of your income? This doesn't mean ignoring money—it means decoupling *earning* from *being*. Your value precedes your revenue.

There's also the daily pressure of spending decisions—each swipe a micro-moral question: "Am I being wasteful?" "Am I buying happiness?" "Is this responsible?" Without a framework, this mental burden compounds. One approach is to install a simple rule: *The 24-Hour Pause*. For any non-essential purchase over a certain threshold—say, £25—pause for a full day. Not as punishment, but as perspective. This single habit introduces distance between impulse and action, allowing you to observe emotional drivers—boredom, status, loneliness—without letting them dictate behaviour. Over time, this micro-boundary reduces regret and builds confidence in your judgement.

Equally important is recognising the role of *micro-decisions* in emotional regulation. People often think money anxiety comes from large events—job loss, debt, emergency expenses. But just as often, it accumulates through dozens of small, unexamined decisions. A cancelled subscription here. A late-night food order there. When these decisions feel unconscious, they corrode your sense of agency. The fix isn't control; it's awareness. Start by tracking three purchases per day—not to shame, but to *witness*. What triggered them? What did they solve? What was their emotional cost or benefit? Simply observing your behaviour restores ownership.

A calm financial mind also requires insulation from noise. Financial advice is everywhere—YouTube, TikTok, Reddit, podcasts. Much of it is contradictory. Some is predatory. The key is not to absorb everything, but to curate *your financial philosophy*. Decide whose voice matters. Choose two or three trusted sources. Build a bookshelf, not a feed. Re-read before you re-scroll. Philosophy brings peace. A curated worldview shields you from the chaos of reactive consumption.

Of course, none of this eliminates stress altogether. Money is inherently linked to uncertainty. But anxiety decreases when uncertainty meets preparation. This is where habits function as emotional shock absorbers. Automating small tasks—weekly savings transfers, categorised expense alerts, investment top-ups—reduces the decision load. The less you have to remember, the more bandwidth you free for reflection. Systems create calm. Not because they eliminate thought, but because they *pre-think* on your behalf.

Finally, perhaps the most transformative mental shift is the redefinition of what financial success actually means. It is tempting to think in absolutes: £X saved, £Y invested, Z passive income streams. But a calm financial mind reframes success as *confidence in your own decisions*. If you can explain your spending without guilt, your saving without shame, your income without panic—you are ahead of the vast majority. That kind of internal coherence is not accidental. It is the result of mental models, emotional boundaries, and daily habits that are chosen, not imposed.

In the end, peace around money is not something you find at a certain net worth. It is something you build—through awareness, clarity, and trust in your process. The world will not become less noisy. But your mind can become quieter. And from that place, financial decisions stop being emergencies and start becoming expressions of your values. That is the real calm: not the absence of tension, but the presence of choice.

Chapter 3
The Real Cost of Being a Teen

The price of adolescence has never been more opaque, nor more entwined with social currents. For Gen Z, growing up involves more than negotiating identity, ambition, and relationships—it requires navigating a financial terrain where merely existing as a teenager carries costs that often exceed awareness, income, and logic. The question isn't only how much is spent, but why, on what, and for whom. The real expense of youth isn't captured in ledgers; it resides in the subtle, constant exchanges between autonomy, expectation, visibility, and belonging.

Today's teenagers inhabit a financial fog. Money flows invisibly through tap-to-pay gestures, automatic subscriptions, in-game currencies, and targeted ads. A £7 streaming service, a £13 outfit, a £5 Uber to avoid public transport, a £4 coffee doubling as a social signal—individually minor, collectively significant. Yet teens rarely learn to see this structural leakage. They track obvious, infrequent purchases while the drip-feed of daily costs goes unnoticed.

Even more insidious is the interplay of spending and signalling. Many purchases aren't about utility but identity. A phone isn't just a device; it broadcasts tech fluency and social inclusion. Labels, festival tickets, skincare, and even monetised hobbies become markers of belonging. Without guidance, spending becomes reflexive, driven by a need to participate rather than by practical value. Not buying can feel like opting out of status or friendship.

Consider a night out with friends. Few adolescents account for the dinner, transport, outfit refresh, and group activity—all of which may fluctuate week to week. Opting out can carry social consequences: exclusion, judgment, or being labelled "cheap." This isn't a flaw in teen judgement; it is a failure of adults to equip them with tools for setting financial boundaries without social cost. The issue isn't that socialising costs money—it always has—but that those costs have become increasingly invisible and unspoken.

Teen income complicates matters further. Many earn through irregular, informal channels: part-time jobs, app-based gigs, parental transfers. Cash flow rarely aligns with expenses. Spontaneous social invitations, limited-edition drops, or group trips demand immediate funds. Traditional budgeting—dividing income evenly across the month—often fails here. What teens need is adaptive budgeting: flexibility, anticipation of unexpected costs, and the ability to act without guilt or panic. Yet, instruction in these skills is rare. Adolescents are expected to "figure it out" alongside school, relationships, identity, and mental health.

Even conscientious teens operate within skewed models. They often categorise spending by type—food, entertainment, clothes—rather than by intention. Was this purchase necessary, or did it soothe discomfort? Did it foster meaningful connection, or merely satisfy comparison? These questions aren't about frugality; they are about freedom. Teens who distinguish purchases that empower from those that entrap reclaim agency over their financial narrative. That insight alone outweighs any budgeting app.

Teen spending is symbolically rich. A gym membership signals transformation. A concert ticket represents memory-making. A fast-food run communicates belonging. None of this is inherently wrong, yet without tools to navigate emotional drivers, adolescents risk choices that erode agency as well as wallets. Money can feel like something happening to them rather than something they shape intentionally.

Earning intensifies the stakes. Income brings pressure to prove, to reward, to signal progress. Teens often succumb to moral licensing—"I earned, so I deserve to spend"—or a YOLO mentality, assuming the future is uncertain, so saving is futile. Both reflect a lack of clarity about purpose: without a guiding sense of what money is for, even earnings become a source of anxiety.

The digital landscape exacerbates the challenge. Ads, algorithmic feeds, and aspirational influencers frame not only products but identities: "Buy this, become this." Highlight reels distort benchmarks, inflating spending, eroding confidence, and compressing self-worth. Decisions shift from "What do I want?" to "What must I do to remain relevant?"

Traditional financial literacy falls short. Knowing compound interest or credit scores is meaningless if anxiety stems from social inclusion, visibility, or comparison. Real education begins in context, teaching teens to assess emotional triggers, social dynamics, and spending patterns with honesty. Hidden costs—£100 sneakers for safety, £6 coffee for routine, ride-share to avoid discomfort—carry stories as well as prices.

The goal is not to shame spending, but to decode it. Spending reflects underlying needs: admiration, belonging, control. Recognising these allows alternative paths that deliver emotional fulfilment without financial harm. Autonomy emerges not from rejecting peer culture, but from selective, intentional participation.

Ultimately, the cost of being a teen is cognitive as well as financial. It is the toll of hundreds of small decisions each week, balancing friendship, identity, independence, and ambition under economic uncertainty. Most critically, it is the erosion of agency when money becomes confusion rather than empowerment.

This can change. With proper tools, frameworks, and guidance, teenagers can shift from reacting to costs to redesigning them. They can understand what purchases truly cost them, unhook identity from possessions, and distinguish joy-driven spending from approval-driven spending. They can budget with foresight rather than constraint.

This chapter is not about minimising expenditure—it is about seeing it clearly. It aims to give teens the mental clarity and emotional confidence to spend in alignment with values, protect energy, and expand choice. This clarity transcends finances; it is a life skill, long overdue.

What Stuff Actually Costs (And Why You Don't Know)

Ask most teenagers how much they spend in a week, and the answer will likely be a hesitant guess. Press further—how much on transport, entertainment, subscriptions, snacks, clothes, apps, and social plans—and the confidence drains even faster. It's not that teens don't care about money. On the contrary, many are more financially anxious than ever before. It's that modern spending has become so frictionless, ambient, and fragmented that awareness gets lost in the flow. And the result is profound: a generation being trained to *spend without seeing*.

Contemporary financial life is structured around *invisibility*. Where once expenses were tactile—cash exchanged by hand, prices rounded and felt—today's economic behaviours happen in micro-moments, on screens, with interfaces designed for speed rather than reflection. The auto-renewing Netflix plan. The daily tap on a contactless card for coffee. The buy-now-pay-later checkout for a hoodie. The £2 upgrade for premium music. All of it bypasses conscious calculation. The transactions accumulate silently, normalised by repetition and obscured by design.

But this is not a technological accident. It is a commercial strategy. Every layer of abstraction—tokens, subscriptions, stored payment methods, bundled services—removes a pinch of pain from spending. Behavioural economists call this the *pain of paying*, and businesses spend billions trying to remove it. When teens swipe without resistance, they are not failing—they are responding exactly as the system intends. And when that system is never named, let alone explained, it becomes internalised as the default. Teens start to think they are simply "bad with money," rather than realising they've been handed tools optimised for spending, not awareness.

Take transport, for instance. Many teens have no idea what their movement costs. If they rely on rides from friends or parents, there's no direct cost visible. If they use public transport, it might be deducted from a prepaid card. If they use ride-hailing apps, the pricing is dynamic and often decoupled from geography or distance. There's rarely a moment of comparison—how much did that Uber cost relative to a bus, or even a bike ride? More importantly, what patterns are forming? Is late-night spending consistently driven by fear of public spaces? Is daily transport being used to bypass boredom, or social discomfort, rather than necessity? These are the questions that budgeting apps don't ask. But they are the questions that shape financial patterns at their root.

Then there's fashion—arguably one of the most psychologically charged spending categories for young people. Clothing is rarely purchased for function alone; it's purchased as a form of expression, affiliation, and aspiration. But the actual *cost* of fashion extends beyond the price tag. It includes the mental churn of fast fashion marketing, the environmental footprint of overproduction, the social toll of outfit comparison, and the algorithmic loop of being constantly re-targeted. A £20 shirt might appear cheap—but if it becomes obsolete in your social circle after two wears, or if it prompts you to buy more to stay "current," the hidden cost is exponential. And again, teens are not taught to deconstruct this. They are sold the idea of "value" without the critical literacy to unpack what value *means*.

The same opacity defines subscriptions. For many teens, subscriptions begin as passive inheritances—added by parents, gifted as trials, included with devices. But over time, they evolve into autonomous financial responsibilities. And unlike one-time purchases, subscriptions operate on a principle of *forgetfulness*. They thrive on inertia. The gym membership you don't use. The editing software you need once a year. The niche content bundle you keep for fear of missing out. Each draws from a bank account invisibly. And because the cost is recurring but low, it rarely triggers the mental audit that a single large expense would. Yet stack enough of them, and a teen can be haemorrhaging £50–100 a month on services they don't even engage with consciously. This is not an issue of irresponsibility—it is an issue of *cognitive load*. When life is full of academic, social, and emotional challenges, remembering to cancel a £4 subscription becomes low-priority, even if it adds up significantly.

Peer expectations compound the problem. While adult financial stress is often tied to housing or childcare, teenage financial stress is often *social*. The pressure to show up, join in, match appearances, or signal independence is omnipresent—and it is rarely acknowledged as a financial issue. But consider the cost of a single Friday night with friends. It might include a new outfit, transport, food, drinks, entry fees, and spontaneous extras. If declining is not framed as a healthy boundary but as antisocial behaviour, the teen faces a no-win decision: spend beyond their means, or risk social exclusion. That's not a budgeting problem—it's a cultural one. And it will not be solved by telling teens to "just say no."

Crucially, many teens *think* they know what things cost because they remember the initial number. But they haven't been taught to trace secondary costs, temporal costs, or opportunity costs. A £200 gaming console may seem like a one-off purchase. But what about the £20–40 games that follow? The £60 headset? The £10 monthly subscription? The time investment that displaces study or sleep? Similarly, a £7 daily coffee may not feel luxurious—but over a year, it totals more than £2,500. These calculations are not meant to shame indulgence. They are meant to illuminate pattern. *The financial choices that feel small often matter more because they are repeated frequently and habitually.*

Another reason teens don't know what things actually cost is because their reference points are distorted. Social media, advertising, and influencer culture compress vast differences in income and background into a uniform aesthetic. A classmate might wear £300 trainers bought with birthday money or parent credit, while another teen with a part-time job assumes that's the "normal" spend. Without transparency, the price becomes the norm. And when norms are aspirational rather than realistic, the psychological burden intensifies. Financial shame sets in—not just about not having, but about not understanding *how* others afford what they do. The reality is, many don't. Buy-now-pay-later schemes, credit misuse, or quiet parental subsidisation often sit behind the scenes. But none of that is visible in the curated feed.

And herein lies the central paradox: teens are both overexposed to spending and undereducated about cost. They watch unboxing videos, product reviews, influencer hauls, and lifestyle vlogs daily—content that normalises consumption as performance. But they rarely see the real financial lives behind those purchases. They don't see debt repayments, or budgeting, or the anxiety of making ends meet. They don't see what's sacrificed to afford what's shown. And without that visibility, their own sense of financial competence deteriorates. They think they're failing because they can't keep up, when in fact, they're comparing their private reality to a public illusion.

To reverse this trend, we must re-teach cost as a *context*, not just a number. Teens need to learn not just "what something costs," but *what it costs them*, personally and psychologically.

Does this purchase expand my freedom or constrain it? Does it express something real or imitate something projected? Can I afford this not just in money, but in mental space, time, or stress? These are the questions that form the basis of financial agency. Not binary ideas of good vs. bad spending, but nuanced reflections on *fit, impact, and sustainability*.

Importantly, teens must be invited into these conversations with respect. They are not "too young to worry" or "too impulsive to learn." They are, in many cases, already worrying—but doing so alone, in silence, and without tools. What they need is not more advice from adults who shame their lattes, but frameworks that *honour the complexity of their spending decisions*. They need tools that help them visualise recurring costs, track peer-driven expenses, and anticipate pop-up demands. They need critical literacy to interpret marketing. And they need space to reflect on the *why* behind each transaction—not just the price.

Ultimately, teaching teens what things actually cost is not about thrift—it's about *truth*. The truth that spending is never neutral. The truth that invisible costs shape financial lives more than large purchases. The truth that awareness is a form of power, and that knowing is the first step to choosing. Not every teen will become a minimalist or a budget wizard. But every teen deserves the chance to spend with eyes wide open.

Spending vs. Signalling

Most financial advice begins with a simple assumption: people buy things because they need them. Yet in reality, that's rarely the full story. Much of modern spending—especially among teenagers and young adults—has little to do with utility, and everything to do with *identity projection*. We don't just buy to use; we buy to *signal*. To belong, to distinguish, to attract, or to deflect. In a hyper-visual world shaped by social feeds and rapid impression cycles, what we own increasingly functions as a language. And if you don't understand that language, you'll misread both your motivations and your money.

At the heart of signalling is a psychological truth: *we care what others think, often more than we care to admit.* This isn't mere vanity—it's evolutionary. For most of human history, survival hinged on group membership. Being accepted by the tribe wasn't a preference; it was a precondition for food, shelter, protection. Though today's threats are more psychological than physical, the need for social validation persists. The modern teenager, standing at the delicate intersection of identity formation and peer influence, is especially vulnerable to this. They are trying to answer one of life's most enduring questions: *Who am I, and how do I matter?* Purchases often become shorthand attempts at answering that.

This explains why someone might choose a £90 hoodie over a £20 one, not for warmth but for logo visibility. Or why AirPods, despite functional competitors at half the price, remain a teen status staple. It's not about sound quality—it's about being seen wearing them. Economists refer to these as *positional goods*—items whose value increases not because they are better, but because they are *perceived* to place the buyer in a better position relative to others. In this framework, the item is not the end goal. The *signal* is.

Crucially, this signalling doesn't require conscious intent. A 16-year-old may not articulate, "I bought this to increase my social capital." But they'll feel it viscerally—when peers comment, when looks linger, when silence suggests disapproval. The reward mechanisms are social and subtle. And this is what makes the pattern so insidious: most teens don't know they're signalling, which means they don't know when they're being manipulated.

Marketers understand this perfectly. Entire industries are built not around meeting needs, but around manufacturing them. Fashion doesn't change because clothes stop working. It changes because status hierarchies must be refreshed. The same is true for phones, shoes, bags, even water bottles. What matters isn't whether the product serves you, but whether it sends the *right message*. And when teenagers internalise this logic, spending decisions become performative. Budgets collapse not under necessity, but under the weight of *impression management*.

Social media accelerates this dynamic. On platforms like Instagram, TikTok, and Snapchat, signalling is not optional—it's baked into the architecture. Every post is a performance. Every comment a cue. The feed doesn't just show you what people own—it shows you *what it seems to mean* about them. This collapses the boundary between the person and the purchase. The person becomes the brand. And the brand must be curated constantly, or else relevance fades. It's not that teens are shallow; it's that they've been socialised into a system where surface is mistaken for substance.

The economic impact of this is rarely measured directly, but its fingerprints are everywhere. A teenager might spend more on an iPhone than they've ever earned in a summer job—not because they misunderstand the value of money, but because they've absorbed the message that *not* having it renders them invisible or less-than. Similarly, consider the rise of streetwear reselling. Teens queue overnight or scramble in digital lotteries to buy limited-edition trainers—not for comfort or practicality, but to access a kind of cultural currency. The resale market flips this into profit for some, but for most, it's a system of escalating cost for shrinking marginal gain.

It's easy to dismiss this as irrational. But it follows a logic—*a logic of belonging*. In environments where confidence is fragile and identity is still fluid, objects can offer temporary anchoring. They become proof points: I am stylish, I am successful, I am worth noticing. But the relief they bring is short-lived. Because signals must be updated. As soon as too many people have an item, it loses its status function. The hierarchy reshuffles. And so begins the churn—spend, post, replace, repeat.

This cycle has deep psychological consequences. For one, it trains young people to attach self-worth to external markers. If your esteem rises and falls with your latest purchase, you are financially exposed—and emotionally volatile. This can lead to a kind of financial dysmorphia, where a person's real economic situation is out of sync with the image they feel obliged to project. Someone may have £20 in their account but feel compelled to wear £200 trainers. Not out of arrogance, but out of fear—of being judged, dismissed, or socially exiled.

There's also the issue of *signalling fatigue*. The constant need to maintain an image is mentally and emotionally draining. It leaves little room for curiosity, experimentation, or financial experimentation. Every purchase must be strategic. Every outfit pre-approved. Every social moment monetised. And when people begin to live for the next post rather than the next experience, their relationship with money narrows. It becomes less about freedom or function, and more about optics.

Of course, not all signalling is toxic. Humans have always used objects to convey meaning. From wedding rings to team jerseys, to religious garments, signalling can also foster connection, pride, and shared identity. The problem is not that we signal. The problem is *when signalling becomes compulsory, unconscious, or disconnected from personal values*. In such cases, spending becomes alienating. Teens buy things they don't care about, with money they don't have, to impress people they don't even trust. The result is not just financial strain, but emotional numbness.

So what's the alternative? Awareness, first. Recognising the difference between *spending for use* and *spending for show* is a powerful psychological shift. It doesn't mean never buying branded goods—it means understanding *why* you want them.

Is it comfort? Quality? Social reassurance? Each answer is valid, but clarity changes the experience. It turns a passive consumer into an active participant. And that's the beginning of financial agency.

Second, teens must learn to identify their personal values—separate from trend cycles or social comparison. What do *you* care about? What kind of life are you building? What signals actually align with your goals, rather than distract from them? For some, that might mean investing in tools or resources that support a side hustle. For others, it might mean spending more on travel and less on tech. The key is coherence—making sure that your financial choices reflect your inner compass, not just external pressure.

Lastly, we need cultural permission to *opt out.* Not every teen can—or should—play the status game. Financial literacy means nothing without *social literacy*: the ability to say, "That's not for me," without shame. Adults play a role here, too. When parents, teachers, and mentors model honesty about money, acknowledge the emotional stakes of consumption, and praise value-aligned spending, they widen the path for teens to follow suit.

At its best, money is a tool for autonomy. But when spending becomes signalling, that autonomy erodes. The buyer is no longer in control—the audience is. And for teens, whose audiences are vast, vocal, and often unforgiving, the stakes are especially high. If we want a generation that spends wisely, we must teach them not just how to budget, but *how to see.* To see through the noise. To see their own patterns. And to see that the most powerful signal of all is *not needing to signal at all.*

When Friends Cost Too Much

The most expensive purchases teenagers make are often not the ones they consciously choose. They're the ones they feel they *can't say no to.* A casual dinner that drains a week's allowance. An impromptu Uber ride home from a party that's "only £12 each." A holiday plan casually floated in a group chat, assumed affordable to all. These moments, rarely discussed in financial terms, are saturated with emotional complexity. They are framed as social opportunities, rites of passage, or proof of loyalty. But underneath the laughter and bonding lies a subtle but powerful current: *peer pressure economics*—the quiet but consistent demand to spend in order to stay included.

Money, in adolescence, is rarely about arithmetic. It's about social coherence. Belonging often has a cost, and the currency isn't just financial—it's psychological. To say "I can't afford it" is, in many teen circles, tantamount to admitting inferiority, to marking oneself as different. And difference, at that age, often feels dangerous. A teenager's sense of self is still forming, and it draws stability from external cues: acceptance, similarity, unspoken rules. When money becomes the ticket to shared experience, saying no is not just a budgeting decision—it's a threat to one's social identity.

The challenge is compounded by the way modern friendships operate. Many social plans are spontaneous, digitally coordinated, and publicly visible. One missed outing can feel like a public exclusion. Worse, financial discomfort is almost never addressed directly. Teens will more readily admit to heartbreak than to being broke. The shame around "not having enough" isn't just economic—it's existential. It challenges the narrative of equality and freedom that friendships are supposed to uphold. But the truth is, financial inequality exists even among close friends. Some families quietly subsidise their children's lifestyles; others stretch to keep up appearances. The tension builds quietly until someone opts out—not from preference, but exhaustion.

And it's not just about big-ticket events. The micro-expenses add up quickly. A daily takeaway coffee "just to hang out." A split bill at a restaurant where you only had a starter. Chipping in for gifts, taxis, drinks, apps, and subscriptions. The costs are often invisible in the moment but brutal in aggregate. Teens rarely track them—and if they do, they often feel conflicted. They fear appearing stingy, uncool, or difficult. So they comply, then compensate by cutting back in private, skipping meals, delaying obligations, or borrowing silently.

This dynamic is not unique to adolescents, but it is amplified for them. Adults at least have income to anchor decisions. Teens rely on allowances, part-time jobs, or parental unpredictability. They often inhabit a paradoxical space: expected to behave like autonomous consumers but without the financial security to do so confidently. This leads to a distortion of financial boundaries. Some become chronic over-spenders to avoid rejection. Others isolate themselves to escape the pressure altogether. Both responses are rooted in the same dilemma: *How do I keep my friendships without losing control of my finances?*

There is, unfortunately, no universal script for resolving this. But clarity begins with recognising the core misunderstanding: that saying no to spending is the same as saying no to friendship. It isn't. True friendship can absorb boundaries. But that truth must be learned—and modelled. If no one speaks up, the illusion persists. Cultural permission is needed. And that begins with small, visible acts of financial self-respect: the friend who offers a cheaper alternative, the one who says, "Actually, I'm saving this month," or the group that rotates between pricey outings and free ones.

Setting boundaries is not a sign of weakness; it's a form of strength. It demonstrates a person's ability to prioritise their future while remaining honest in the present. For teens, this is difficult because the skill is rarely taught. Schools don't cover it. Parents often sidestep it, either out of discomfort or lack of insight. And peers don't reward it—at least not immediately. But over time, boundary-setting fosters a kind of integrity that both protects and clarifies relationships. The friends who respect your financial limits are more likely to respect your personal ones too.

This doesn't mean all financial peer pressure is malicious. Often, it's thoughtless rather than cruel. The person suggesting an expensive plan might have no idea it's burdensome to others. In groups, spending norms evolve quickly, and silence is easily mistaken for agreement. Which is why *someone speaking up* is so powerful. It breaks the trance. It opens the door for others to admit similar hesitations. Financial honesty is contagious—but someone has to go first.

Digital tools offer partial solutions. Apps that track spending, split bills, or facilitate group budgeting can reduce friction. But they can't replace conversation. What's missing isn't technology—it's *language*. Teens need scripts, not software. Simple phrases like "That's out of my budget," or "Could we find a cheaper option?" may feel awkward initially, but they normalise transparency. Over time, these microboundaries create macrochange. They rewire social expectations, making room for authenticity without austerity.

There's also a broader cultural conversation to be had here—about how society frames generosity, fun, and worth. Too often, spending is conflated with care. The person who "always pays" is admired. The one who declines is questioned. But generosity that depletes is not generosity—it's sacrifice. And when that sacrifice is driven by fear of exclusion, it's not noble; it's unhealthy. Young people must learn the difference between showing up emotionally and overextending financially. True connection doesn't demand financial proof.

For some teens, the answer may lie in finding more values-aligned circles. Not all friendships are meant to last, and some are simply too economically mismatched to sustain without pain. Recognising this doesn't mean abandoning people—but it may mean broadening one's social ecosystem. Seeking out friends who share similar financial attitudes can reduce the pressure to perform. These relationships tend to be more grounded, more reciprocal, and less emotionally expensive.

Ultimately, the most valuable lesson is this: *your financial wellbeing is part of your overall wellbeing*. If maintaining a friendship is consistently harming your ability to save, plan, or feel at ease, it is not a friendship—it is a transaction. And healthy relationships are not transactions. They are spaces where honesty is allowed, difference is respected, and personal growth is encouraged.

Helping teens internalise this requires adult support. Parents should avoid shaming spending patterns and instead engage in open-ended conversations: "How did that outing feel for you financially?" or "Was there anything you wished you could've done differently?" These discussions foster awareness without judgement. Teachers and mentors can reinforce the idea that financial boundaries are part of emotional intelligence. And media can play its part too, by showcasing characters and stories where saying no is celebrated, not mocked.

There is dignity in discernment. And when a young person learns to honour their own limits, they don't just protect their bank account—they protect their sense of self. In the long run, that self-respect will serve them far more than any outfit, dinner, or digital moment ever could. Because real friends don't just split bills. They make space for each other's truth—even when that truth is, "Not this time."

Budgeting for the Unpredictable

Most financial advice is built on the fantasy of predictability: steady paycheques, fixed expenses, and a clean, linear path between income and outgoings. But for teenagers and young adults—especially those relying on part-time jobs, side hustles, parental stipends, or gig work—income is rarely consistent. It's lumpy, seasonal, or sporadic. Expenses, meanwhile, often arrive unannounced: a friend's birthday dinner, a broken phone screen, an urgent textbook, or an impromptu festival ticket that "everyone" is going to. This mismatch between financial planning and financial reality creates a gap that conventional budgeting tools are ill-equipped to bridge. *What's needed is not just a budget, but an adaptive system—one that treats unpredictability not as a glitch, but as a given.*

The problem with most budgeting frameworks is that they assume financial life follows a stable rhythm. Income is treated as known, and expenses as controllable. But for most people under 20, neither assumption holds. A 17-year-old doing shifts at a café may earn £320 one month, £120 the next. A 19-year-old tutoring GCSE maths may land five students in February and zero in April. Even those with regular allowances face fluctuation when parents tie payment to behaviour, performance, or household contributions. In short, cash flow at this stage of life is not just inconsistent—it's structurally volatile. Yet few financial education models account for that volatility. Instead, they present monthly budgets as sacred, encouraging guilt when reality doesn't match the spreadsheet.

This disconnect breeds frustration. Many young people attempt budgeting, only to abandon it after a few weeks, convinced they've failed. But the failure isn't personal—it's architectural. They're applying a rigid model to a fluid environment. What's needed is a mindset shift: *move from precision to resilience.* Rather than aiming to track every pound perfectly, adaptive budgeting focuses on developing flexible habits, tolerances, and contingency planning that reflect how real financial lives unfold.

At the heart of adaptive budgeting is the idea of variable baselines. Rather than building your spending plan around a fixed income figure, you budget around *minimum guaranteed income.* If you know your worst-case monthly earnings are

£150, then your core expenses—transport, essentials, phone bill—must fit within that. Anything beyond is treated as surplus, not baseline. This way, your financial system becomes sustainable even in a bad month. When extra income arrives, it's a bonus, not a lifeline. This doesn't mean you live permanently restricted—it means you decouple *needs* from *nice-to-haves*, allowing flexibility without fragility.

Another critical tool is *percentage-based allocation*. Instead of assigning absolute numbers to categories ("£50 for food, £100 for fun"), you assign proportions of income to broad zones. For instance: 50% to essentials, 30% to flexible spending, 20% to saving or investing. If you earn £300 one month, that's £150, £90, and £60 respectively. If you earn £100 the next, the same ratio holds, just scaled down. This method mirrors the way most bills and needs behave in early financial life—relative rather than fixed. It allows for mental consistency across inconsistent cash flows, reducing planning stress and emotional volatility.

But adaptive budgeting also requires a change in temporal focus. Rather than budgeting by calendar month, many teens benefit more from *event-driven budgeting*. For example: "I'll set aside £40 for food until my next shift," or "This £100 must last until the end of the school break." This approach mirrors the way income is actually received—irregularly and tied to life rhythms. It shifts budgeting from a passive spreadsheet activity into an active, real-time decision-making skill. Instead of being something you check at the end of the month, your budget becomes something you *live through*, adjusting as conditions change.

This is especially powerful when dealing with pop-up costs. Pop-up costs are the expenses that never make it into formal budgets because they don't feel like part of "normal life." Yet they arrive with ruthless regularity: club dues, exam fees, friend emergencies, social pressures, limited-time offers. These are not aberrations—they are the very texture of youth finance. A resilient budget builds for them in advance, not in hindsight. This is where *buffer accounts* and *rolling categories* become useful. Rather than labelling every pound in advance, you maintain an "unassigned" category—essentially a small pool of idle cash designed for the unknown. The goal is not perfect allocation, but strategic slack.

Yet even with buffers and flexible categories, psychological discipline is needed. One of the least discussed aspects of budgeting is the emotional turbulence of variable income. When a teen gets paid £200 unexpectedly, it doesn't feel like *income*—it feels like *found money*. Behavioural economists call this "mental accounting": the tendency to treat different pools of money differently depending on how they arrive. Found money is spent faster, with less scrutiny. This is why *pre-committing allocations*—even rough ones—can dramatically improve outcomes. Before a windfall hits your account, decide: 20% to fun, 20% to short-term goals, 20% to savings, and the rest as flexible. Having a template preserves clarity in moments of excitement.

Another underappreciated challenge is the *emotional impact of lulls*. When income dries up—whether due to exams, illness, or seasonal gaps—young people can experience financial shame or anxiety that far exceeds the actual inconvenience. The feeling of "having no money" becomes a story about failure. Here, language matters. Teaching teens to distinguish between being *temporarily low on cash* and being *financially unstable* is critical. A dry week is not a disaster if it's expected and planned for. Normalising dry periods as a routine part of youth budgeting reduces panic and prevents desperate decisions (like selling possessions, taking on unnecessary debt, or cancelling long-term plans).

Peer dynamics complicate the picture. Inconsistent income is invisible, but social expectations are public. A teen might be between gigs or saving for university, but their friends are still going out. Declining invitations, explaining limits, or opting for cheaper alternatives takes courage. This is why budgeting is not just a private act—it's a *social skill*. Adaptive budgeting includes scripts, boundaries, and emotional rehearsals. It teaches not only how to manage money, but how to communicate your choices without shame.

Technology can support these habits but not replace them. Budgeting apps like YNAB (You Need A Budget) or Monzo's pots feature can help users allocate money dynamically, but the mindset has to precede the tool. Digital solutions work best when they are paired with reflective practices: weekly money check-ins, journaling financial feelings, setting micro-goals. Adaptive budgeting is not about rigid compliance—it's about staying emotionally engaged with your money in real time, without spiralling into either neglect or obsession.

Finally, there's a philosophical shift worth embracing: *budgeting is not about control—it's about clarity*. Most people abandon budgeting because they expect it to guarantee order. But in a life phase filled with flux, that's an unrealistic demand. A good budget does not eliminate chaos; it helps you navigate it with fewer blind spots. It won't make your income predictable, but it will make your responses intelligent. That alone is transformative.

Young people who internalise adaptive budgeting early enter adulthood with a powerful advantage. They learn that money is not static, that plans are not sacred, and that flexibility is not failure. They begin to see themselves not as victims of unpredictability but as designers of systems that *account for unpredictability*. And that lesson—that uncertainty doesn't preclude agency—is not just financial. It's foundational.

Chapter 4
How to Earn Before 20

Most young people first encounter money through allowances, summer jobs, or—more recently—TikTok side hustles. Yet these familiar entry points obscure a deeper truth: earning today is rarely linear. It is platform-dependent, mediated by algorithms, and often governed more by virality than merit. For teenagers attempting to grasp how money actually reaches their accounts, the rules are unclear, benchmarks fluctuate wildly, and the risks—wasted time, digital traps, misjudged value—are real. What is required is not a rigid map, but a new perspective on earning itself.

The modern challenge of income isn't simply "how to make money young"; it is incoherent access. There is no single gateway into the economy. Some resell items on Depop, others manage social media for a café, some offer niche skills on Fiverr, and yet others chase crypto or affiliate marketing schemes that yield nothing. Earning has become decentralised—no HR departments, no fixed schedules, no salary ladders—just a tangled spectrum of opportunity, distraction, and illusion. The first skill Gen Z must cultivate is discernment, not hustle.

A misleading narrative persists: that early earning is a lottery. Tales of teens making six figures overnight create distortion, setting the outlier as the benchmark. Consequently, a young person earning £80 dog-walking may feel behind, despite the experience being educational. Early earnings are feedback loops, not accolades. What worked? What didn't? Was it sustainable? Monetisation is not magic; it is reflection.

Meaningful earning is relational rather than transactional. It is not about extracting value from a platform, but offering solutions to someone's problem. The question shifts from "What hack can I try this week?" to "Whose life can I improve using my skills or knowledge?" This reframing transforms earning from ego-driven hustle to service-oriented creation, the bedrock of enduring business, freelance, or entrepreneurial ventures.

Yet many young people inherit a mindset shaped by optics rather than substance. Side hustles are judged on shareability, not sustainability. Teenagers brand themselves before creating real value. Performance eclipses learning. The Instagrammable hustle gets more attention than the profitable one.

This tension between signalling and producing is perilous in an era where visible activity often masks financial fragility. Teens may edit videos, post motivational content, and promote Etsy stores endlessly—yet never achieve net profit. Effort is visible, income invisible, and activity mistaken for earning. A quiet tutor charging £30 an hour may be more financially secure than a flamboyant "digital entrepreneur" with thousands of followers and no stable cash flow.

The antidote is grounded experimentation. Early earners treat each opportunity as a micro-laboratory, tracking time, outcomes, and energy. They do not chase scale but clarity. They monetise overlooked skills—teaching coding, editing essays, offering lessons, managing communities—not to dazzle, but to prove that skills can become solutions, and solutions are always valuable.

Even skill-based earning demands mental reframing. Many undervalue their abilities because they come easily. Video editing or Canva design may feel trivial, yet the market rewards outcomes, not effort. The skill lies in identifying friction in someone else's life and charging for resolving it—far more valuable than algorithm mastery.

Caution is essential. Youth earning is littered with half-truths, manipulative offers, and aesthetic scams. MLMs masquerade as "communities," dropshipping pipelines are "freedom blueprints," courses sell hope over substance. The constant? They frame income as acquired through alignment with gurus, not through marketable skill. Early discernment is armour: if the product is fantasy, walk away. Genuine opportunities are modest, imperfect, yet anchored in reality.

Even legitimate opportunities can flounder without a coherent framework. The objective is not just money, but cultivating an earning identity. Confidence in spotting problems, offering solutions, pricing time, and negotiating agreements matters more than immediate gain. Recognising busywork versus deep work, growth versus stagnation, short-term income versus long-term skill-building is a lifelong asset.

This challenges the notion that earning belongs after formal education. Early earning is a form of learning, offering lessons no classroom replicates: understanding client priorities, pricing impact, recovery from rejection, time management, coping with ambiguity and failure. Economic maturity grows through action, not theory.

Most importantly, early earning dismantles financial fatalism. Teens internalise the idea that money is reserved for parents, influencers, or professionals. Earning the first £40 through cleaning cars or building a landing page collapses that myth: money is value in motion, accessible to anyone offering solutions. It is a truth that requires experience to internalise.

This chapter does not list side hustles or promise shortcuts. It offers a lens: viewing earning as craft rather than chase, habit rather than hack. Platforms matter less than principles. And above all, it recognises the economic agency of teenagers—even before their twentieth birthday. Because that agency is real, and it is now.

The Income Problem No One Prepares You For

A teenager earning their first pound today is more likely to do so through a screen than a payslip. Gone are the days when early income was limited to paper rounds, retail jobs, or washing cars on weekends. In their place has emerged an economy that rewards digital fluency, platform agility, and algorithmic favour. For today's youth, income doesn't arrive neatly in envelopes on Fridays—it trickles in through online marketplaces, gig apps, creator dashboards, and peer-to-peer platforms. This shift has not merely changed how young people earn; it has upended what earning even means. Yet almost no one prepares them for this terrain—neither schools nor guardians, nor most mainstream financial advice. The disconnect is as much cultural as it is practical: young people are handed yesterday's economic vocabulary to navigate today's economic reality.

The structural scaffolding of teenage income has undergone a profound transformation. Where prior generations were socialised into the workforce through part-time employment—where responsibility, negotiation, scheduling, and interpersonal dynamics were all cultivated in embodied environments—young earners today are ushered into fragmented and gamified ecosystems that reward attention over consistency, virality over skill, and brand over effort. They are expected to build incomes from digital micro-roles: pet-sitting via apps, flipping vintage trainers on Depop, streaming gameplay for tips, or doing bite-sized tasks on Fiverr. While these may sound empowering on the surface—and in many ways they are—such fluid ecosystems also generate instability, invisibility, and emotional complexity that the "make and save" advice of traditional budgeting frameworks does not account for.

The psychological effects of gig-based or platform-tethered income are quietly shaping the financial habits of an entire generation. Irregularity becomes normalised: payments arrive late, unpredictably, or are subject to arbitrary platform rules. Earnings become detached from hours worked, as creative labour and algorithmic favour skew perceived input-output ratios. A TikTok creator might earn nothing for a week, then get a sponsorship deal worth £500 overnight. Conversely, a digital artist might log thirty hours of client outreach to land one commission worth £75. This detachment erodes the internal metric of value-for-effort—a core tenet of financial confidence. When income feels opaque and unstable, planning becomes harder, and self-doubt easier. Even accomplished young freelancers often report a background hum of uncertainty: *Will this last? Is this even real income? What do I do with it once I've got it?*

This is not just a psychological hurdle; it is a pedagogical vacuum. Most financial education, where it exists at all, is still structured around salaried paradigms: regular income, predictable tax deductions, employer pensions, monthly budgeting. There is scant instruction on how to price freelance work, navigate payment platforms, handle delayed invoices, or budget in weeks where income is zero. Nor is there much moral vocabulary for talking about this new kind of labour. Are you "working" if you edit videos at midnight for your YouTube channel that might, someday, generate ad revenue? Is it a "side hustle" if it doesn't pay yet, or is it self-exploitation in hope of imagined reward? Such questions are not incidental—they shape identity, effort, and financial risk tolerance in crucial ways.

Moreover, the mythology around early digital income is wildly polarised. On one side, social media celebrates teen entrepreneurs making five-figure dropshipping incomes or "quitting school to become creators," presenting platform earnings as democratic goldmines open to anyone with hustle. On the other, critics dismiss gig work as exploitative and hollow, painting all early income as unstable and soul-crushing. Both positions flatten the complexity of what it means to earn today. The truth lies somewhere between: many teens do earn real income in digital spaces—sometimes more than they could through formal part-time jobs—but often with higher volatility, less protection, and more emotional investment than adults appreciate.

The broader economic structure compounds the problem. Many platforms thrive by outsourcing risk onto their users. Whether you're selling products, delivering takeaways, or building an audience, the infrastructure benefits from your labour without guaranteeing your reward. Unlike employment contracts, these models offer no sick pay, no minimum wage, no protections. For a teen just beginning their financial life, this can blur crucial lines: between effort and return, between self-worth and algorithmic reach, between autonomy and precarity. Some will adapt quickly, learning to diversify platforms, price their work well, or build niche audiences. Others will internalise their income volatility as personal failure, misreading structural instability as a lack of talent or discipline.

Another complication lies in the tax and legal grey zones of early income. Teens making £200 a month through digital resales or social media services are often unaware of when income becomes declarable, or what counts as a business. Parents may not know either. Schools rarely mention it. Meanwhile, platforms—by design—frame the experience as "side" or "fun" work, downplaying its economic and legal implications. The result is a strange tension: a 17-year-old might earn more than a minimum wage worker but have no employer, no payslip, and no understanding of income tax thresholds. They are earners without employment, entrepreneurs without paperwork, taxpayers without guidance.

So, how should we make sense of this? First, by acknowledging that early income is no longer an appendage to the formal economy—it is a distinct economy, with its own rules, cultures, and pitfalls. We need frameworks that help young people read this space critically, not just navigate it transactionally. This means teaching adaptive budgeting, yes, but also emotional regulation, digital resilience, contract negotiation, and even platform ethics. It means helping teens distinguish between *earning* and *appearing to earn*—a difference that matters in online cultures that often monetise perception more than skill. It means preparing them for the loneliness of self-directed work, the vulnerability of public-facing income, and the reality that not all gigs scale—or should.

Secondly, we must shift how we value early income itself. Earning £30 from an online course you built yourself may be more educationally valuable than earning £300 at a one-off brand shoot, not because of the money but because of what you learned about product design, customer feedback, or ownership. Similarly, earning sporadic sums from several small clients can teach more about professional communication, resilience, and workflow than a single predictable paycheck. Yet such learning is often invisible to parents, teachers, and even the teens themselves, who have been taught to value stability over self-direction, consistency over experimentation.

Finally, we need to build a vocabulary around earning that is nuanced, respectful, and future-focused. Not all income is good income; not all hustle is healthy. At its best, early earning can be an on-ramp to independence, creativity, and competence. At its worst, it can become a treadmill of self-marketing, self-doubt, and burnout before adulthood even begins. Helping young people tell the difference is not just an economic imperative—it's a civic one.

The income problem no one prepares you for is not just about where the money comes from. It's about how you understand yourself in relation to it. Whether you're uploading a logo to a freelance site or babysitting for the neighbours, every act of early earning is also an act of identity-building. That means the question is never just *how do I earn more?* but also, *who am I becoming through the way I earn?* The sooner we start asking that, the better prepared we all will be for the economy ahead.

Side Hustles vs. Side Scams

Every generation discovers new ways to earn, but few have faced the volume of options—and illusions—that Gen Z now navigates. At first glance, the digital economy appears democratised, meritocratic, and brimming with possibility: start a dropshipping business from your bedroom, earn through affiliate links on TikTok, launch a course on Gumroad, or get paid to "just post content." But beneath this hyper-accessible surface lies a thicket of half-truths, monetised hype, and outright deception. For young people chasing early income, the central challenge is no longer just earning—it's discerning. What separates a legitimate income opportunity from a costly mirage? What's the difference between building a skill-based hustle and becoming collateral in someone else's funnel? These questions are urgent, and they're not theoretical. They shape the financial trajectory, mental health, and critical thinking of millions of young people trying to earn in an economy where the line between entrepreneur and exploited user is razor-thin.

The contemporary gig landscape is saturated with what could be termed *mirage work*: tasks or ventures that look like income paths but function more as digital decoys—offering appearance without substance, motion without progress. A 17-year-old might spend weeks promoting a cryptocurrency coin on Telegram thinking they're building a marketing portfolio, only to find themselves unpaid and ghosted. Another might enrol in a pricey "side hustle academy" only to discover it's 200 pages of recycled internet advice. These aren't fringe occurrences; they're part of the economic atmosphere. According to a 2023 survey by Morning Consult, nearly 60% of Gen Z say they plan to start a side hustle—but only 14% report consistent income from one. The gap between aspiration and outcome is wide, and the mechanisms behind that gap are often commercially engineered.

One of the most under-acknowledged drivers of the "side hustle illusion" is social media itself, not just as a promotional vehicle but as an ideological amplifier. On platforms like TikTok and Instagram, side hustles are aestheticised: visually curated, deceptively compressed, and emotionally persuasive. A 30-second clip might show a creator "making £2,000 in a week" by flipping products, but omit the context—capital investment, hours spent sourcing, the failure rate of listings, or even whether it was a one-off. What appears as hustle is often theatre. This isn't just misleading; it reshapes how young people internalise what work *is*. Instead of work being understood as a disciplined application of skills toward value creation, it becomes equated with short-term hacks, minimal effort, and algorithmic luck. *If you're not making easy money online, you're doing something wrong*—that's the implicit message.

To evaluate opportunities clearly, we need sharper criteria—less about aesthetics and more about structure. A genuine side hustle typically exhibits three core characteristics: *value exchange, skill development,* and *economic clarity.* In contrast, a side scam often depends on opacity: revenue models are vague, "success" stories are cherry-picked or faked, and the primary product is often not a good or service, but *belief in the system itself.* Multi-level marketing (MLM) schemes, for instance, cloak themselves in entrepreneurial language but often generate income primarily from recruitment rather than product sales. Similarly, paid online "mentorships" promising seven-figure results often sell confidence rather than competence—targeting aspiration rather than offering structure.

The epistemology of scams is worth unpacking. A scam today doesn't need to be illegal to be corrosive. Many so-called side hustles are legal yet economically irrational, relying on the new user's ignorance of opportunity cost. A young person who spends £80 on a "how to start an e-commerce empire" course might not be defrauded in the legal sense, but if that course merely regurgitates free YouTube content and yields no realistic outcomes, the damage is intellectual: it wastes time, flattens critical thinking, and replaces real learning with lifestyle mimicry. *You believed you were building capacity, but you were consuming a fantasy.*

There's also a generational vulnerability at play. Gen Z came of age in an era where the labour market was destabilised and wages decoupled from productivity. The promise of stable employment, rising wages, and employer-supported growth has all but evaporated. In its place are algorithmically-driven markets and platform economies that reward flexibility, branding, and short-termism. Against this backdrop, side hustles are not just income strategies—they are survival logic. So when a young person jumps at a chance to earn £500 quickly, even if the path is opaque or inflated, that decision often stems from economic precarity, not gullibility.

Complicating matters is the fact that many legitimate side hustles *begin* as unpaid efforts. A graphic designer might take on free projects to build a portfolio, or a writer may guest-post for visibility. This makes it harder to distinguish between strategic unpaid labour and exploitative ventures that rely on idealistic beginners. The test, then, lies in trajectory. Is the activity building transferable skill? Is there a clear economic mechanism for eventual payment? Are you learning how value is created—or simply burning energy to maintain the appearance of progress?

To cultivate discernment, young earners must adopt what might be called a *structural lens*: instead of asking "Is this easy money?", ask "What is the underlying model—and who benefits from my participation?" A YouTuber making £200 a month from ad revenue has a clear value path: views generate monetisation. A person selling used trainers on Depop knows the margin between cost and price. But a crypto project that pays you in its own token for posting promotional content? That's circular logic disguised as income. Similarly, a paid community where members sell "how to hustle" guides to each other is less a marketplace than an echo chamber.

There's a larger philosophical tension worth noting here: the collision between *self-actualisation* and *financial desperation*. The best side hustles emerge from interests aligned with market needs: a teen who loves photography starts charging for portraits; someone who enjoys writing builds a newsletter. But the internet often flips this relationship—encouraging people to chase money first and figure out skills later. This creates a culture of economic cosplay: adopting the posture of success without the substance. Over time, this undermines confidence. If every "grindset" influencer seems to be earning thousands by doing less than you, it's easy to feel like you're missing something—or failing. But often what's being missed is reality itself.

This makes mentorship vital—but not just from any source. Look for mentors who emphasise *process over promise*, who are transparent about failure, and who define success as cumulative skill-building, not isolated paydays. The most credible voices in the digital economy often speak modestly about their early earnings, admit to learning curves, and avoid hype. They treat income as a by-product of value—not as the product itself.

Importantly, the goal is not to scare people away from side hustles, but to help them approach the landscape with clarity and agency. The modern economy demands entrepreneurial experimentation. But experimentation without critical filters leads to burnout, sunk costs, and cynicism. A good side hustle should stretch your capacity, reward your curiosity, and make you smarter over time. A bad one will distract you, inflate your expectations, and leave you chasing phantoms.

At its best, a side hustle is not just income—it's rehearsal for autonomy. It teaches you to recognise patterns, manage risk, and trust your judgement. But that judgement must be informed. Not every low-barrier income stream is a scam, but *anything that promises high returns with low clarity deserves scrutiny*. The internet rewards speed, but earning rewards depth. And those who learn to slow down, ask hard questions, and see the mechanics behind the hype will not only avoid scams—they'll outlast them.

The First $100: A Skill-Test, Not a Jackpot

A hundred pounds. It's not a life-changing sum. It won't pay for university, buy a car, or even cover a week's groceries in many cities. And yet, for a teenager trying to earn money for the first time, that first £100 can carry the weight of something far greater than its face value. It represents the proof of possibility—the moment the abstract notion of "earning" becomes concrete. But only if that hundred is earned, not gifted; created, not clicked; built through skill, not luck. The first £100 is not a windfall. It is a stress test of ingenuity, discipline, and value creation. It is a psychological milestone dressed up as a financial one.

The cultural narrative around money has become distorted by extremes. On one side, social media platforms are flooded with stories of teens going viral, flipping NFTs, or trading crypto to "six figures before 18." On the other, the traditional advice still clings to lawn-mowing and babysitting as if the digital economy never happened. What's missing is a framework that treats early income not as a jackpot or a gimmick, but as a laboratory—a controlled environment to test what someone can offer to the world that's worth being paid for.

The first £100 you earn matters more than the next thousand, because it forces you to reckon with value, not volume.

Earning early is not about proving maturity; it's about learning leverage. When a young person makes their first £100 through a skill—design, tutoring, coding, writing, editing, reselling, or any honest service—they build the internal scaffolding for how money is generated. They stop seeing income as a fixed salary or a parental allowance and start recognising it as the result of solving a problem. This shift is subtle but profound. It changes the locus of control from external to internal, from dependency to initiative.

One of the most overlooked aspects of this early financial milestone is *the feedback loop it establishes between effort and outcome*. When a teenager realises that their time can be converted into money through something they already know or are learning to do, money stops being abstract. It becomes an output variable. This cognitive shift rewires how future opportunities are evaluated. Is this task scalable? Can it be repeated? Would someone else pay for this? These are entrepreneurial questions born not from textbooks, but from the lived experience of earning that first bit of income.

Compare this with the opposite scenario: a teen falls into a micro-scam that promises £100 in exchange for "clicking links" or promoting affiliate codes with no clear product. Or perhaps they spend hours on an online platform performing tasks that pay pennies per click, never quite understanding what they're part of. Yes, they may technically earn something. But what they walk away with is not confidence—it's confusion. They haven't learned a skill. They haven't created value. They've become participants in a game designed to use their time, not reward their talent. The lesson? *Not all income is instructional. Some is purely extractive.*

The genius of focusing on the first £100 as a skill-test lies in its bounded ambition. It sets a goal that is achievable without being trivial. It avoids the trap of grandiose earnings fantasies, while also rejecting the notion that young people can't or shouldn't earn. More importantly, it invites teens to start from where they already are. The most overlooked starting point in youth earning is not access to capital, mentorship, or platforms. It's inventory of skill.

Take, for example, a 16-year-old who has been using Canva to design social media graphics for their personal TikTok. They might not think of themselves as a designer. But their aesthetic sense, tool familiarity, and instinct for trends is *already* a skill set. What happens when that teenager offers to design three Instagram posts for a local café or tutor a friend in maths for a small fee? They're not just monetising their time—they're testing demand, building confidence, and gathering signal. The £100 they earn isn't just a reward. It's feedback from the world that says, *this skill matters enough to be paid for.*

This kind of early monetisation doesn't need to be perfect. It doesn't need to be formalised into a full-fledged business. But it *must* be anchored in authenticity. What is the person already good at, interested in, or asked about by others? What problem can they solve—however small—that is worth a modest payment? When the goal is £100, not £100,000, the scale becomes manageable. The process becomes instructive rather than overwhelming.

The platform economy complicates this, of course. Teens are now surrounded by monetisation options that blur the line between effort and illusion. YouTube ad revenue, affiliate marketing, print-on-demand stores, stock trading apps—these are often presented as quick paths to passive income. But most of them are deeply misleading when treated as entry points. They are not *starting lines*; they are *multipliers*. They require an underlying skill, audience, or asset to amplify. Without that, they don't teach value creation—they simulate it.

This is why the early earning phase must be reframed as *active learning, not passive hoping.* When young people are encouraged to approach their first earnings as a diagnostic—

What am I good at? What do people want? What am I willing to improve for pay?—they avoid the mental traps of both desperation and delusion. They also begin to develop what behavioural economists call "internal attribution bias": the belief that outcomes stem from one's own actions, not external randomness.

This is particularly important in a world where luck is frequently mistaken for merit. Viral videos, one-time flips, or algorithmic wins may look like skill. But without replicability, they don't build confidence. They build dependence on volatility. By contrast, when a teenager charges £10 for editing a podcast episode, and then gets hired again based on that quality, they are experiencing *earned validation*. The £100 that accumulates from repeatable, improvable effort creates not just income—it creates narrative. A personal sense of economic agency.

Educational institutions rarely teach this. Schools are structured around assessment, not value creation. Students are trained to seek marks, not markets. That makes the first £100 all the more crucial. It is the bridge between structured learning and self-directed application. It is the moment a young person realises that money doesn't just come from employment—it can also come from insight, usefulness, and trust.

And here's the secret: it doesn't matter if the skill that earns the first £100 is *the* skill they use for the rest of their lives. What matters is the *framework* they build from it. That framework asks questions like: What am I solving? Who am I helping? How can I improve? What do I charge—and why? These are foundational earning questions. And answering them early creates not just confidence, but discernment. It helps young people avoid scams, self-doubt, and the lure of passive-income fantasies. They no longer ask, "How do I make money fast?" They ask, *"What's worth doing that also pays?"*

The first £100 is not just about economics. It's about *identity integration*. It gives a teenager the proof that their interests, skills, and actions can align with financial outcomes. That alignment is rare. Most people spend decades chasing it. But those who experience it early develop a kind of financial intuition that is hard to teach and harder to fake. They stop being afraid of asking for money. They stop underpricing themselves. They start experimenting with higher-value skills, better clients, and smarter systems.

And so, we come back to the central premise: *the first £100 is a test, not a trophy.* It's not supposed to feel like a win. It's supposed to feel like a window. A view into the landscape of earning where every pound is a signal: of demand, trust, usefulness, and persistence. Teenagers who treat this first milestone with seriousness—not pressure, but intentionality—begin the process of earning not just money, but self-trust. And that, in the long run, is worth far more than the currency itself.

Building a Value-First Earning Mindset

The most transformative shift a young person can make in their relationship with money is to stop asking, *"How do I make more?"* and start asking, *"Who am I helping?"* That pivot—subtle in phrasing, radical in outcome—separates the fleeting illusion of hacks from the enduring force of value. Earning is not a scavenger hunt for loopholes. It is a process of relevance. And relevance begins with solving real problems.

In today's landscape, young earners are bombarded with monetisation schemes dressed in glamour: viral content, affiliate marketing pipelines, dropshipping promises, day-trading theatrics. Each claims to bypass effort, automate income, and generate passive streams with minimal friction. What these models rarely clarify is their dependence on *audience, access, capital,* or sheer algorithmic luck—factors that are neither teachable nor controllable. Worse still, they embed the wrong question into the mindset: *How can I extract?* rather than *How can I contribute?*

A value-first mindset inverts the dynamic. It begins not with platforms but with problems. Every pound earned becomes the byproduct of someone else's gain—something better, faster, easier, safer, more beautiful, more functional because you intervened. *Money, then, becomes a signal of usefulness, not cunning.* This reframing restores dignity to the act of earning and removes the performative anxiety that so often shadows today's young economic participants.

The shift is psychological before it is practical. It demands that teens and early earners let go of the fantasy that there is a *right trick*—a silver bullet, hidden method, or secret algorithm waiting to be cracked. It replaces that with a deeper inquiry: *What problem can I solve that someone will gladly pay to have resolved?* This is not a question answered overnight. But it is one worth living with.

Take, for instance, the difference between trying to "monetise a following" versus teaching GCSE revision skills online. The former often chases vanity—likes, impressions, surface-level attention. The latter identifies a specific need, offers targeted help, and charges for clarity. One depends on mass scale; the other on precise usefulness. One is fragile; the other, replicable. The mindset that produces the latter is not anti-ambition. It is anti-delusion.

Value-first earners understand something most people miss: *you don't need to invent a product to offer value—you need to identify friction.* Where are people stuck? Where are they overwhelmed? Where are they wasting time, making mistakes, or missing out? Every friction point is a potential source of income. Not because you trick someone into a transaction, but because you *reduce suffering or expand capacity.*

This mindset also invites humility. It acknowledges that early work will not be glamorous. The first problems you solve may be small: proofreading essays, helping a local business update their website, running errands for busy neighbours, or designing simple graphics. None of this will make headlines. But all of it is rooted in the same formula: *understand a need, offer a fix, build trust, get paid.* With each cycle, you strengthen the muscle of discernment—spotting real-world inefficiencies and pairing them with your own growing competence.

It's easy to scoff at this approach when the online world rewards spectacle. A teenager boasting "five income streams" from selling digital templates might seem like the new normal. But look closer. Often those income streams are thinly spread, highly volatile, and contingent on being early to a trend. They lack durability. They scale only when luck and timing align. In contrast, a teen who understands how to make a product photo look 20% better through lighting, styling, and editing—*and knows how to sell that service to five clients*—is operating from a stable base of value. Not only can that be repeated, it can be improved, taught, and scaled.

This leads us to another underdiscussed principle: *value creation precedes value capture.* Too many young earners skip this. They attempt to price, pitch, or monetise before they've even clarified what, exactly, they're making better. A value-first earner is not afraid to give away early effort in exchange for signal. They offer a free design, a demo session, or a short audit—not because they undervalue themselves, but because they want to learn what lands. They understand that *market feedback is more valuable than imaginary pricing confidence.*

In traditional education systems, students are rarely taught to think this way. Value is defined by grades, test scores, or conformity to rubrics. But in the economic world, value is asymmetric. One person's throwaway skill is another person's critical shortcut. The teenager who loves Excel may find it boring—but to a small business owner drowning in inventory spreadsheets, that same skill is worth £25 an hour. The mismatch between perceived effort and perceived relief is where pricing power lives. And recognising it requires *seeing through someone else's lens.*

This form of empathy—economic, not emotional—is a core pillar of value-first earning. It demands attention. Not to trends, but to people. What are they stuck on? What do they wish was easier? What tasks do they procrastinate on, outsource, or complain about? These are not abstract curiosities. They are indicators of monetisable friction. And noticing them builds a deeper type of financial literacy—one rooted in *problem fluency,* not product obsession.

There is a quiet confidence that develops in those who adopt this lens. They stop bouncing between side-hustle trends and start building a catalogue of solved problems. Each time they earn, it is with clarity: *This is why I was paid. This is what improved. This is what I can do again—better, faster, at higher rates.* The unpredictability of the gig economy becomes less scary when you are not blindly applying to tasks, but actively offering known value.

Importantly, this mindset also protects against burnout. Hacks and hustle culture teach you to "stack income streams" without teaching you to think about *personal bandwidth*. But when you are solving problems in ways that align with your strengths, energy flows differently. A value-first earner calibrates what they offer not just based on what people want, but also on what they can sustain. That self-awareness is a form of integrity. It prevents you from becoming a performer trapped in a game you didn't mean to join.

The long-term implications of this mindset cannot be overstated. A teenager who earns their first £500 by solving five different types of problems for real people has more earning intelligence than someone who made £2,000 from a one-time viral drop-shipping win. Why? Because their model is legible. Teachable. Expandable. They can hire, delegate, train, or scale based on what they've built. Their income is no longer a fluke—it's a function.

It's also worth noting what this mindset rejects. It rejects entitlement. No one is owed income because they are clever, passionate, or willing to work hard. The market doesn't pay for potential. It pays for relevance. That can be frustrating. But it is also liberating. Because it means *anyone*—regardless of age, background, or academic credentials—can enter the earning arena by paying attention and being useful.

This kind of mental architecture is rare. It is not taught in schools, nor easily found in mainstream influencer content. But it is what every enduring freelancer, entrepreneur, or service provider ultimately learns: *the money you make is the byproduct of the problems you solve.* And when you commit to solving real problems, you no longer need to chase the next hack. You've built something better: a career, however small, that starts with others and ends with you.

The value-first mindset is not a mindset of scarcity or purity. It's not about rejecting ambition or refusing to charge. It's about sequencing: create value *first*, then ask for money. This order builds trust, longevity, and reputation. And for a teenager navigating a sea of hype, that order is everything.

So if you're starting to earn, start here: what can I fix for someone else? And how well can I do it? If you answer that consistently, you will not only make money—you will become the kind of person who *knows how to earn it again.*

Chapter 5
How to Spend Without Screwing Yourself

Every time we part with money, we're casting a vote—not merely in pounds and pence, but in values. Yet few young people are taught to see spending this way. Lessons usually focus on what not to do: avoid overspending, save diligently, perhaps consider investing. Rarely is the conversation about how to spend deliberately, with awareness, and enough structure to safeguard both finances and joy. The predictable outcome? A generation oscillating between impulsive online purchases and guilt-laden restraint, all while puzzled at how money seems to disappear despite good intentions.

The issue is not spending itself. It is spending without a coherent system for deciding. Cultural narratives frame it in extremes: indulgent versus prudent, reckless versus wise. This binary is not merely outdated—it is corrosive. Discipline becomes synonymous with denial, pleasure is suspect, and logic battles emotion in a zero-sum fight. There is little space left for confident, balanced choices. The reality is that responsible spending is not about abstinence; it is about alignment.

Alignment demands clarity—not only about cost, but about meaning. What does this purchase signal about me? What need is it meeting—comfort, status, belonging, escape? What trade-offs are implied? What am I foregoing by saying yes? These are not abstract musings; they are practical prompts that shield earners from the quiet accumulation of regret that often follows thoughtless transactions. Modern spending is designed to bypass reflection: one tap, one swipe, one Face ID—and the money is gone, frequently without conscious memory.

Financial systems have traditionally prioritised tracking and budgeting over cognition and emotion. Yet psychology is where most spending battles are truly won—or lost. Consider the subtle distinction between "I deserve this" and "I'll regret this." Both arise from the same inner voice, seeking reward or comfort. Yet one is grounded in entitlement, the other in foresight. The challenge is not to eliminate emotional spending, but to refine it—to cultivate the ability to distinguish genuine self-care from self-sabotage masquerading as indulgence.

This becomes especially pertinent in a digital economy, where money increasingly feels intangible. Contactless payments, embedded wallets, and auto-renewing subscriptions have stripped away the tactile feedback once offered by handing over cash—a moment that naturally invited reflection. Today, purchases occur in frictionless spaces: the choice between shoes and savings vanishes; you just click. And that difference is consequential.

Rejecting technology is not the answer. The solution lies in building mental frameworks robust enough to withstand its seductions. This chapter introduces one such approach: the Four-Question Filter—a tool to slow the interval between desire and transaction. Its purpose is not to halt spending, but to shape it thoughtfully. Each purchase becomes a choice rather than a compulsion. Money becomes a tool for self-definition rather than self-deception.

We will also examine the "swipe habit"—those small, often invisible transactions that appear trivial individually but accumulate into significant structural leaks. Teenagers and young adults face a paradox: irregular income, unstable budgets, yet constant exposure to platforms optimised for addictive ease. Combine that with social pressures, algorithmic nudges, and the pressures of identity formation, and you get chronic misalignment. Discipline alone is insufficient; awareness is indispensable.

Yet awareness need not translate to guilt. Intentional, thoughtful spending can be joyous, restorative, and expressive. Money, when directed consciously, communicates priorities, strengthens relationships, amplifies learning, and signals self-respect. The issue is not spending itself, but spending unconsciously, reflexively, or from fear—fear of missing out, of not keeping pace, of appearing cheap or uninspired. The antidote is not austerity, but autonomy.

Spending well requires precision—not merely in numbers, but in motive. It demands a shift from arithmetic to reflection, from restraint to expression. When young people learn to interrogate the why behind every what, they begin to rewrite the script of consumption. They spend less on what others admire, more on what genuinely matters. They choose function over flash, presence over panic, and, crucially, they protect the future without sacrificing the present.

This chapter is not about rules. It is about cultivating wisdom. It is for those exhausted by overspending and underthinking, ready to examine habits without self-reproach, and willing to see that money—like time—is more than a resource; it is a mirror. How you spend reveals what you value. Look closely, ask honestly, answer clearly—and you will do more than spend wisely. You will understand yourself more profoundly.

The 4-Question Filter for Every Purchase

Modern spending rarely feels like a decision. It feels like a reaction—swift, ambient, and emotionally justified in the moment. A £4 coffee because you're running late. A £12 streaming subscription you forgot you had. A £90 pair of trainers because they were 20% off, and you told yourself you'd regret not getting them. What's more troubling is that, in hindsight, few of these choices ever feel worth revisiting. There's no critical audit. No reflection. Just accumulation—of transactions, of clutter, of a quiet anxiety about where your money keeps going. This is not a budgeting issue. It is a thinking issue. More precisely, a *decision design* issue. And the tool to solve it begins not with an app, but with four deceptively simple questions.

But first, why questions? Because unlike rules, questions don't impose—they reveal. They encourage autonomy, reflection, and pattern recognition. They equip you to confront desire without dismissing it. They make space for nuance, rather than relying on binary labels like "need" versus "want." And when used consistently, they build a form of internal calibration—one that resists manipulation from marketing, trends, or the emotional volatility of your worst day. *Every purchase you make is an identity claim.* The question is whether it's a conscious one.

1. Does this purchase reflect my values, or my mood?

This is the fulcrum. Most spending happens as a response to *how we feel*, not to *what we believe*. You buy takeout not because you lack food, but because you're stressed. You splurge on skincare not because it's urgent, but because you're anxious or seeking control. Emotions are not inherently dangerous. But unexamined, they override clarity. When you pause to ask if a purchase reflects your values—say, health, learning, self-expression, generosity—you bring intention back into the transaction. If it doesn't align, you don't necessarily need to say no. But you'll be saying yes with eyes open. *Mood-based spending is impulsive. Values-based spending is deliberate.*

Consider someone who deeply values creativity but finds themselves endlessly buying convenience-driven tech accessories or fast fashion. The issue isn't the cost—it's the misalignment. They're consuming things that reflect how they feel temporarily, not who they want to be sustainably. This dissonance creates regret. Not because the item was objectively bad, but because it pulled them further from their self-concept.

2. What is the real cost—beyond the price tag?

The price is never the full cost. Every purchase also has an *opportunity cost*—what else that money could have gone toward. It may also have an *emotional cost*—guilt, distraction, clutter, or the discomfort of misalignment. Then there's the *time cost*—not just how long you worked to earn the money, but how much time you'll spend maintaining, justifying, or worrying about the thing once you own it.

Take the example of a £60 impulse buy on a weekend trip. The monetary cost seems minor. But you worked three hours to earn that £60 after tax. You spent ten minutes deciding to buy it. You'll spend perhaps another hour over the next few weeks deciding where to store it, whether to return it, or why you don't feel as excited about it anymore. All in, the "small" decision consumed over four hours of your life. When you start measuring purchases in time, not just currency, your sense of value sharpens. *Money is fungible. Time is not.*

3. Am I buying this for its function—or for what it signals?

Status is a quiet, relentless driver of modern consumption. Much of what we buy signals something—taste, success, tastefulness, independence. And that's not inherently wrong. But when the signal *replaces* the function as your primary reason for purchasing, you're entering dangerous terrain.

Take fitness gear. There's a difference between buying a pair of quality trainers because you run every morning and buying them because they're trending on TikTok. One is a functional enhancement of a habit. The other is a symbolic gesture—often to others more than to yourself. Of course, many purchases can be both. A MacBook can be both a design tool and a prestige object. A designer handbag can be both a practical item and a cultural flex. The question is whether you're aware of which reason is dominant. *If your spending is driven more by what it says than by what it does, your finances are likely performing for others, not serving you.*

4. What will this look like in 30 days—useful, neutral, or regrettable?

Future pacing is one of the most powerful antidotes to impulsive spending. This question forces you to zoom out—beyond the excitement, the sale countdown, the novelty. It asks you to imagine the item once the dopamine wears off. Will it still hold value? Will you be using it, wearing it, benefiting from it? Or will it join the graveyard of near-new possessions collecting dust, acting as silent reminders of your fragmented attention?

Most regret is not from *big* purchases—it's from the low-level noise of continual *small*, emotionally-driven purchases that age poorly. By asking this question, you compel your future self into the decision room. And that self tends to have better perspective. *Impulse serves the present. Wisdom defers to the future.*

These four questions aren't just filters. Over time, they become habits of mind. They teach you to pause—not in paralysis, but in presence. In a world designed to monetise your impulses, the ability to slow down, to interrogate your wants, and to align your money with your values becomes a radical act of autonomy.

It's also worth noting what these questions are *not*. They're not rigid rules. They don't shame pleasure or reward only frugality. They don't reduce spending to a cold calculus of need. Instead, they make spending *visible*. They bring you back into relationship with your money—so it becomes a tool for self-knowledge, not self-avoidance.

In application, the questions don't need to take long. With practice, they become near-instant. You see an ad. You feel the pull. But instead of tapping "Buy Now," you ask, "Wait—do I want this, or do I just want to feel better right now?" Often, that's enough to create space. And in that space, better choices emerge. More aligned ones. Ones that reinforce your identity instead of dilute it.

Ultimately, the four-question filter is not about saying "no" more often. It's about saying "yes" with clarity. To things that matter. To purchases that endure. To choices that reflect *you*, not your feed, your stress, or your surroundings. And once you build that muscle, spending becomes not just a financial act—but a moral one. Not in the sense of good or bad, but in the deeper sense of *who you are choosing to be* with every pound you send out into the world.

"I Deserve It" vs. "I'll Regret It"

Few phrases are more seductive—and more financially hazardous—than "I deserve it." It cloaks desire in the language of self-worth, implying that restraint would somehow be self-denial. It appears virtuous, even therapeutic. After all, who could argue with rewarding oneself for hard work, perseverance, or emotional turbulence? Yet, beneath this seemingly empowering mantra often lies a dangerous conflation of *reward* and *relief*, of *value* and *validation*. The real test isn't whether you "deserve" to spend, but whether the act of spending will actually deliver what you're hoping to feel. This is where regret enters the picture—not as a moral reprimand, but as a signal of misalignment between impulse and intention. The distinction between healthy self-reward and reckless self-justification is not philosophical—it is practical, and it often begins with timing, clarity, and emotional honesty.

Consider the behavioural dynamic. When someone says, "I deserve this," it's almost never in a calm, well-resourced state. It's uttered when tired, overextended, anxious, or emotionally depleted. It is often a plea, not a plan. What's being sought is not the item itself, but an emotional state—comfort, control, relief, validation. This makes the transaction less about consumption and more about compensation. You are buying to *fix* something, not to *enrich* something. The item becomes a stand-in for needs that are rarely financial: boundaries, rest, recognition, affirmation. But credit cards don't provide closure. And most purchases acquired from this psychological space do not age well.

The problem isn't emotional spending per se—emotions are involved in all decisions, even the most rational ones. The problem arises when *emotion becomes the justification* rather than the context. Let's say you've had a difficult week at work. You're drained, irritable, and the thought of cooking dinner feels Herculean. So you order from an expensive restaurant and scroll for a new gadget while you wait. Your internal monologue whispers, "You've earned this." And maybe you have. But the deeper question is: *What are you actually trying to resolve?* Is it hunger? Exhaustion? The sense that your efforts go unrecognised? If the purchase is meeting a real, present need—nutrition, downtime, convenience—then it's fair game. But if it's a proxy for unmet emotional needs, you're paying a premium for a fleeting illusion of relief. *True self-care doesn't require debt.*

Let's flip the script. What happens when you ask, instead, "Will I regret this?" It's a sobering pause. Regret requires projecting yourself into the future and imagining the emotional residue of a decision. This activates the prefrontal cortex—responsible for planning and long-term thinking—rather than the limbic system, which drives immediate gratification. The question doesn't moralise the purchase. It simply tests its durability. Will this object, subscription, meal, or experience still feel worth it when the mood has passed? If the answer is yes, the decision has integrity. If not, the purchase becomes a transaction with your future self—who, unlike your present self, will not be grateful for the bill or the clutter.

Emotional spending becomes particularly fraught in an age of algorithmic nudges. Social media and e-commerce platforms are designed to trigger emotional reactivity—offering the dopamine hit of a quick buy as a solution to existential fatigue. The "Treat Yourself" culture capitalises on the discomfort of restraint, spinning discipline as repression and indulgence as empowerment. But here's the paradox: the more often you buy something to feel better, the less effective it becomes. Dopamine habituates. What felt like a reward yesterday becomes baseline expectation tomorrow. The £20 splurge becomes £50. The exception becomes the norm. *The cost of short-term comfort is often long-term ambiguity about what truly brings you joy.*

To complicate matters, not all regret is equal. Some is immediate—realising you didn't need what you just bought. Some is delayed—only noticing the impact when your bank statement reminds you. And some is ambient—an ongoing sense of dissatisfaction that's hard to trace to any one decision, but rooted in an overall pattern of misaligned consumption. This last form is the most insidious because it doesn't feel like an event; it feels like background noise. You're always spending, never satisfied, always slightly guilty. And the most dangerous part? You start believing that's normal.

So how do you distinguish healthy emotional self-reward from reckless self-justification? Start by asking *when* you feel compelled to spend. Is it during moments of stress, loneliness, or boredom? Or is it after moments of effort, growth, or creativity? The former often leads to regret, the latter to reinforcement. Also observe *how* the decision unfolds. Does it feel expansive or urgent? Are you curious or compulsive? Are you seeking to celebrate your life or escape it? These aren't rhetorical questions—they are diagnostic tools for financial clarity. *You don't need to avoid emotional spending. You need to understand the emotion behind it.*

There's also a cultural dimension to the "I deserve it" narrative. It is disproportionately targeted at those conditioned to feel they must justify every indulgence: women, caregivers, working-class earners, perfectionists. When society teaches you to prioritise others, any act of self-investment can feel radical—and thus dangerous. Marketers exploit this by framing consumption as rebellion, as empowerment. But self-worth should not be contingent on consumption. You do not need to prove your value by spending money on yourself. *The strongest expression of self-respect is not how much you can buy—it's how aligned your purchases are with what you truly value.*

That's not to say you shouldn't buy things that feel good. You should. But the best self-rewards are those that honour both your present emotions and your future priorities. A massage after a long month? Excellent. A solo day at the cinema? Beautiful. A meal with friends to mark a milestone? Essential. The difference is in the *integration*—where the purchase is an extension of how you live, not a detour from how you wish you felt. Spending becomes generative rather than compensatory.

It helps to build rituals of intentional reward. Decide in advance what constitutes a meaningful treat. Set a self-care budget that allows you to enjoy pleasure without guilt. Curate a list of non-monetary ways to recharge—journaling, walking, reconnecting with someone. These are not restrictions; they are reinforcements. They protect you from spending that undermines your wellbeing under the guise of serving it.

To spend intentionally is not to be joyless. It's to be discerning. It's to recognise that you are not your cravings, and that treating yourself should not feel like a betrayal once the receipt arrives. *Mature spending isn't austere—it's anchored.* It reflects not just what you want, but what you want to remember about your choices. Regret, in this context, becomes not a punishment but a teacher. It shows you the cost of unexamined desire and invites you to choose again—this time, with more presence.

In the end, the question isn't whether you deserve it. You probably do. The question is whether that deservingness is best honoured by spending—or by something deeper, quieter, and ultimately more nourishing. When the answer to that question becomes instinctive, you're no longer at war with your wallet. You're in conversation with it. And that is where financial peace begins.

Breaking the Swipe Habit

There is something disarmingly frictionless about a digital wallet. A tap, a blink, a chime—and a transaction vanishes into the cloud. No cash exchanged, no signatures required, no receipts unless you go looking. You might walk away from a purchase without even noticing you've spent money at all. This frictionless convenience is precisely the problem. It has decoupled the *experience of spending* from the *awareness of cost*, creating a behavioural blind spot that drains wealth quietly, gradually, and often invisibly. In a world optimised for speed and automation, the challenge is not just to spend less—it is to *remember* that we are spending at all.

This is the silent tax of swipe culture: the erosion of financial mindfulness in exchange for convenience. Studies in behavioural economics consistently show that we spend more when paying with cards than with cash. Digital wallets intensify this effect, introducing not only psychological distance from money but also temporal distortion. When a £7 subscription renews silently in the background, or a coffee costs £5 via Apple Pay and no physical note changes hands, the experience of financial loss is muted. The transaction feels less like a decision and more like a default—part of the ambient hum of life. *You are not overspending because you are reckless. You are overspending because the system is designed to make you forget you're spending.*

This isn't conjecture. Data from the Bank of England and fintech platforms consistently show that contactless and mobile-based spending is less frequently tracked by consumers and more likely to result in over-budgeting errors. And it's not just large purchases—it's the repetition of small, unconscious ones. The late-night takeaway ordered with a facial scan. The £3.99 app trial you forgot to cancel. The round of drinks you authorised with a watch tap. Each of these is individually negligible. Collectively, they shape a financial narrative built not on extravagant mistakes but on micro-failures of attention.

The psychology behind this is well understood. When you swipe or tap to pay, you bypass the physical cues of loss. There is no wallet being opened, no notes being handed over, no tactile moment to pause. The human brain evolved to assess loss based on sensory and emotional cues. When those cues are dulled, so is our sense of consequence. Digital interfaces exploit this by making payment a design feature, not a decision point. UX design, intended to enhance user satisfaction, paradoxically removes the very friction that prompts restraint. You're not just paying quickly—you're *paying mindlessly*.

This becomes especially problematic for younger earners, many of whom have never developed the habits of physical money management. A teenager who earns money via a digital platform and spends via a digital wallet may never encounter a ten-pound note in the process. They live within a closed loop of transactions that feel intangible, even abstract. Budgeting in this environment is like navigating a landscape without gravity—fluid, fast, and disorienting. Financial literacy must therefore begin not with spreadsheets but with *perception training*—the art of noticing what has been intentionally made invisible.

To break the swipe habit, one must first understand that it is not merely a payment method—it is a behavioural system. It is a design-driven environment built on subtle cues, default settings, and cognitive blind spots. Breaking the habit doesn't mean abandoning digital tools altogether. It means *reinstating friction* where it has been removed, restoring pause points in an ecosystem optimised for unconscious flow.

One of the most effective interventions is the reintroduction of manual tracking. Not via automation, but by *requiring yourself to log every expense*. This transforms a passive tap into an active entry. The act of writing—by hand, by voice, or even in a notes app—forces you to re-engage with the reality of cost. It makes spending conscious again. A £5 snack entered manually has more behavioural weight than a £10 impulse buy forgotten by evening. You cannot change what you do not register.

A second method is delaying digital approvals. Instead of enabling one-tap payments, set devices to require biometric confirmation or manual code input—even for minor purchases. This momentary friction acts as a speed bump, not a blockade. It's not about inconvenience for its own sake; it's about *anchoring attention* in the decision. When you need to pause for a password or confirm your face ID, the mind has a chance to ask: *Do I actually want this?* A five-second delay can recover a five-pound loss.

Subscription management is another front in this behavioural battle. Most digital wallet users carry dozens of micro-subscriptions—streaming platforms, learning apps, fitness tools, cloud storage, in-game upgrades—each one trivial on its own but cumulatively significant. These payments often renew without review, protected by inertia and apathy. Break this pattern by setting monthly "subscription audits"—a recurring calendar event that forces review of all active services. If you cannot remember the last time you used it, cancel it. If it's bundled with emotional guilt ("I should be using this more"), cancel it anyway. *Money tied to shame is not value. It is procrastination disguised as self-investment.*

The swipe habit is also fed by reward structures. Loyalty schemes, cashback offers, gamified interfaces—all are built to reward frequency, not discernment. You get points for spending, not saving. The psychological effect is that spending feels like winning. This perverts the logic of money, where accumulation, not activity, creates strength. To recalibrate this, consider implementing your own inverse rewards: every time you *don't* buy something you were tempted by, transfer that amount to a separate savings pot. Call it "the no-thanks fund." Over time, this not only builds savings—it builds discernment, by showing that *restraint has outcomes, too*.

There is a philosophical dimension here, as well. In traditional economies, money was both tool and symbol. It carried social weight, moral framing, and physical form. The digitisation of finance has stripped it of all but utility. But in doing so, it has also stripped away the rituals that once reinforced responsibility. Swiping, by design, is ritual-less. To restore discipline, we must restore ritual—moments of reflection, decision-making, and narrative. This doesn't mean romanticising cash. It means embedding meaning back into money. A cup of coffee bought with full attention tastes better, lingers longer, and is remembered tomorrow. A swipe is over before the espresso cools.

The solution is not technophobia. It is techno-literacy. The tools are not the enemy. The enemy is autopilot. And autopilot is most dangerous when you don't realise it has been activated. A digital wallet, when used with awareness, can be a powerful budgeting ally. Real-time alerts, spend categorisation, and instant transfers can empower the user. But *these benefits must be chosen, not assumed*. Passive spending leads to passive living. If you cannot feel your finances, you cannot fix them.

To break the swipe habit is to reclaim authorship over your choices. It is to say: I do not want my financial life dictated by interface design and impulse frequency. I want it guided by memory, clarity, and alignment. Every tap is a sentence in the story of your money. When those sentences are written unconsciously, the story veers off course. But when written with presence, the story becomes coherent. And that coherence is not only financial—it is existential. For how we spend is ultimately how we live. And swiping may be seamless, but a life without seams is a life without structure. Better to feel a little friction than to feel nothing at all.

Making Room for Joyful Spending

For all the guidance offered about cutting back, tightening belts, and living below one's means, it is striking how rarely personal finance advice gives sustained attention to one of its most human questions: *What makes spending feel good, and why should we make space for that?* The prevailing narrative frames joy as suspect—pleasure as indulgent, spontaneity as financially reckless, and enjoyment as something to be explained away with guilt. But this is not prudence; it is economic puritanism. And it doesn't work. The refusal to acknowledge that spending can and should generate happiness leads not to discipline, but to repression—one that erupts, inevitably, in unplanned, unconscious bursts of compensation. If the budget is all sacrifice and no soul, it will be ignored. Not because the person is irresponsible, but because the plan was inhumane.

Making room for joyful spending is not a loophole in the system. It is *part of the system.* A sound, durable financial philosophy must accommodate the psychology of motivation. People are not machines optimised for maximising utility. They are narrative-driven, emotion-saturated creatures who must find meaning in what they do with their money. To spend without joy is to budget like a robot. To spend with guilt is to lose twice—once in funds, again in spirit. True financial maturity is not just knowing how to save; it is knowing *when to spend with purpose and delight.*

The starting point is redefining the concept of "deservedness." Much of consumer marketing is predicated on the logic of emotional reward: "You've worked hard—treat yourself." But this is a blunt instrument. It collapses all forms of effort and fatigue into a single justification for spending, often bypassing questions of intention, value, or consequence. Worse still, it casts spending as an emotional salve, rather than a conscious choice. This is where joyful spending diverges from reflexive self-reward. *Joyful spending is not compensation. It is connection—between money and meaning, action and identity.*

To make space for that kind of spending, the first task is to *define your values with specificity*. Generic financial goals—"save more," "spend less," "be responsible"—are unhelpful because they lack emotional resonance. In contrast, when people articulate what they actually want their money to *do*, decisions become far clearer. For one person, joyful spending might mean regular solo travel that creates memories and fosters independence. For another, it might mean splurging on high-quality cookware to nourish a daily ritual of home-cooked meals. The critical shift is from asking, "What can I afford?" to "What adds value to my life?" *Cost without context is meaningless. Spending aligned with values becomes sustainable because it is grounded.*

This clarity makes it possible to separate short-term cravings from long-term nourishment. Not all pleasures are equal in impact. A new gadget may offer dopamine for a week, but attending a live event that speaks to your identity—music, sport, literature—can linger in memory and self-conception for years. Joyful spending, therefore, is not merely about what feels good in the moment. It's about *spending that resonates beyond the moment*. Its value is not just transactional but experiential and existential. And because it feels fulfilling, it *reduces the urge to spend unconsciously elsewhere.*

Behavioural science supports this idea. Studies on happiness economics consistently show that experiences yield more lasting satisfaction than material goods. But the principle extends further: even within material purchases, the degree of personal alignment determines how joyful the spending feels. Buying a stylish, well-made bag that reflects your personal aesthetic and supports an ethical manufacturer can deliver more enduring satisfaction than three cheaper bags bought on impulse during a sale. The lesson is not to avoid spending on things—but to *spend like an editor, not a collector*. Be deliberate. Be personal. Be slow enough to be sure.

This brings us to another critical point: joyful spending requires *deliberate budgeting*. Not because joy needs restriction, but because *room must be created for it*. Just as a good diet makes space for indulgences that matter—desserts shared, wines appreciated—so too should a financial plan include a category for intentional delight. Call it your "joy fund" if you like. The point is to *budget for happiness proactively*, not retroactively justify it. That reframes joy not as an accident, but as a principle. And that makes the practice sustainable.

The difference is palpable. When joy spending is pre-allocated, it feels light and expansive. There's no internal debate, no guilt negotiation, no self-manipulation. The money is there, and its purpose is clear. You can spend freely *within defined bounds*. This reinforces both autonomy and trust in your financial system. On the other hand, when spending is reactive—triggered by emotion or exhaustion—the experience is often tainted by ambiguity: Was this worth it? Did I just sabotage my goals? Will I regret this tomorrow? Joyful spending removes the ambiguity because *the rules are known and the intent is sound*.

Another point often missed in traditional finance literature is that *joyful spending is deeply personal and sometimes socially subversive*. What makes one person light up may strike another as trivial or foolish. That's precisely why your spending plan must be anchored in your own values—not in others' expectations. A young person may derive real satisfaction from upgrading their home desk setup with ergonomic tools and design elements. To others, that may seem excessive. But if the setup improves daily focus, physical health, and a sense of personal investment in their work, then the expense is not frivolous—it is meaningful. *Money should not serve the illusion of wealth. It should serve the reality of meaning.*

To defend joyful spending is also to resist two common traps: performative frugality and status mimicry. In the former, people deny themselves reasonable pleasures out of performative virtue—saving for saving's sake, abstaining from coffee or meals out not because they can't afford them, but because austerity has become their identity. This is a form of emotional rigidity masquerading as discipline. In the latter, people spend not from joy but from imitation—purchasing what peers value, what influencers display, or what the market signals as aspirational. This creates a loop of anxiety, where spending is never satisfying because it is never fully *yours*.

True joyful spending breaks both patterns. It asks not "What would others admire?" or "What would make me seem responsible?" but "What deepens my experience of being alive?" This can be as small as a morning pastry from your favourite local café or as large as a weekend retreat that restores your mental health. The amount is not what makes it joyful. *The intent and alignment do.* And that's the point. When money flows toward what matters, it flows with meaning.

To reach that state, however, we must cultivate not only permission, but *attention*. Many people have no idea what actually brings them joy because they've never studied their spending history for emotional impact. Try reviewing the past three months of expenses. Which purchases do you remember fondly? Which do you regret or not remember at all? What patterns emerge? Joy leaves a trace. Regret often does not.

Learning to distinguish these signals is a skill, and like any skill, it sharpens with practice.

The final insight is philosophical. Joy is not the opposite of discipline. It is what makes discipline worthwhile. Saving is not a virtue unto itself. It is the act of preparing to say yes to the right things. And when you say yes at the right time, to the right thing, with the right mindset, there is no guilt to be found. There is only alignment. That is the essence of joyful spending. It is not hedonic. It is not mindless. It is *intentional happiness*, funded by clarity and sustained by design. To make room for it is not to betray prudence. It is to prove that prudence can support a life worth living.

Chapter 6
Saving Without Feeling Deprived

The challenge with saving is rarely laziness, shortsightedness, or irresponsibility. For many young people—teenagers and twenty-somethings just beginning to grasp financial agency—saving can feel like stepping to the sidelines of life's main event. The world encourages "living in the moment," peers spend openly and often, and the benefits of saving are abstract, distant, or invisible. Saving, as it is usually framed, feels less like empowerment and more like loss dressed in responsibility.

But perhaps that framing is precisely the obstacle. What if saving were not about sacrifice, but about amplifying what matters—both now and in the future? Shifting this perspective requires rethinking both the mechanics and the meaning of saving. This isn't about trickery or enforcing discipline for its own sake. It is about redesigning the emotional architecture of money so that setting funds aside feels energising, not punishing—a reflection of identity rather than austerity.

At its core, money is a time machine. It allows today's effort to create tomorrow's freedom. Yet time machines are difficult to appreciate without a clear vision of the destination. For many Gen Z earners, uncertainty clouds the horizon—economic, environmental, social. Asking them to "delay gratification" without a sense of what they are waiting for is like urging someone to walk into fog on the promise of a castle ahead. Abstract goals fail to motivate; tangible ones compel.

Effective saving strategies, therefore, rely on structure rather than restriction—systems that mirror the rhythms of actual life. The classic "save what's left" approach is too vague and punitive. A teenager navigating side gigs, freelance work, or seasonal employment needs more than guilt; they need a framework that reflects how money moves in and out of their lives. The 3-Bucket Saving Method offers one such system, dividing income into short-term, mid-term, and long-term categories—each with a defined purpose, a clear horizon, and an emotional payoff. Saving for next month's essentials is not the same as saving for a summer trip or five years down the line. Blurring these goals breeds confusion; separating them cultivates clarity, momentum, and motivation.

Structure alone, however, is insufficient if the process feels cold. Humans—especially young savers—are wired for feedback. Progress must be visible, goals tangible, and small wins celebrated. Gamifying saving—through visual trackers, tiered challenges, or incremental milestones—transforms abstract discipline into a concrete experience. Watching a savings tracker grow week by week engages the same reward circuitry as a fitness app or game level. It is not trivial; it is neurobiologically sound. Visibility renews motivation.

Equally important is defining what counts as an emergency. Generic admonitions to save for the unexpected often miss the mark. A burst tyre may be irrelevant if you don't drive, but a broken laptop during exam season, a last-minute train fare to a funeral, or an urgent medical copay are genuine crises. Teaching young people to identify actual vulnerabilities—and plan for them—creates compliance through clarity. Vagueness encourages avoidance; precision fosters action.

Yet even the best system falters if saving feels like deprivation. The necessary mindset shift is from seeing saving as sacrifice to recognising it as self-authorship. Every pound set aside is not withheld from joy—it is allocated to a deeper, more enduring form of it: the joy of readiness, the pride of resilience, the quiet authority of prioritisation. Saving is not merely a financial skill; it is a psychological stance, a declaration that your future self deserves preparation, not wishful thinking.

In a culture dominated by instant gratification and performative consumption, the choice to save intentionally may feel countercultural—and that is no accident. Resisting the default is not self-denial; it is self-definition. Nothing accelerates this transformation faster than witnessing your savings grow, observing options expand, and realising that financial control is not a limitation, but a lever for shaping life.

This chapter does not preach thrift. It provides a blueprint for financial self-empowerment that avoids fear, shame, or vague promises of "someday." It explores why saving feels emotionally taxing despite logical benefits, presents a functional system for categorising funds, demonstrates ways to make progress visible and rewarding, and clarifies what real-world emergencies look like for under-25s. Most importantly, it teaches a skill often absent from financial education: how to align saving with identity, desire, and emotional experience.

Saving is not about having less now. It is about choosing more—with freedom, foresight, and sometimes even immediacy. When approached correctly, it does not feel like sacrifice; it feels like a quiet revolution.

Why Saving Feels Like Losing

Ask a teenager to save £50, and you'll likely be met with resistance—not because they can't do it, but because it *feels* wrong. Ask a twenty-year-old to transfer £200 into a long-term savings account, and they might do it, but with the internal friction of giving something up. This resistance is not about ignorance, laziness, or bad character. It's *psychological.* Saving, for many, is a transaction that feels emotionally negative—even when it's financially positive. *We are evolutionarily and socially wired to favour immediacy, visibility, and reward—all of which saving often lacks.*

To understand why saving feels like losing, we must first understand the mental models that underpin financial decision-making. Human beings are present-biased creatures.

Decades of behavioural economics research—especially the work of Daniel Kahneman, Amos Tversky, and Richard Thaler—have shown that we systematically overvalue rewards that are available now and undervalue those that are delayed. This phenomenon, known as hyperbolic discounting, means that even when we intellectually understand the long-term benefits of saving, *our emotional system still favours immediate consumption*. This is not a flaw in logic—it's a function of how brains evolved in environments where "now" mattered far more than "later."

Modern consumer culture exploits this bias to perfection. Every tap of a contactless card, every one-click purchase, every push notification from a retailer is designed to collapse the gap between desire and acquisition. Saving, by contrast, asks us to *intentionally create a gap* between income and spending—an act that feels like artificial deprivation in a world where gratification is optimised for speed. *The emotional cost of not buying is amplified by the psychological design of the environments we inhabit.* It's not just that saving is hard—it's that spending is engineered to feel good.

There's also the problem of *invisibility*. When you spend money, you get something tangible: a shirt, a ticket, a meal, a dopamine hit. When you save money, the reward is abstract. A number on a screen. A vague sense of responsibility. A future that may or may not unfold the way you hope. For young people especially, whose futures are marked by uncertainty—financial, environmental, political—*saving for the future can feel like investing in fog*. The lack of emotional resonance with distant outcomes means that saving lacks the narrative pull that drives behaviour.

Social comparison only deepens this disconnect. In the digital age, the financial choices of others are made hyper-visible—curated through social media, celebrated in influencer culture, and normalised through peer circles. Spending becomes a performance, and opting out looks like disappearing. If your friends are all buying new tech, eating out three times a week, or travelling on budget flights, saying no and saving instead doesn't just feel like restraint—it feels like *social exclusion*. The choice to save is framed not just as a personal decision, but as a quiet deviation from a visible norm. *And in adolescence or early adulthood, deviation feels like loss of belonging.*

Culturally, the narrative of saving is also poorly constructed. For decades, the dominant rhetoric around saving has been one of guilt and discipline—"Don't be wasteful," "Be responsible," "Think about your future." This language may be well-intentioned, but it reinforces the idea that saving is a moral obligation rather than a *strategic act of self-respect*. It positions saving as the opposite of pleasure, the adversary of indulgence, rather than an enabler of choice, autonomy, or readiness. *When saving is cast as a virtue rather than a power tool, it loses emotional traction.*

There's also a cognitive distortion at play: the pain of paying. Behavioural economist Ofer Zellermayer coined the term to describe the emotional discomfort people feel when parting with money. Intriguingly, this pain is often stronger when the money is directed toward less tangible outcomes. Paying for a dinner delivers immediate pleasure and social experience. Setting that same money aside for an undefined future? The same neural pathways that register loss light up. Saving triggers a *loss frame*, even though it's a gain in disguise.

The problem compounds when savings goals are too far removed from real life. Asking a 17-year-old to save for retirement is like asking them to pack for a trip to a country they've never heard of. The timeline is too long, the relevance too vague. But ask them to save for something concrete—a travel fund, an emergency cushion, a self-funded course—and the equation changes. *The more immediate and personal the benefit, the more tolerable the delay.* When saving is de-abstracted—when it becomes a story rather than a sacrifice—its psychological resistance weakens.

Part of the solution, then, lies in *reframing* the act of saving itself. Rather than viewing it as an act of withholding, it must be seen as an act of building. This means reengineering the context in which saving occurs. Automated transfers, visual goal trackers, app-based gamification—all help make the act of saving feel like progress, not punishment. But even more important is how saving is *framed narratively*. When framed as a choice to secure future agency, rather than a denial of present pleasure, saving becomes less about what you're giving up and more about *what you're giving yourself access to later*.

It also helps to inject immediacy into saving by tethering it to small, near-term milestones. Instead of "Save £10,000 by age 30," try "Save £50 by Friday." The latter creates a feedback loop that the brain can engage with now. Each small win reinforces the identity of someone who saves. *Identity-driven behaviour is far more sustainable than rule-based behaviour.* If you see yourself as someone who respects your own future, the act of saving becomes an expression of who you are, not just a strategy for some distant event.

Yet even identity isn't enough if your financial environment works against you. Many young people today operate in precarious economies—part-time jobs, freelance gigs, platform work—where income is irregular and expenses can feel unpredictable. For them, the idea of "saving a fixed percentage" every month is not just unrealistic; it's naive. What's needed is *adaptive saving logic*, where the amount saved flexes with the rhythm of earnings, not against it. This aligns savings behaviour with lived experience, not idealised financial advice.

There's also an overlooked emotional truth: *saving is hardest when you've never had money before*. For someone earning their first real income—especially from a working-class or resource-stretched background—the temptation to spend is not just about materialism. It's about finally tasting options.

Spending feels like proof that the hustle worked. That you've made it. That you matter. Saving, by contrast, reintroduces restraint at the exact moment freedom has become newly available. Unless it is framed differently—*not as the cancellation of freedom, but as its compounder*—it will feel like a cruel bait-and-switch.

The irony is this: those who master the emotional side of saving early build the deepest foundation for long-term wealth—not because they saved the most, but because they *trained their mind to see delayed rewards as valuable, even exciting*. That mental shift ripples into how they invest, plan, and spend for the rest of their lives. It's not the amount saved that changes everything—it's the internal logic behind it.

Saving doesn't feel good at first because most of us were never taught to *feel ownership of our future selves*. We treat tomorrow's version of us as a stranger, not a stakeholder. But that version of us is real. They will need shelter, opportunities, health, stability. Saving is the only dialogue we have with them. And the more fluently we speak that language, the better we treat ourselves—not just now, but later, where the stakes are higher, and the costs of short-sightedness less forgiving.

To make saving work, then, we must stop treating it as an act of punishment and start seeing it as a profound act of *respect*. Not just for money, but for the unfolding story of who we are becoming. And that shift—from loss to authorship—is where financial maturity truly begins.

The 3-Bucket Saving System

One of the most common reasons people fail to sustain a savings habit isn't laziness, ignorance, or lack of access—it's vagueness. When saving is treated as a monolithic activity—"just put some money aside"—it lacks direction, purpose, and feedback. Money pooled in a single savings account blurs together into an undifferentiated mass, untethered to real-life objectives. It becomes easy to dip into, hard to grow, and nearly impossible to prioritise. *The result is a savings system that feels abstract, reactive, and fragile.* What's needed instead is a structure that brings clarity to intent, stability to discipline, and adaptability to life's evolving demands. Enter the 3-Bucket Saving System.

At its core, the 3-Bucket model is not a budgeting trick—it's a conceptual operating system. It divides your savings into three distinct categories: short-term, mid-term, and long-term. Each bucket is defined not just by time horizon, but by emotional tone and functional purpose. This segmentation gives your money *meaning*, your goals *architecture*, and your decision-making *precision*. It transforms saving from an amorphous virtue into a set of actionable behaviours, each calibrated to serve a different kind of future.

The short-term bucket is about *resilience*. This is your buffer against life's everyday volatility: a cracked phone screen, an unplanned trip home, an urgent dental visit, or the sudden cost of replacing a laptop charger the night before a deadline. These are not catastrophes—but they're the kind of small shocks that, when unbuffered, send people spiralling into debt, panic, or regretful spending. A short-term fund, properly built, isn't about growing wealth—it's about buying stability. For most people, this fund should aim to cover at least one to three months' worth of essential personal expenses. *Its job is not to make money—it's to stop you from losing it unnecessarily.*

The mid-term bucket is about *freedom*. This is where your next one to five years live—the wedding you'll attend abroad, the professional course you want to fund, the moving costs for relocating to a new city, the deposit for your first flat, or the sabbatical you're daring to dream of. This bucket protects your aspirations from being swallowed by routine. It allows you to say yes to opportunities, not just emergencies. Crucially, mid-term savings often determine whether you feel constrained or empowered in key transitional life moments. *It's not just money—it's momentum.* Without a mid-term fund, every desire feels like a debt risk or an irresponsible indulgence.

Then comes the long-term bucket: the most misunderstood, neglected, and emotionally distant of the three. This is about *legacy*. Not in a grandiose, empire-building sense, but in the quiet power of compound preparation. This bucket holds the funds you won't need for 10, 20, even 40 years—your retirement savings, your investment accounts, your generational safety net. It is here that compound interest becomes not just a financial phenomenon but a *philosophical one*—a living testament to patience, belief in the future, and the slow accrual of advantage. Long-term savings don't feel urgent, but they are deeply strategic. *They are not about predicting the future—they're about giving your future self optionality.*

Segmenting your savings in this way shifts not only how you manage money but *how you think about time*. Each bucket demands a different psychology. The short-term is about control and liquidity: the money should be accessible, low-risk, and instantly usable. The mid-term requires a balance of growth and flexibility: savings accounts with higher interest, premium bonds, or short-term fixed-income investments. The long-term demands commitment and resilience to volatility: diversified stock market investments, pensions, or index funds. Each time horizon carries with it not just a different financial product—but a different version of yourself that you are honouring.

Critically, this system also guards against a common trap: over-saving for the distant future while under-preparing for life's current complexity. Too many people are told to "start early with retirement" (which is sound advice), but do so at the cost of neglecting their mid-term goals. They contribute diligently to a pension, yet have no financial plan for a career pivot, a sabbatical, or the cost of moving countries. *A 65-year-old version of you may thank you for your diligence—but your*

28-year-old self might feel trapped, burnt out, and unable to act on your own curiosity. The 3-Bucket System forces us to recognise that a full life needs layered savings—each bucket sustaining a different dimension of experience.

The system also acts as an antidote to impulsive borrowing. Without a short-term buffer, an unexpected bill becomes a credit card transaction. Without a mid-term fund, an opportunity becomes a loan. This is how debt accumulates—not from laziness, but from a lack of structured foresight. Savings are not just about accumulation—they are about *avoiding unnecessary financial entanglement.* Each bucket, properly funded, keeps you from trading your future time and autonomy for the illusion of present ease.

A well-structured 3-Bucket system also promotes better self-awareness. It forces you to articulate what your goals actually are. Many people fail to save effectively not because they can't, but because they haven't clearly defined what they're saving *for.* Abstract goals create abstract discipline. But when you look at your mid-term bucket and know it's for a sabbatical in Lisbon, or a design course in Amsterdam, or the down payment on a place that lets your parents retire early—*that's when the act of saving becomes emotionally fuelled.* It moves from a sterile task to a value-driven practice.

The flexibility of the 3-Bucket model is also part of its strength. It can scale up or down depending on your income, your needs, and your life stage. A teenager earning from weekend gigs can start with £5 in each bucket. A graduate on a modest salary might direct 50% of savings to mid-term goals, 30% to short-term, and 20% to long-term. A freelancer with variable income might prioritise the short-term bucket during lean months and pour surplus into long-term investments in flush periods. The point is not rigid percentages—it's *structured intentionality.* This framework invites you to treat savings as a *strategy,* not a leftover.

Perhaps most importantly, the 3-Bucket system offers a psychological benefit that flat saving cannot: *a sense of progress across multiple dimensions.* When all your savings live in a single account, progress can feel slow and demoralising. But when each bucket is its own narrative—each milestone reached its own reward—you gain the motivation of small wins across short, medium, and long horizons. *It mirrors how real life unfolds—not as one linear path, but as overlapping arcs of readiness, opportunity, and legacy.*

We often say that money should serve your life, not the other way around. But to make that real, you need to design a system that translates that principle into behaviour. The 3-Bucket Saving System does exactly that. It is deceptively simple, infinitely adaptable, and deeply clarifying. It gives your savings a skeleton. Your choices, a rhythm. Your future, a scaffolding. And for anyone navigating the uncertainty of early financial independence, that clarity may be the most valuable currency of all.

How to Make Saving Feel Like Winning

A peculiar paradox lies at the heart of modern financial behaviour: while we understand that saving money is good for us, it rarely *feels* good in the moment. Unlike spending—which offers instant gratification, sensory pleasure, and social visibility—saving is often quiet, slow, and emotionally opaque. There's no dopamine hit from transferring £50 into a long-term fund. No applause for declining an Uber. No badge for skipping the takeaway. The psychological reward mechanisms that make us repeat behaviours are often absent in saving. And when progress is invisible, motivation withers. *If saving feels like deprivation, it will eventually lose to consumption.* The solution is not to moralise harder or budget more strictly, but to rewire how saving interacts with our emotions. This is where the gamification of saving becomes a serious idea—not a gimmick, but a strategic intervention in human psychology.

At its core, gamification is not about playing games—it's about structuring behaviours to tap into our brain's reward systems. Well-designed games offer frequent feedback, clear goals, rising levels of difficulty, and the possibility of progress. These principles—if applied thoughtfully to saving—can convert what feels like sacrifice into something far more motivating: a sense of achievement. The goal is not to trivialise saving but to *energise it*. This approach doesn't ask people to suppress their instincts; it asks them to channel them.

The most effective gamified saving systems start with visual progress tracking. Humans are wired to respond to visible advancement. It's why we cross days off a calendar, celebrate fitness streaks, and track steps with wearable devices. When saving is made visible—via charts, streak counters, milestones, or even colour-coded visuals—it ceases to be abstract. A digital savings app that shows a mountain being climbed with each contribution activates parts of the brain associated with achievement. A thermometer graphic that fills as you approach a target makes progress tangible. *People don't save more just because they know it's important—they save more when they can see that it's working.*

Beyond visuals, introducing incremental challenges keeps the process engaging. Much like levels in a game, small, time-bound saving tasks create bite-sized wins. A "No Spend Weekend" challenge, a "£5-a-Day for 10 Days" sprint, or a "Double Your Rounding Ups This Week" micro-goal gives people something to *do*, not just to avoid. The key is to create achievable challenges that compound into confidence. These tasks should be self-contained yet cumulative—each building the belief that saving is both possible and worthwhile. Over time, they generate the emotional loop of success: *I did this, so I can do more.*

Crucially, effective saving games respect the individual's context. They are not competitive in the traditional sense—they are personalised. Unlike social media-driven financial challenges that encourage performance for external approval, true gamified saving is *intrinsic*. It doesn't matter whether someone else saved more. What matters is that *you beat your own baseline*. In this sense, the most powerful metric is not the total amount saved—but the consistency of action over time. A person who saves £1 a day for 60 days is cultivating a saving identity. That identity, once established, becomes sticky.

One of the most overlooked aspects of gamified saving is *celebration*. We tend to celebrate earnings—bonuses, promotions, passive income—but rarely acknowledge the quiet victories of restraint. This is a missed opportunity. Even a modest goal—like hitting the £100 mark in a short-term emergency fund—deserves recognition. Not necessarily with more spending, but with reflection. Write it down. Share it with a trusted peer. Allow it to register. Just as a game gives you badges, levels, or titles for progress, so too should your saving practice give you moments of affirmation. *Celebration is not frivolous—it reinforces identity.*

Technology can help, but it's not the only way. While apps like Monzo, Plum, or Cleo have built-in saving features, even a handwritten journal, physical stickers, or a hand-drawn savings ladder can be effective. The point isn't sophistication—it's visibility and feedback. Some of the best savings streaks start not with automation but with attention. When someone sets a challenge, tracks it with intent, and reflects on it weekly, they're building a personal financial dashboard in their mind.

To gamify saving is also to reframe its narrative. Instead of treating it as a postponement of pleasure, we begin to see it as a builder of options. *Every pound saved is not withheld joy—it is stored freedom.* When that freedom is named—"my next flat deposit," "my three-month sabbatical," "my startup runway"—the emotional tone of saving shifts. It becomes generative, not restrictive. In this way, gamification is not just a behavioural trick but a cognitive one—it helps us reassign emotional value to future readiness.

However, the gamified approach is not without its risks. If taken too far, it can become performative or mechanical. Saving should never become a source of guilt or self-worth comparison. Nor should it displace deeper financial reflection. A challenge-driven saving model should always be tethered to *why* the saving matters. The mechanics—progress bars, challenges, streaks—are there to serve the meaning, not replace it.

Additionally, gamified saving should resist the temptation of gimmickry. Cashback rewards, promotional stunts, or lottery-style savings incentives offered by some fintech companies often blur the line between motivation and manipulation. While these tactics can attract short-term engagement, they rarely build long-term discipline. The most sustainable saving habits are those rooted in autonomy and self-efficacy, not external bribes. *Saving that is enjoyable is good. Saving that is dependent on tricks is fragile.*

There is also a cultural dimension to this approach. In societies where consumerism is both normalised and glamorised, saving can feel like swimming upstream. By gamifying the act of saving, individuals begin to write a counter-narrative. They become players of a different game—one that rewards patience, strategy, and intentionality over speed, spectacle, and status. In this way, gamification becomes subversive: *it turns a private discipline into a form of personal power.*

Some of the most impactful applications of this philosophy come from unexpected places. For instance, among Gen Z communities on TikTok, the "100 Envelope Challenge"—where participants label 100 envelopes with amounts from £1 to £100 and randomly select one to fill each day or week—has gained traction not because it's financially optimal, but because it *feels like a game.* It provides randomness, anticipation, and visual satisfaction. It makes the abstract concrete. And it turns saving into something people want to share—not because they're showing off, but because they're proud of their engagement.

What all of this underscores is a central truth: *saving isn't just a financial behaviour—it's an emotional and cognitive experience*. And like any experience, it can be shaped. It can be designed to reward rather than punish, to reinforce rather than nag. When saving is positioned as an active, skill-building, identity-affirming process, people begin to stick with it—not out of guilt or fear, but out of pride and progress.

To make saving feel like winning is not to trivialise it. It is to give it back the attention, emotion, and feedback that spending has stolen for too long. When saving becomes visible, measurable, and meaningful, it stops feeling like waiting. It starts feeling like preparing. Like building. Like winning—on your own terms.

Emergency Funds for the Real World

Most people don't build an emergency fund until life demands it—and by then, it's too late. But for teenagers and young adults, the issue isn't urgency, it's *relevance*. Emergencies, to them, are often framed in adult terms: job loss, car repairs, or medical bills. Yet that framing misses the mark. It teaches them to delay thinking about saving for emergencies until they encounter "real" adulthood. In reality, emergencies already exist in teenage life—they just look different. A cracked phone that disrupts schoolwork, a friend's last-minute birthday dinner you can't afford, or a forgotten sports fee due the next morning. These are not trivial—they are immediate, stressful, and financially destabilising when unprepared for. To ignore these realities is to alienate a generation from the concept of emergency saving before they've had the chance to internalise its purpose. *To make saving stick, it must first feel personal.*

Part of the reason teens don't build emergency funds is because the term itself feels distant—something for later, like pensions or wills. Yet redefined correctly, an emergency fund is nothing more than *a tool for agency*. It says: "When life throws something unexpected at me, I can respond without panic, shame, or reliance." That's not a financial luxury—it's a psychological necessity. Teens today already face high levels of anxiety around money, often intensified by social comparison and unstable economic messaging. Creating a personal emergency buffer is one of the simplest, clearest acts of self-respect they can make. It doesn't just shield them from surprise expenses; it affirms their ability to take care of themselves in unpredictable situations.

This reframing requires a cultural shift. Adults often mischaracterise young people as reckless spenders, but what is commonly seen as frivolity is more often the absence of financial infrastructure. You can't expect someone to budget for emergencies if they don't have a system for anticipating them. This is where tactical clarity matters. Instead of telling young people to "save just in case," we must ask them to *define* what counts as an emergency in their current context. A school laptop left on the bus. A bus pass renewal they forgot was due. A sibling's birthday when they want to contribute to a gift. These are *emotionally urgent* events. And when people are emotionally unprepared for financial pressure, they borrow, overdraw, or opt out. *The cost of not being prepared isn't just financial—it's social, academic, and psychological.*

Once emergencies are grounded in real-world relevance, the next barrier becomes behavioural. Saving for something that *might* happen is a hard sell, especially when impulse-driven spending is rewarded immediately. Therefore, building an emergency fund must not be framed as a punishment or test of willpower—it must be made easy, visible, and satisfying. The best tactic is automation with micro-contributions. A recurring £1 transfer into a dedicated "Uh-Oh Fund" requires no decision-making but builds consistency. Over time, it creates a resource with psychological utility that exceeds its monetary value. A teen who sees £25 in their emergency pot isn't just seeing money—they're seeing a safety net, a source of calm, and a form of autonomy.

This automation should be paired with clear, flexible rules. One of the reasons emergency funds often fail is because users either raid them impulsively or hesitate to use them at all. The solution is to define *your own rules* in advance. For teens, this might mean: "I can use this fund only if (a) something breaks, (b) I forgot something essential, or (c) saying yes would make me proud, not anxious." This criterion builds both boundary and confidence. It encourages reflection without paralysis. When someone dips into their emergency fund under conditions they've set, they feel relief, not regret. *And when they refill it after use, they reaffirm their own reliability.*

It's also essential to talk about *scale*. Many financial guides suggest emergency funds should cover 3–6 months of expenses. This is appropriate for working adults with recurring liabilities—but absurd for a 16-year-old with no rent and fluctuating income. For teenagers, an emergency fund of £50 to £200 is often more than enough. This amount can cover a broken school calculator, a last-minute Uber, a forgotten uniform fee, or a social obligation. More importantly, it teaches scale-relative saving. The principle is not to hoard money, but to match preparedness to context. Over time, as responsibilities grow, so does the target amount. The key is to *build the habit before the need expands.*

In practice, many young savers find it helpful to treat their emergency fund as *a named, visible account*. Labelling it something like "Rainy Day," "Break Glass," or "Peace of Mind" creates psychological distance from their main spending pool. Even better is keeping it in a separate savings account or digital wallet with a slight friction barrier—accessible, but not too convenient. This small design tweak reduces impulsive transfers and protects the fund's purpose. In behavioural finance, this is known as *mental accounting*: the tendency to treat money differently based on its intended use. Naming the fund and making it slightly harder to access works with our biases instead of against them.

One of the most powerful moments in financial maturity is when a young person uses their emergency fund for the first time and *doesn't feel shame*. Instead of scrambling, asking parents, or avoiding the situation, they solve it themselves. That act is a form of identity-building. It whispers, "You're someone who handles things." And that identity becomes sticky. They begin to trust themselves. They realise that financial discipline is not just about denial—it's about design. About putting small systems in place that make big problems smaller.

This emotional shift is especially vital in a world where unexpected costs are rising, and financial shock is a leading cause of adolescent stress. According to a 2023 report by the UK's Money and Pensions Service, nearly 40% of teens experience anxiety when thinking about how to pay for unexpected costs. Yet only a small fraction report having a personal savings plan. The gap is not just informational—it's architectural. Schools rarely teach it. Parents rarely model it. Apps rarely emphasise it. But when young people are given the *tools* and *language* to anticipate their own emergencies, they don't just save more—they stress less.

Emergency saving is not the same as financial perfection. It's not about being invulnerable or having a bulletproof budget. It's about being responsive, not reactive. It's about recovering from small hits without going into crisis mode. And it's about *redefining what control looks like in a world that's often chaotic.* For teens, especially those from lower-income backgrounds or unstable households, an emergency fund can be the only buffer between them and a downward spiral. And for those with privilege, it's a reminder that security is not a given—it's cultivated.

Ultimately, building an emergency fund is one of the most mature acts a young person can take. But it shouldn't be wrapped in solemnity or financial jargon. It should be spoken about like an everyday skill—like brushing your teeth or packing an umbrella. A basic form of self-care. Something normal, something proud. When teens are taught that they're allowed to prepare—not because they're scared, but because they're smart—they begin to understand money not just as currency, but as capacity. They're not saving to avoid disaster. They're saving to protect their momentum.

The adult world often teaches money through crises. But if we want the next generation to be resilient, we should teach them how to prevent crises—not just respond to them. Emergency funds are not about what might go wrong. They're about what you can make go *right* when you're ready. And readiness, in personal finance, is a form of quiet confidence that compounds faster than interest.

Chapter 7
Investing 101—Without the B.S.

The word "investing" has been so mythologised, overexposed, and commodified that by the time most young people approach it seriously, their expectations are already skewed. For Gen Z in particular—raised amid TikTok tips, crypto hype, and meme-stock mania—it is all too easy to conflate investing with a personality trait or a get-rich-quick ritual. Strip away the spectacle, however, and the concept is remarkably straightforward: allocating money today in anticipation of growth tomorrow. No magic. No manipulation. No lottery ticket cloaked in jargon. Simply a tool—a lever designed to amplify time, effort, and strategy. The problem is not disinterest; it is an overdose of fantasy paired with too little clarity.

Investing is less about money and more about how someone negotiates time and uncertainty. Every allocation—whether purchasing a share in a global index or putting £50 into Bitcoin—carries two invisible variables: patience and tolerance for unpredictability. Much of the advice culture complicates this relationship unnecessarily, fetishising technicalities like price-to-earnings ratios and candlestick charts before ever considering readiness. But readiness is not mastery of vocabulary—it is cultivating a mindset attuned to trade-offs. If saving demands restraint, investing demands trust—not blind faith in markets, but informed confidence in navigating risk over time.

The issue with much beginner-focused investing content is not that it is wrong, but that it is patronising. Telling someone to "just buy index funds" or "crypto is the future" without context is abdication, not guidance. It overlooks the psychological weight of watching balances fluctuate, the complications of living at home or earning irregular income, and the challenge of imagining a distant retirement. Thriving versus panicking is rarely about luck or intelligence; it is about matching assets to goals, not to FOMO.

Take stocks. Often presented as the gold standard of investing, they are indeed stable—but stability manifests over decades, not days. Their short-term volatility contrasts with long-term resilience, a nuance critical for anyone navigating different time horizons. A three-year plan is not a thirty-year plan, yet most platforms display identical interfaces, identical graphs, and "trending now" metrics. The result is confusion and panic during inevitable dips. Sound investing demands not only the right asset selection but also realistic expectations.

Crypto, by contrast, merges speculation, ideology, and storytelling. Its technological innovation is real, but its volatility is profound. For young investors, it offers cultural belonging, a sense of participation in a movement. This is intoxicating—and risky. Investing driven by tribalism or aesthetics turns financial decisions into loyalty tests: "Am I still one of them?" rather than "Is this allocation sound?" True risk assessment requires honesty about drawdowns, scams, and asymmetrical access—lessons rarely found in YouTube thumbnails or Discord threads.

Index funds, while lacking flash, offer structural humility. Buying into an index fund is not a bet on a single company or trend, but an acknowledgement that markets reward long-term consistency. Exposure to an entire economy reduces narrative risk and provides liberation: the investor need not outsmart the market, only stay invested. Here, patience—not brilliance—is the most valuable skill. For a generation conditioned by algorithms to engage constantly, the discipline of non-intervention is formidable.

What often unnerves young investors is ambiguity, not loss. Traditional education teaches avoidance, not navigation of uncertainty. But investing is probabilistic, not perfect. Losses are inevitable; the relevant questions are magnitude, frequency, and whether they are strategic. Risk is not the enemy—uninformed risk is. A 30% dip in a twenty-year holding is not a crisis; a similar drop in rent money is. Context is inseparable from investing.

Engagement begins with small, intentional steps. A thoughtful £10 investment teaches more than a £1,000 leap into hype. Early engagement rewires relationships with time: compounding occurs not only in accounts but in behaviour. Each choice informs the next. The real dividend is calm—the certainty that today's decisions serve tomorrow's self.

Investing, properly understood, is disciplined optimism. It affirms: "The future exists, and I intend to meet it prepared." It demands clarity, humility, and consistency, not spreadsheets or six-figure portfolios. It requires resisting the allure of headlines in favour of steady, repeatable actions. Perhaps dull, but infinitely more rewarding.

This chapter does not aim to produce derivative experts or entertain with overnight success stories. Its goal is sharper: to cultivate fluency, replace fear with understanding, and provide a mental framework that treats investing as an extension of values, priorities, and time horizon.

If you leave this chapter still seeing investing as a game to be won quickly, the lesson has not taken hold. But if you understand it as a long-term relationship offering options, agency, and resilience, you have gained more than knowledge. You have gained leverage over your future—and clarity about the kind of investor you wish to become.

What Investing Actually Means (And Doesn't)

It is both a triumph and a tragedy of the modern world that the word *investing* is now used so promiscuously that its meaning often vanishes beneath layers of abstraction, aspiration, and algorithmic hype. To the uninitiated, it may sound like a sophisticated form of gambling, or a privileged domain reserved for financial elites whispering in tickers and dividends. For Gen Z, bombarded by TikTok stock gurus and crypto-fuelled Reddit threads, it frequently arrives preloaded with emotional baggage—confusion, intimidation, and above all, the unspoken assumption that investing is something you either master fast or stay away from forever. But the truth is far more grounded. *Investing is simply the act of putting your money to work to grow over time.* It is not an exclusive club. Nor is it a game of genius. It is a deliberate, disciplined relationship with time, uncertainty, and intention.

To understand investing, we must first dismantle the cult of complexity. Financial jargon thrives on opacity. Terms like "market capitalisation," "beta volatility," or "yield curves" may sound authoritative, but they often serve as smoke rather than substance. At its core, investing isn't about understanding exotic vocabulary; it's about grasping *a few durable principles* and applying them with rigour and patience. The essence of investing lies in the trade-off between risk and reward, between present-day certainty and future possibility. You part with money now—not for instant gratification, but for the hope that it will return to you amplified by time. That's it. Everything else is commentary.

But clarity demands more than definitions. It requires a distinction between what investing *is* and what it is *not*. First and foremost, investing is *not* the same as speculating. When you invest, you make a calculated decision grounded in data, strategy, and time horizon. You may invest in a diversified index fund because you believe that the economy, over decades, tends to grow. You may invest in a start-up because you understand its business model and have reason to believe in its potential. But if you throw £500 into a meme stock because it's trending on social media, you're not investing—you're speculating. That doesn't make it wrong; it just makes it risky in a fundamentally different way. *Speculation thrives on timing and narrative. Investing is built on evidence and discipline.*

Second, investing is *not* saving. Saving is about preservation—keeping your money accessible and safe. Investing is about growth, and with that growth comes volatility. Money in a savings account earns minimal interest but offers near-total security. Money in the stock market can rise or fall dramatically, depending on when and where you've placed it. The confusion between these two creates frustration. People who expect investing to feel like saving often panic when values fluctuate. But to expect stability from an inherently unstable instrument is to misunderstand its purpose. *Volatility is not a flaw in investing—it is its engine.*

Investing is also not a shortcut to wealth. The most effective investors rarely chase windfalls. Instead, they rely on consistency, time, and an understanding of compounding—the quiet arithmetic of exponential growth. Consider this: if you invest £100 every month from age 18 to 30 and then stop entirely, your money will likely outperform someone who starts at 30 and contributes until 60, assuming typical market returns. Why? Because time, not talent, is the most underrated force in finance. The longer your money stays invested, the more it earns on itself—not just on your initial contributions. *The miracle of investing is not speed. It is endurance.*

This endurance, however, demands a mental model that accommodates delayed gratification and tolerates uncertainty. For many, especially those accustomed to the instant feedback loops of digital life, this is profoundly unnatural. Social media, gaming, and ecommerce platforms reward immediate engagement. Investing punishes it. Checking your portfolio every day is not a strategy—it's a stressor. The daily ups and downs of markets say very little about long-term value. But because we are emotionally wired to react to loss more intensely than to gain—a bias known as loss aversion—even minor market dips can trigger disproportionate panic.

Recognising this cognitive distortion is essential. *To invest well is to learn emotional resilience, not just financial literacy.*

The modern investing landscape doesn't make this any easier. With the rise of digital platforms, the barrier to entry has fallen—but so has the barrier to overreaction. Apps now allow anyone to buy and sell assets with a swipe, often gamifying the process with confetti and push notifications. But investing is not meant to be thrilling. When it becomes entertainment, risk becomes invisible. And yet, the problem isn't the technology—it's the absence of context. A trading app without an understanding of financial principles is like handing a scalpel to someone who's never studied anatomy. The tool is powerful. But power without clarity invites chaos.

So what does investing actually look like in practice? It means choosing assets that align with your goals and timeframes. A teenager might invest in a broad-market index fund, not because it's glamorous, but because it offers diversified exposure to the economy with relatively low fees. Someone with higher risk tolerance might allocate a portion to emerging markets or new technologies, understanding these may swing wildly in value. And those who truly grasp the long game may even invest during downturns, knowing that *buying when others are fearful*—to borrow Warren Buffett's famous phrasing—is often where long-term gains are born.

Critically, good investing is not about predicting the future. It is about preparing for a range of possible futures. This is why diversification matters. By spreading your investments across asset classes—stocks, bonds, real estate, perhaps even crypto in moderation—you reduce your vulnerability to any single failure. Think of it less as hedging your bets and more as *building resilience into your financial system*. No one knows which sectors will thrive in ten years. But we do know that betting everything on one of them is more fragile than betting modestly on several.

We must also confront a final misconception: that investing requires wealth. In fact, the opposite is true. Wealth is often *the result* of investing, not the prerequisite. With fractional shares and low-cost platforms, you can begin with as little as £10. The key is not how much you start with, but *how soon* and *how consistently*. Even modest amounts, compounded over time, become meaningful. More importantly, starting early builds habits. It teaches you to weather uncertainty, to delay consumption, and to make decisions based on future value, not current mood. These are not just financial skills—they are life skills.

In a world that markets immediacy, investing teaches patience. In a culture obsessed with trends, it rewards principle. And in an age where information is abundant but wisdom is rare, *understanding what investing actually means* is more than financial hygiene—it is intellectual independence. It's the ability to distinguish noise from signal, to resist the tyranny of urgency, and to operate with clarity where others chase spectacle.

The young investor who grasps this is not just preparing for a financially secure future—they are practicing the mindset of someone who knows the difference between performance and substance. Between hype and strategy. Between activity and progress. And ultimately, *between what investing looks like, and what it actually is.*

Stocks, Crypto, Index Funds: A Reality Check

For a generation raised on algorithmic feeds and financial memes, investment options arrive not through textbooks or formal education, but through Twitter threads, Discord rooms, and YouTube thumbnails that flash urgent words like "moon," "bull," or "rug pull." Against this cultural backdrop, choosing where to put your money has become not only a financial decision but a performative act—something visible, shareable, and often emotionally loaded. The danger is not that young investors are enthusiastic, but that enthusiasm is routinely mistaken for clarity. In this climate, a sober, intellectually honest breakdown of the three dominant entry points—individual stocks, cryptocurrencies, and index funds—is less a luxury and more a public service.

Let's begin with the most historically grounded: *stocks*. When you buy a share in a company, you are quite literally buying a slice of ownership in that business. If the company grows, becomes more profitable, or pays dividends, your investment may grow accordingly. But this logic, while structurally sound, is increasingly lost beneath the noise of day-trading subcultures. The idea that stocks are bets to be timed, rather than assets to be held, has distorted the public understanding of equity investing. Platforms like Robinhood (in the US) or Freetrade (in the UK) gamify access to stocks, framing them less as strategic decisions and more as reflexive reactions. Yet if investing is meant to be a long game, *trading stocks like football stickers undermines the entire premise*.

That isn't to say individual stocks should be avoided altogether—but they must be approached with a degree of epistemic humility. Most people overestimate their ability to pick winners. This is not merely a matter of intelligence, but of access. Retail investors, especially beginners, typically lack the data, context, and strategic tools available to institutional players. Even among professional fund managers, the vast majority *fail to beat the market* over time. So when an amateur investor declares that they've found the next Tesla or Amazon, what they often possess is not insight, but narrative—usually borrowed from someone else's confidence, delivered with algorithmic reach.

This brings us to *cryptocurrencies*, the most polarising and poorly understood asset class of the 21st century. To its advocates, crypto represents the future of decentralised finance, programmable money, and digital sovereignty. To its critics, it is a speculative bubble powered by hype, fraud, and technological overreach. The truth, as always, is less binary. Cryptocurrencies *do* introduce innovative models of financial exchange, and some of them—like Ethereum—have utility that extends beyond price speculation. But investing in crypto today is functionally closer to venture capital than traditional equity. It is a high-risk, high-volatility play that can offer enormous upside but also wipe out capital with astonishing speed. Anyone who treats it like a savings account is confusing ambition with prudence.

Crypto's main appeal lies in its psychological profile—it offers narrative, community, and radical upside. But these same features can also turn it into a cognitive trap. Because prices can double or collapse overnight, crypto exploits every psychological bias known to behavioural finance: *FOMO (fear of missing out), recency bias, confirmation bias*, and the illusion of control. The platforms that facilitate this trading—many of which operate outside traditional regulatory frameworks—often amplify these effects through gamified interfaces and social engineering. For Gen Z investors raised in a culture of real-time feedback, crypto feels familiar. But *familiarity is not the same as safety*. To engage with crypto intelligently, one must acknowledge both its transformative potential and its structural fragility.

The antidote to all this noise is found not in a guru or a hidden gem, but in the quiet reliability of *index funds*. These are diversified portfolios that track broad sections of the market—like the FTSE 100 or the S&P 500—and aim to *match* the market's performance rather than beat it. They are not sexy. They do not promise overnight returns. But they embody the most evidence-backed investment strategy available to the average investor. Index funds are low-cost, low-maintenance, and structurally diversified. Because they are designed to hold a basket of assets, they reduce exposure to the failure of any single company. For someone starting young and thinking long-term, they are as close to a "smart default" as investing gets.

What makes index funds particularly powerful is not their innovation—there's nothing flashy about them—but their alignment with how markets actually behave. Over time, broad markets tend to grow, reflecting overall economic expansion. This growth is not linear or smooth, but it is consistent enough that, with a long enough time horizon, the odds overwhelmingly favour patient investors. This is why Warren Buffett has repeatedly advised most people to simply invest in a low-cost index fund and forget about it. Not because it's exciting, but because it works. *Index funds reward consistency over cleverness.*

But this logic only holds if investors can resist the urge to interfere. The human impulse to tinker—to sell in downturns, to rotate into what's "hot," to abandon the plan in favour of novelty—is the real enemy. Index investing demands emotional discipline, not financial wizardry. It is not a hack. It is a habit.

Comparing these three options reveals a deeper truth about investing: it is less about the specific vehicle and more about the mindset you bring to it. Individual stocks require deep research, emotional detachment, and a clear thesis. Crypto demands an even higher tolerance for volatility and the humility to admit what you don't know. Index funds require patience, consistency, and a willingness to embrace the boring. None of these are wrong; all of them can work. But *only if you understand the rules of the game you're playing*.

Too many new investors adopt multiple strategies at once without understanding the internal contradictions. They buy index funds for "safety," then FOMO into a meme coin after watching a YouTube video. They follow financial influencers on TikTok, then panic when the S&P dips 3%. This incoherence is not just a failure of knowledge—it is a failure of alignment. Before choosing an investment, you must ask: *What is this money for? When will I need it? How much volatility can I emotionally tolerate?* If your answers are vague, your strategy will be, too.

And while comparison is inevitable, the real enemy of smart investing is envy. Seeing others post screenshots of windfall gains—real or fabricated—can make even the soundest portfolio feel inadequate. But investing is not a performance for others; it is a commitment to your own future. You do not need to hold the most impressive assets. You need to hold the ones that serve your goals, fit your temperament, and align with your time horizon. *There is no prize for complexity—only for clarity and consistency.*

Ultimately, each of these options—stocks, crypto, index funds—represents a different set of assumptions about the world. Stocks reward belief in individual enterprises. Crypto rewards belief in transformation. Index funds reward belief in the system as a whole. There is no universally "correct" belief. But there are better questions. What do you value? How much uncertainty are you willing to absorb? And are you building a system that you can maintain—not just during the highs, but especially during the lows?

The fantasy of investing is that you can time the market, pick winners, and double your money with flair. The reality is that smart investing is often invisible. It happens quietly, month after month, without fanfare or screenshots. It's not a bet—it's a system. And the sooner you understand the trade-offs between these tools, the sooner you can stop chasing the illusion of mastery and start building something real. *Not flashy. Not viral. Just real.*

Why Risk Isn't the Enemy (Uninformed Risk Is)

Risk is not the villain it is so often made out to be. In fact, the complete absence of risk—at least in the context of money—almost always guarantees stagnation, not safety. The greater threat to financial health, especially for young investors, is not risk itself but the *misunderstanding* of it: mistaking volatility for danger, mistaking temporary setbacks for failure, and mistaking hype for opportunity. Risk, when understood, can be a strategic ally. When it's misread or ignored, it becomes a silent saboteur.

The word "risk" carries heavy psychological baggage, largely because it signals the possibility of loss. But loss, in economic terms, is rarely absolute. The stock market crashing doesn't mean it disappears. A coin's value falling does not delete the network it was built on. A start-up failing doesn't render the skills you gained from investing in it irrelevant. Yet because most people define risk as "the chance something goes wrong," they tend to overreact emotionally and underreact strategically. What's far more useful is to redefine risk in terms of *likelihood and consequence*—not merely what could happen, but how much it would matter if it did.

There's a critical distinction between *volatility* and *permanent loss*, yet the two are often conflated. Volatility is the natural movement of prices—sometimes rapid, sometimes erratic—but usually temporary. Permanent loss, on the other hand, is when value disappears entirely and cannot be recovered: think of investing your savings in a fraudulent scheme, or buying into a stock that goes bankrupt. Volatility feels scary, but it's not inherently dangerous if your timeline is long. Permanent loss, however, is devastating—especially when caused by ignorance or overconfidence. This is why *informed patience beats blind optimism*. Time cushions volatility; education cushions loss.

The financial media, driven by engagement metrics, thrives on amplifying volatility. Every market dip becomes a crisis; every rally becomes a revolution. The result is a distorted emotional landscape where short-term fluctuations are mistaken for structural failure or golden opportunity. In such an environment, rational investors are punished not by the market itself, but by their own reactions to it. *The most common financial losses among new investors stem not from the market's behaviour, but from the investor's inability to sit still.*

Consider this: if you buy a diversified index fund and its value drops 10% next month, have you lost money? Technically, yes—on paper. But if you don't need to sell for another decade, and the underlying companies remain fundamentally sound, what you've actually experienced is a price adjustment, not a loss. It only becomes a true loss if you panic, sell, and lock in the downturn. The same logic applies to buying individual stocks or even alternative assets. The risk is not in the drop; it's in the response.

One of the most overlooked factors in evaluating risk is *time horizon*. A risky asset in the short term might be relatively safe over the long haul, and vice versa. Stocks, for instance, can lose 30% of their value in a year but gain 300% over a decade. A savings account, by contrast, offers near-zero volatility—but also near-zero growth, and if inflation outpaces interest (as it often does), you're losing money in real terms. So the relevant question is not "Is this risky?" but "How long am I giving this to work?" *The shorter your timeline, the lower your tolerance for fluctuation must be—but that's a trade-off, not a moral judgement.*

Understanding risk also means understanding *your own risk profile*, not just the asset's. How would you feel if your investment halved in value next week? Could you hold firm or would you sell immediately? Do you need access to the money in two years or twenty? Is your job stable, or are you relying on these funds for emergency liquidity? The right amount of risk is not defined by what's "smart" or "dumb" in the abstract—it's defined by *what you can emotionally and practically tolerate without compromising your larger goals*. Misalignment here—between the volatility of the asset and the volatility of your temperament—is where most financial pain is born.

The danger of uninformed risk is that it disguises itself as courage. It rewards early wins with unjustified confidence. A teenager who triples their money on a meme stock might believe they've found a repeatable system, when in reality they've stumbled upon a statistical outlier. Once that confidence calcifies, it resists correction, and the next inevitable downturn feels not like a learning moment, but a personal betrayal. By contrast, *informed risk begins with humility*. It acknowledges that no one can predict markets consistently, that luck often masquerades as skill, and that resilience is a more useful trait than brilliance.

Behavioural economics has long demonstrated how humans are hardwired to fear losses more than they enjoy equivalent gains—a phenomenon known as *loss aversion*. This bias makes it harder to hold investments during downturns, even when logic dictates doing so. But awareness of this bias is half the battle. Knowing that your brain is primed to overreact can help you build systems to counteract it—automated investing, diversified portfolios, and the refusal to check your account every hour. In this way, *self-awareness becomes a form of financial risk management*.

It's also worth distinguishing between *idiosyncratic risk* (specific to a single investment) and *systemic risk* (affecting the broader economy). Putting all your money in one tech stock is idiosyncratic risk. Spreading it across many sectors through a fund reduces that exposure. But no amount of diversification can eliminate systemic shocks—like a global pandemic or banking collapse. What you can do, however, is prepare psychologically and structurally: maintain an emergency fund, don't invest money you need within the next two years, and keep your allocation in line with your age and goals. Risk doesn't disappear, but it becomes *contextualised*.

The cultural narrative around investing—especially online—often glorifies high-risk, high-reward bets. But these stories are usually told backwards. We hear about the person who made £200,000 from crypto, not the 10,000 others who lost half their savings chasing the same dream. Survivorship bias is rampant, and unless you actively seek out the losses, you'll mistake volatility for genius and risk for opportunity. *Real investing wisdom is boring, methodical, and under-celebrated.*

This isn't to discourage ambition. High-risk investments can play a role in a well-balanced portfolio, especially if you're young and have time on your side. But they must be approached *as part of a broader strategy*, not as stand-alone gambles. If 80% of your money is in diversified, long-term assets, and 20% is allocated to riskier ventures, you're not avoiding risk—you're managing it. That's the key. *Good investors don't fear risk—they price it.* They ask: What's the worst-case scenario? How likely is it? Can I recover from it? And is the upside worth that trade?

In the end, risk is the price you pay for opportunity. There is no version of a financially free life that does not involve it. But the right kind of risk—calculated, conscious, aligned with your goals—can accelerate that freedom rather than endanger it. Uninformed risk, on the other hand, is just speculation in a costume. It feels bold but builds nothing.

So stop asking how to avoid risk. Ask how to *understand it, absorb it*, and *leverage it intelligently*. Risk isn't a storm to be weathered—it's a current to be navigated. Not all currents are safe, but none can be crossed by those who freeze at the first wave.

Start Small, Think Long

When it comes to investing, scale is overrated and consistency is underestimated. The cultural script around wealth tends to glorify the outsized bet—the "all-in" play, the overnight success, the unicorn outcome. It seduces with the fantasy that one bold move can bypass the slow grind and deliver instant elevation. But when you pull back from the headlines and look at real financial outcomes over time, what emerges is something far less dramatic and far more reliable: those who accumulate the most, and keep the most, tend to do so by starting small and persisting. Not by betting big and hoping.

This truth is neither sexy nor viral. But it is mathematically sound, psychologically sustainable, and historically validated. Investing isn't a test of bravado; it's a test of behaviour. What you do consistently—especially with small amounts—will almost always beat what you do once with a large amount. And that difference compounds.

To appreciate why, consider how compound growth actually works. At its core, compounding is not magic. It's time, multiplied by repetition, shaped by reinvestment. The earlier and more frequently you feed it, the more potent it becomes. But if you delay because your starting amount feels "too small to matter," you sabotage the very advantage that makes compounding work in your favour. The beginner who invests £50 per month from age 18 will often end up wealthier than the latecomer who starts with £10,000 at 30. Not because they saved more overall, but because they started sooner and built the habit before the stakes were high. *The most powerful financial advantage is time, not timing.*

Small, consistent contributions are also easier to sustain. One-time windfalls may feel empowering, but they tend to distort your expectations. A big investment can create emotional turbulence: you watch it obsessively, overreact to every dip, and risk abandoning the plan at the first sign of trouble. Low-stakes, repeated investing, by contrast, normalises fluctuation. You get used to the rhythm. You care less about the daily swings because your identity isn't tied to a single trade. Over time, this builds not just wealth, but *resilience.*

There's also a psychological phenomenon known as the "unit bias"—the tendency to believe that actions must feel substantial to be valuable. This bias convinces people that investing £10 is pointless, that they need hundreds or thousands to get started. But that's a fundamental misunderstanding of scale in the investing world. Most reputable investing platforms now allow fractional investing, meaning you can buy £5 worth of a £300 stock. There are no more legitimate excuses for waiting. *The new barrier to entry is not money—it's mindset.*

Yet even in a world of accessible platforms and zero-commission trades, the emotional resistance persists. Why? Because small investing doesn't feel "real." It lacks drama. It doesn't make for a compelling story at parties. It doesn't scratch the same itch as speculation. This is where behavioural discipline becomes essential. You must learn to override the temptation for excitement in favour of the much quieter satisfaction of long-term alignment. *Boring is where wealth builds.*

The irony is that the same people who dismiss low-stakes investing as insignificant often think nothing of spending £10 on fast food or £30 on a subscription they forgot about. In those moments, small amounts are casually disposable. But when the same amount is earmarked for investing, suddenly it feels "too little to matter." This contradiction isn't rational—it's emotional. The act of spending offers immediate gratification. Investing, on the other hand, is a deferred payoff. That psychological tension—between present comfort and future gain—is precisely why most people delay starting. *But the discipline of starting small is the antidote to financial procrastination.*

One of the most productive mental models for consistent investing is to treat it as *rent you pay your future self.* It reframes saving and investing not as a sacrifice, but as a service—to the version of you who will need options, time, and freedom. And the price of that service isn't enormous. It's not hundreds of pounds every month. It's a few coffees skipped. A few rides walked. A few upgrades forgone. When framed this way, investing becomes not just financially feasible but *emotionally logical.*

It's also worth noting that smaller investments make it easier to learn. Mistakes made with £20 are far less painful than mistakes made with £2,000. And you will make mistakes—everyone does. The market will drop. You'll buy something at the wrong time. You'll misunderstand a trend. But if your early entries are modest, you'll earn education at a discount. That learning compounds, too.

There is another benefit to starting small: it builds identity. Each contribution reinforces the idea that you are an investor. Not someday, not "when you have more money"—now. And identity drives behaviour. The more you see yourself as a long-term thinker, the more naturally you'll act like one. You'll be less tempted by fads. Less shaken by headlines. Less reactive to temporary losses. *The earlier you adopt the investor mindset, the easier it becomes to think beyond the next payday.*

Of course, this does not mean that you should never take bigger financial swings—just that they should be built on a foundation of routine. If your default is consistent low-stakes investing, then you can afford to selectively take larger risks *with surplus capital,* not with your safety net. That discipline ensures that when big opportunities arise, you're not gambling with your future, but leveraging from a place of strength.

Consider the analogy of physical fitness. You don't start by bench-pressing 200 pounds. You start by showing up. Doing push-ups. Learning form. Avoiding injury. The strength comes from repetition, not heroics. Investing is no different. The world is full of financial injuries sustained by people who tried to "skip leg day" and jump straight to the heaviest weights. *The sustainable gains come from mastering small, repeatable actions.*

For those worried that small investments won't yield enough, a practical counterpoint: £25 invested weekly at an average 7% return becomes over £50,000 in twenty years. That's the cost of a new car. A business startup. A down payment. And if you increase that to £50 a week, you cross six figures. All of it built from amounts that felt, at the time, like "not enough to bother."

That's the long game. Not a lottery ticket. Not a viral crypto bet. But a steady, boring, quietly compounding machine that works while you sleep, study, travel, and work. The point is not that you become rich instantly. It's that you build a base so solid that when real opportunities come—whether it's launching a venture, moving cities, or taking a sabbatical—you can afford to say yes.

Starting small doesn't mean thinking small. It means refusing to let size dictate seriousness. Every empire began with a single brick. Every fortune began with a single deposit. Every seasoned investor began by being new. *What separates those who succeed from those who stall is not access—it's action.*

So don't wait to be "ready." Start with what you have, automate what you can, and increase when it's natural. Keep your eye on the runway, not the scoreboard. The game of wealth isn't about making the biggest move. It's about staying in the game long enough to let your smartest ones count.

Chapter 8
Digital Money Traps

Financial self-sabotage rarely arrives with fanfare. It doesn't need maxed-out credit cards or extravagant splurges to wreak havoc. Increasingly, it looks like a perfectly ordinary month: nothing lavish, nothing headline-worthy, yet your bank balance is inexplicably lower than expected. There are no luxury holidays, no impulsive online hauls—just a slow, almost imperceptible bleed of money through tiny, repeated deductions: one-tap purchases, forgotten auto-renewals, small treats that quietly accumulate far beyond your intention. This subtle erosion is the main stage of modern financial life for Gen Z, digital natives for whom money often flows invisibly.

The nature of spending has transformed. In the analogue era, a transaction demanded attention: you reached for your wallet, counted the notes, made a conscious decision. Digital design has stripped away these pauses. Convenience, speed, frictionless interfaces—all engineered to make spending almost effortless—have created a paradox: the easier it is to pay, the less real it feels. A fingerprint now substitutes for a PIN; a swipe substitutes for consent; money vanishes quietly through app interfaces and notifications, only revealing its absence later in overdrafts or missing funds.

Subscriptions are emblematic of this shift. Once a niche for magazines or gym memberships, they now pervade entertainment, meal kits, wellness apps, and more. Their danger lies not in their existence but in their invisibility. Many users forget what they subscribe to, or fail to engage with it consistently. A 2023 study by C+R Research revealed that 74% of millennials underestimated their monthly subscription expenditure by over 100%. That gap between perception and reality is where money quietly escapes, a drain that dulls awareness rather than warning you with dramatic splashes.

Gaming ecosystems offer another example. Free-to-play platforms thrive on microtransactions—small, seemingly harmless purchases. But "micro" is misleading: one £3 cosmetic skin often leads to another, until £100 vanishes with no tangible value. Behavioural design is deliberate. Humans are loss-averse; developers exploit this by creating streak-based rewards and limited-time offers, nudging players to spend now or miss out. The boundary between leisure and exploitation is engineered to be slippery.

Culture, too, conspires. Influencer finance, crypto promotion, and TikTok money advice saturate the online space with self-styled experts. While some provide value, many peddle oversimplified tactics, risky strategies, or outright scams—cloaked in confidence and anecdotal success. The danger is not just misinformation but emotional manipulation. FOMO is weaponised; young viewers, navigating economic uncertainty, are pressured to "act now" or risk being left behind by peers. This cocktail of urgency and insecurity distorts both spending and identity.

Scams often masquerade as opportunity: get-rich-quick schemes, dropshipping courses, secret investment blueprints, and affiliate funnels rely on aesthetic credibility and social proof. They may not always be illegal, yet they prey on desperation and confusion, particularly among those eager to bypass traditional financial constraints. The antidote is not cynicism but literacy. Thriving financially in a digital world demands intelligence, not rejection—an ability to out-think the system rather than fall victim to it.

Digital hygiene is essential. Just as you would lock your door, you should shield your financial identity. Password reuse, public Wi-Fi banking, and lax privacy settings remain commonplace among those assuming they are too insignificant to target. Modern fraud does not require fame—only access. Data breaches, phishing attempts, and spoofed payment links are routine threats. The remedy is protocol, not paranoia: two-factor authentication, transaction alerts, spending caps, and granular permission controls are the foundations of digital-age financial self-defence.

The traps of digital money are as psychological as they are technical. They exploit speed, decision overload, and cognitive fatigue, making "yes" the easier default than "why." Fragmented attention allows money to slip away unnoticed. Awareness alone is insufficient; the architecture of your financial environment matters. Disable auto-renewals, choose banks with transparent insights, curate feeds that influence spending decisions. Discipline is only part of the equation; intelligent design is the rest.

This chapter unpacks the mechanics of these traps: how they are constructed, why they work, and how to respond. Technology is not the enemy; obfuscation is. Every interface has intent. Every frictionless payment carries economic purpose. True financial freedom in a digital age starts not with radical austerity but with informed agency.

There is no returning to analogue simplicity. Yet it is possible to move forward with control, precision, and skill. The key is recognising that digital spending is engineered behaviour. Only then can you construct a system that safeguards your money, empowers your choices, and ensures that the tools you use serve your goals, rather than quietly subverting them.

Subscription Sinkholes

No single transaction in a typical subscription model feels significant. That's precisely the problem. The modern digital economy thrives not on the magnitude of purchases, but on their *persistence*. £4.99 for music. £7.99 for streaming. £2.49 for cloud storage. £11.99 for "premium" fitness. On their own, these recurring charges appear harmless—modest investments in lifestyle and convenience. Yet collectively, they behave like financial termites: quiet, consistent, and structurally damaging over time. The average Gen Z user now holds over six active digital subscriptions without fully realising it. The real cost of this isn't just monetary—it's cognitive and behavioural, reshaping how we relate to our finances and what we consider "normal" spending.

Subscription models are not inherently deceptive, but they are *incentivised* to be forgettable. Their economic power lies in what behavioural economists call *passive frictionlessness*: a state where the consumer has to do *nothing* to continue paying. This is a reversal of traditional commerce. In the past, purchasing something required repeated intent. Now, cancelling is the labour, while continuing is the default. This asymmetry exploits cognitive laziness, optimism bias, and decision fatigue—especially among younger consumers who are managing increasing numbers of digital accounts across platforms.

Consider the design of cancellation interfaces. Numerous studies have shown that digital services often implement "dark patterns"—manipulative UX strategies that make unsubscribing harder than signing up. These can range from buried settings to mandatory feedback loops and misleading buttons. Amazon Prime was investigated by the Norwegian Consumer Council for exactly this, with findings showing how users were deterred from cancellation by a labyrinth of choices and psychological nudges. These tactics aren't bugs—they are features. They are engineered to maintain revenue by capitalising on inertia.

Yet it's not merely the interface that causes trouble—it's the *illusion of utility*. Subscription fatigue doesn't always stem from services we never use, but from those we use just enough to justify keeping. A young user might log into a meditation app once a week and tell themselves it's "worth it," despite having dozens of free alternatives. The calculus shifts from actual value to perceived guilt: *if I cancel, am I giving up on my better self?* This gamifies identity, not just consumption, and leads people to maintain subscriptions less out of need than aspiration. In such cases, the product being sold isn't content or service—it's *potential.*

This is where the economic trap deepens. When money is spent regularly in small increments, the human brain fails to compute long-term cost intuitively. £12.99/month doesn't *feel* like £155.88/year. That psychological disconnection makes budgeting porous. Most people don't sit down and calculate annualised subscription costs; they mentally anchor each service as a minor, justifiable indulgence. But stack six to ten such "minor" services, and you've quietly constructed a second rent. A 2022 survey in the UK found that the average young adult spends more than £300 a year on subscriptions they forgot they had—an amount equal to a new smartphone or a decent emergency fund.

More insidiously, subscription pricing often conceals deeper financial vulnerabilities. In low-income households or among students, these recurring charges are frequently paid on autopilot—even when it means incurring overdraft fees or cutting back on essentials. Because subscriptions are billed automatically, they quietly take precedence over discretionary spending. There's no warning, no budget checkpoint. For someone juggling rent, transportation, and groceries, a forgotten streaming charge can mean the difference between stability and stress. *This isn't indulgence—it's design-induced financial precarity.*

It's also generational. Millennials and Gen Z are the first cohorts to grow up in a subscription-dominant economy. From software to social media tools, from education platforms to dating apps, they are taught that *access* matters more than ownership. In many ways, this mindset is modern and efficient. But it also erodes the instinct to audit, to question, and to cancel. Subscription services thrive because they offer continual convenience in exchange for perpetual micro-debt. They turn fixed costs into ambient ones—painless at the point of purchase, but corrosive over time. And they encourage passive engagement with money: a worldview where spending is not a choice, but a background condition of life.

One of the most under-acknowledged issues with subscription sinkholes is their tendency to mask financial agency. People often know they should cut back but don't know where to start. The emotional toll of cancellation—especially for services tied to well-being, productivity, or social connection—creates a paralysis of choice. Should I cancel the fitness app I barely use? The language-learning tool I abandoned after two weeks? The "premium" news site I skim once a month? These are not trivial dilemmas. They are *identity decisions* masquerading as financial ones.

The solution is not to demonise subscriptions but to recalibrate our relationship with them. A healthy financial system includes recurring services—when chosen with clarity and reviewed regularly. The key lies in converting passive decisions into active ones. One proven method is the *subscription audit*: a quarterly exercise where every recurring charge is surfaced, evaluated, and either retained, paused, or cancelled. More advanced users may adopt "subscription fasting" for a set period—cancelling all non-essential services and reintroducing them one by one based on actual demand. These aren't extreme tactics; they are practical defences against engineered forgetfulness.

Technology itself can be repurposed for this awareness. Several fintech apps now offer automated subscription tracking, alerts for duplicate services, and even one-tap cancellations. But the deeper shift must be psychological: a recognition that small, recurring costs are not small over time—and that *default spending is still spending*. The act of unchecking a renewal box or pausing a trial is not petty frugality; it's financial authorship. It's the difference between being a user and being a strategist.

Ultimately, the question isn't "Can I afford this subscription?" but "Does this subscription still serve a purpose worth paying for today?" That mental reframing reasserts control in an economic model designed to minimise it. The goal is not to live a subscription-free life—only a *subscription-conscious* one. Because when money drains in drips, the danger isn't the flood—it's that you never notice the leak.

Gaming, Gifting, and Microtransactions

One of the most misunderstood forces shaping the financial behaviour of Gen Z isn't a new credit card product or a fintech startup. It's the psychological machinery embedded within mobile games, streaming platforms, and gifting ecosystems. In an age where physical wallets are vanishing and digital spending is frictionless, the smallest monetary interactions often leave the deepest impressions. Microtransactions—defined by their low cost and high frequency—have transformed the economics of entertainment and, more subtly, the architecture of decision-making. When spending no longer feels like spending, control becomes an illusion, not a strategy.

Microtransactions began innocently enough: a dollar here for an in-game skin, a few pounds there for bonus lives or aesthetic upgrades. But they've since metastasised into a trillion-dollar economy built on behavioural manipulation. The design is deliberate. Game developers, e-commerce platforms, and social media giants now rely heavily on variable reward schedules—what psychologists refer to as "intermittent reinforcement"—to create compulsive engagement. Users are rewarded unpredictably, keeping them in a cycle of hopeful tapping, scrolling, or swiping. This is the same behavioural loop exploited by slot machines. The difference is that this one fits in your pocket, not a casino.

This system is sustained by a powerful financial illusion: decoupling money from meaning. In many platforms, users do not spend real currency directly. Instead, they convert it into in-app tokens, gems, coins, or credits—units with no intuitive sense of value. A £5 top-up might buy 500 gems, but what is a gem *worth*? This obfuscation severs the emotional link between cost and consequence. It allows users—especially younger ones—to spend recklessly while feeling like they're managing points, not pounds. The design language is light, colourful, and playful. The financial reality is not.

More critically, microtransactions thrive on social psychology. In multiplayer games or social platforms, paid enhancements aren't merely functional—they're status symbols. Cosmetic items, exclusive skins, badges, and digital gifts signal identity and hierarchy. In communities where visibility equals value, *not paying* can feel like opting out of social relevance. Teenagers and young adults in particular are susceptible to this dynamic. To them, refusing to participate can feel like self-exclusion, even invisibility. The pressure to spend becomes ambient, not overt—a constant background hum rather than a single sales pitch.

This is where gifting enters the equation. Digital gifting, whether in the form of Twitch donations, TikTok roses, or Discord boosts, has reframed generosity itself as a transactional gesture. It offers immediate validation—applause, emojis, leaderboards—in return for money. But it also gamifies affection, support, and admiration. The more you spend, the more visible your gesture. This isn't new (the wealthy have long used money to command attention), but the scale and subtlety of digital gifting normalises this logic among all users, not just the affluent. Even a £0.99 virtual sticker becomes a small lever in a social economy that equates spending with care.

This behaviour has economic ripple effects. As gifting becomes a common feature of youth culture, its presence distorts budgeting habits. A young person may resist buying lunch to avoid overspending, but think nothing of sending digital gifts to influencers or streamers. The distinction lies not in logic, but in *emotional immediacy*. Microtransactions are emotionally charged and temporally compressed—they happen in moments of excitement, not contemplation. They are usually prompted by impulse, not intention. This makes them extraordinarily difficult to resist, especially for those whose prefrontal cortex—the brain's impulse-control centre—is still developing.

To understand the gravity of the issue, one must examine the economic incentives of the platforms themselves. Games like *Clash of Clans*, *Fortnite*, and *Genshin Impact* generate billions in revenue annually, not from upfront sales, but from sustained microspending. Their monetisation models are not ancillary—they are foundational. Every element of game design is tuned to drive transactions: difficulty spikes that can be bypassed with purchases, time delays that can be shortened with payments, characters locked behind randomised loot boxes. These are not neutral mechanics. They are psychological traps engineered for monetisation.

One particularly pernicious mechanism is the loot box—a form of digital gambling disguised as gameplay. Users pay for a chance to win rare items, often with odds undisclosed or obfuscated. Studies have shown strong correlations between loot box spending and problem gambling behaviour, particularly among adolescents. The UK's House of Lords has even called for regulating loot boxes under gambling legislation, recognising the potential for addiction and financial harm. Yet in many countries, this form of monetised chance remains legal and largely unregulated. The players lose; the platforms win.

This landscape is not without resistance. Parents, educators, and some regulators have begun to raise alarms. But awareness alone is insufficient. What's needed is a new form of *personal literacy*—a cognitive toolkit for recognising when digital environments are shaping financial behaviour without consent. The ability to name the tactic—"this is a variable reward schedule," or "this is an artificial time gate designed to drive urgency"—is the first line of defence. Naming breaks the spell. It restores agency.

From a financial standpoint, the solution is not abstinence, but awareness. Microtransactions can be harmless entertainment when bounded by conscious limits. The problem arises when boundaries are blurred by design. One practical tactic is the use of prepaid wallets or capped digital spending accounts. Another is time-delay systems: apps or settings that force a 24-hour buffer before in-app purchases are processed. These introduce *friction*, which is the enemy of impulsive financial behaviour and the ally of considered spending. The goal is to *interrupt automation*—to ensure that spending is a choice, not a reflex.

More broadly, there is a need for cultural reframing. Within many peer groups, especially among youth, there is a subtle valorisation of spending as engagement. "Whales"—the small percentage of users who account for the majority of microtransaction revenue—are often revered in digital communities. But this glamorisation masks economic fragility. In truth, overspending on microtransactions is often a proxy for unmet emotional needs: status, belonging, recognition. Teaching financial intelligence must therefore include *emotional awareness*. Ask not just "what are you buying?" but "why now?"

Digital platforms will not voluntarily curtail their most profitable mechanics. That leaves individual users to become their own regulators. This isn't a cry for cynicism, but for *lucid scepticism*. Assume that every reward, every limited-time offer, every animated pop-up is optimised to extract money. Assume that convenience is rarely neutral, and friction is often your financial ally. In a world where platforms profit most when you think least, awareness becomes a revolutionary act.

The psychology of microtransactions is not limited to gaming. It spills into dating apps, learning platforms, health tools, and social media. It rewires expectations for how money is spent, what value looks like, and how decisions are made. For a generation coming of age in this digital terrain, financial literacy must evolve. It is no longer enough to know what a budget is. One must understand *how the architecture of choice is constructed around them*—and how to deconstruct it when necessary.

True financial control in the age of microtransactions does not mean refusing to spend. It means learning to *see*—clearly, calmly, and critically—what you're being asked to trade, and whether the reward is worth the cost. That awareness is not innate. It must be cultivated. And it begins with recognising that when a platform tells you your next reward is "just one tap away," what they're really saying is that your money, your attention, and your judgement are all on the line.

Influencer Finance and Scam Culture

There has never been a time in history when financial advice was so accessible and yet so dangerous. On TikTok, Instagram, and YouTube, millions of followers are just one swipe away from someone claiming to unlock "the secrets of passive income," "crypto goldmines," or "side hustles that make £10k a week." These messages often come wrapped in a carefully staged aesthetic—high-rise apartments, leased luxury cars, foreign getaways, and captions that blend urgency with familiarity: "If I can do it, so can you." But what's being sold here isn't merely information—it's aspiration packaged as authority. And for a generation raised on social media, *the line between expert and entertainer has almost entirely collapsed.*

The term "influencer" was once reserved for those in beauty, fashion, or lifestyle, but it has now metastasised into finance—a domain where stakes are higher, errors more costly, and regulation largely absent. The consequences of this shift are profound. Financial influencers (or "finfluencers") operate in a market that rewards visibility over rigour, confidence over competence, virality over validity. There is no barrier to entry, no certification process, no standard of accountability. One can be an overnight expert with nothing more than Canva, CapCut, and a persuasive tone of voice. The result is a digital Wild West in which charisma becomes currency, and misinformation spreads faster than due diligence.

What makes influencer finance uniquely problematic is not just the *lack* of credentials—it's the *illusion* of them. Finfluencers frequently mimic the aesthetics and language of authority. They present charts, data, and acronyms, often borrowed without comprehension. They reference books they haven't read and markets they barely understand. They flash screenshots of brokerage accounts as if wealth itself were proof of wisdom. This is not education—it's performance. And it works, especially on those least equipped to tell the difference.

At the heart of the problem is a psychological phenomenon known as *social proof*. Humans are evolutionarily wired to follow perceived consensus. When thousands of others appear to endorse a person or idea—through likes, shares, or comments—we instinctively assign it credibility. The more engagement a financial influencer garners, the more legitimate they seem, regardless of substance. This creates a feedback loop: popularity breeds trust, trust breeds investment, and investment—when fuelled by poor information—breeds loss. By the time the bubble pops, the influencer has moved on to the next shiny opportunity, while their followers are left with sunk costs and silent regret.

The tactics used by financial influencers mirror those of traditional scam artists, but updated for the digital age. They rely heavily on *FOMO*—fear of missing out. Urgency is a staple of their script: "The market's about to explode," "Only 12 spots left," "You can't afford to wait." These aren't just calls to action—they're psychological triggers designed to bypass rational analysis. Scarcity is manufactured. Deadlines are fabricated. The goal is not to inform, but to incite. When urgency overrides critical thinking, people don't ask hard questions—they reach for their wallets.

Then comes the upsell. Once trust is established, influencers often funnel followers into higher-priced offerings: private Discord groups, paid courses, affiliate programmes, or even subscription-based "alpha signals." Some offer "consultations" that are little more than pre-recorded sales pitches. Others promote trading platforms or digital coins from which they earn undisclosed commissions. Transparency is rare; conflicts of interest are rampant. These ecosystems are not designed to elevate the follower—they are engineered to extract maximum lifetime value from them, all under the guise of empowerment.

The consequences of this model are already visible. Teens are taking out loans to "invest" in pump-and-dump crypto tokens. University students are gambling tuition money on forex trades endorsed by Instagram mentors with no track record. Young workers are skipping employer-matched pensions because they're chasing higher short-term returns via high-risk altcoins. *This is not financial empowerment—it is misdirected ambition disguised as savvy investing.* It reflects a broader cultural shift in which speed is prized over strategy, optics over outcomes.

To be clear, not all influencers operating in the financial space are malicious or incompetent. Some provide genuine value, share thoughtful insights, and disclose their limitations. But the problem lies in the inability of most audiences to distinguish credible guidance from curated illusion. Algorithms are indifferent to accuracy. They reward engagement, and nothing spreads faster than confidence laced with controversy. This structural bias turns the financial education of millions into a popularity contest where the loudest voice, not the wisest, wins.

One of the most effective antidotes to this landscape of misinformation is *contextual awareness*. A legitimate financial educator will not promise guaranteed returns, shortcut strategies, or "secrets the banks don't want you to know." They will talk about risk, nuance, and long-term trade-offs. They will welcome questions, acknowledge uncertainty, and explain concepts without jargon. Their goal is not to impress you—it's to equip you. *That is the fundamental difference between persuasion and pedagogy.*

Developing the capacity to spot financial fakery requires more than just scepticism—it demands a new form of *digital literacy*. It means asking the right questions: What are this person's qualifications? Are they selling something? Do their claims align with evidence from trusted sources? Is their advice reproducible, or entirely dependent on timing and luck? Have they disclosed risk, or just potential upside? Most importantly, do they benefit more from your belief than your success?

One instructive example is the rise and fall of "crypto gurus" during the 2021 bull market. Many of them amassed huge followings by showcasing early wins, hyping new tokens, and declaring fiat currency obsolete. Their communities swelled, driven by speculative euphoria. But when the market corrected, followers were left with heavy losses, and influencers simply pivoted to the next trend. No apologies. No restitution. Just rebranded advice under a new buzzword—AI, NFTs, or "Web3 real estate." This is not evolution. It is evasion.

Scam culture is broader than individual influencers. It is an ecosystem that thrives on ambiguity. Fake brokers, phishing schemes, and deepfake "endorsements" from celebrities now circulate freely across platforms. In this environment, trust is not only misplaced—it's weaponised. Influencers lend credibility to dubious projects. Dubious projects boost the visibility of influencers. And somewhere in that cycle, a 17-year-old empties their savings into a scheme that vanishes overnight.

The educational response to this crisis cannot be passive. We must teach not just *what to think about money*, but *how to think about financial information*. This means fostering *epistemic humility*—the ability to say "I don't know enough yet to act"—as a legitimate, even admirable, stance. It means reintroducing *delayed gratification* into the conversation, not as moralism but as pragmatism. And it means cultivating *financial independence* as something earned through understanding, not bought through algorithms.

Gen Z is not naïve. They are curious, connected, and more financially aware than many give them credit for. But they are also navigating a digital economy where the incentives are misaligned and the loudest signals are the most misleading. The answer is not to shame or shelter them, but to equip them—with frameworks, filters, and the fluency to ask, "Who benefits if I believe this?"

In the end, financial literacy in the influencer age must go beyond balance sheets and compound interest. It must become *cultural literacy*—an ability to decode not only financial products, but the narratives, aesthetics, and incentives behind them. To recognise when someone is selling you a future they themselves don't believe in. To walk away when urgency is synthetic and authority unearned. And most of all, to understand that real financial strength is not about keeping up. It's about seeing clearly, thinking slowly, and choosing deliberately.

Protecting Your Money Online

The average internet user today manages more financial information on a smartphone than bankers did on desktop terminals twenty years ago. Savings accounts, investments, budgeting tools, credit histories, payment apps, cryptocurrency wallets—all are now housed in devices that fit in a pocket. This unprecedented convenience comes at a cost: exposure. While the tools have become smarter, so have the threats. Cybercriminals no longer need to pick locks or forge cheques; they exploit weak passwords, phishing emails, leaked data, and digital complacency. *The paradox of modern finance is that you can be financially literate yet digitally vulnerable—and one undermines the other.*

Young people, in particular, often mistake technical fluency for security. Comfort with using apps, streaming content, and managing notifications doesn't equate to an understanding of encryption, malware, or digital hygiene. They are fluent users, not necessarily informed custodians. As financial activity migrates entirely online, this gap becomes a lucrative opportunity for bad actors. Identity theft, account takeovers, SIM-swapping, keylogging software, malicious browser extensions—these aren't rare or Hollywood-style threats; they are commonplace tactics, refined daily by people who make their living off digital recklessness.

One of the most overlooked facts in personal finance is that *your financial resilience begins with your information security*. It's not enough to save and invest wisely if the access to your accounts can be compromised through a weak point—a reused password, a lost phone without two-factor authentication, or a poorly vetted browser plugin. The difference between a future of compounding wealth and one of painful setbacks can be as simple as whether your phone's lock screen is secured by biometric authentication or an easy-to-guess code like 1234.

Consider the most common entry point for attackers: the human one. Phishing scams no longer come in broken English from obscure addresses. They mimic real companies, replicate login pages, and use personal details scraped from social media to create messages that feel familiar, even urgent. A notification from your bank asking you to verify a transaction. An email from your favourite streaming service requesting password confirmation. A message from a payment app about suspicious activity. These aren't crude guesses—they're engineered hooks. And once you click, your credentials are harvested, your access compromised, and the cascade begins.

The underlying vulnerability here is not just digital ignorance—it's behavioural laziness. People reuse passwords across platforms. They delay security updates. They store sensitive notes in unencrypted apps. They disable two-factor authentication because it's inconvenient. *The irony is stark: users will spend hours trying to optimise their budgeting strategy while ignoring the simplest, most effective form of financial defence—basic security hygiene.*

Let's define what that hygiene entails. First, there's the issue of authentication. A strong password is not one you can remember—it's one you store in a secure password manager and never reuse. Two-factor authentication (2FA) is not optional; it is the modern equivalent of locking your front door. It should be enabled for every financial service you use. Preferably, that second factor is not SMS-based—which is vulnerable to SIM-swapping—but app-based (like Authy or Google Authenticator) or hardware-based (like a YubiKey). Biometric logins such as fingerprint or facial recognition add another layer of friction for unauthorised access, especially if your phone is lost or stolen.

Second, device hygiene is essential. Keeping your software up to date isn't cosmetic—it's strategic. Many updates contain patches for vulnerabilities that hackers actively exploit. A six-month-old operating system can be the equivalent of leaving your vault door ajar. The same applies to apps: update them, vet them, and delete those you no longer use. Each app on your phone is a potential entry point. Only download financial tools from reputable sources, and take a moment to read what permissions an app is requesting. If a calculator wants access to your location, microphone, or contact list, uninstall it immediately. These are red flags, not design quirks.

Then there's the issue of public networks. Free Wi-Fi in cafés, airports, or libraries is tempting, but it is also notoriously insecure. Connecting to a financial account or entering sensitive information over such a network is akin to having a private conversation on a loudspeaker. Use a Virtual Private Network (VPN) if you must access anything sensitive on a public network, or better yet, wait until you're on a secure, trusted connection.

Another emerging risk is the use of autofill features in browsers. While they offer convenience, they also create a single point of failure. If your browser is compromised—say, via malware or a rogue extension—everything stored within it, from card numbers to logins, becomes accessible. The convenience of saved credentials is not worth the cost of breached accounts. Rely instead on standalone password managers with encryption and compartmentalisation. They don't just store your keys—they keep them in a vault the browser can't automatically unlock.

Let's address a misconception: cybercriminals don't need to target you specifically for you to become a victim. They operate by exploiting systemic weak points and casting wide nets. If your password appears in a leaked data set from a retail hack, your email and login may be tried on hundreds of other platforms through a method called credential stuffing. If you're using that same password for your bank, brokerage, or digital wallet, you're already compromised—it's just a matter of when.

For this reason, it's vital to monitor your own data footprint. Use breach notification tools like HaveIBeenPwned or enable dark web monitoring features through your bank or credit agency. These services scan for your data in known breaches and alert you when your credentials appear in the wild. The earlier you know, the faster you can reset access and contain the fallout.

Beyond technical practices, digital money protection also requires psychological discipline. *Learn to question urgency.* Scammers exploit impulse, not reason. If you receive a message urging you to act fast—whether to claim a prize, stop a charge, or avoid suspension—it is likely manipulative by design. Take a breath. Check the sender. Visit the official site independently instead of clicking through the message. Treat all unsolicited financial requests as guilty until proven innocent.

Privacy also plays a role. Oversharing on social media isn't just unwise—it's exploitable. Birth dates, pet names, graduation years, and phone numbers are commonly used in passwords or as identity verification questions. The more personal data you post publicly, the easier it is for attackers to reset your accounts or impersonate you to your bank. What feels like harmless content can become a toolkit in the wrong hands.

An often-overlooked frontier is the realm of connected devices. Smartwatches, voice assistants, even smart TVs are becoming nodes in our digital ecosystem. Many of these devices are poorly secured and rarely updated. If they're connected to the same network as your phone or computer, a breach in one can offer a path to another. Think of your home network as a chain: its strength depends on its weakest link.

In financial terms, the return on investment for digital hygiene is enormous. It costs nothing to enable 2FA, change your passwords, or update your software—but it can prevent thousands in potential loss, not to mention the psychological and logistical toll of identity theft. Cybersecurity isn't merely a technical discipline; for individuals, *it is risk management in its most immediate form.*

Teaching this is no longer optional. It must be embedded into every financial literacy programme, every personal finance curriculum, and every conversation about money in the digital age. The modern definition of wealth must include *control over access*. It's not just about what you earn or invest—it's about what you can keep secure. And in a world where the average person juggles dozens of online accounts and handles payments through a touchscreen, the difference between safety and exposure often comes down to habits, not hardware.

Ultimately, digital hygiene should not be treated as a checklist but as a mindset. A healthy scepticism toward unsolicited messages. A commitment to regular audits of your security settings. A recognition that trust is earned, not assumed—especially in the domain of money. The tools exist. The risks are known. What remains is the choice to act not out of fear, but from the maturity of understanding. And in that choice lies the most powerful form of protection: awareness sharpened by action.

Chapter 9
Your First Bank (and What They Won't Tell You)

The first encounter with a bank rarely registers as a deliberate financial choice. It feels more like navigating bureaucracy: ID checks, forms, and terms you skim but don't truly absorb. A card arrives in the post, a mobile app promises "financial freedom," and suddenly you're enmeshed in the global banking system. Yet, unlike most major institutions—education, healthcare, government—banks are not designed to prioritise your best interests. They are profit-driven by default, and every interaction you have—from selecting an account to swiping a card, or even overdrawing—presents them with an opportunity to earn, often at your expense if you're inattentive. Recognising this asymmetry early is not cynicism; it is a mark of financial maturity.

Banks are not neutral custodians of your money. They are gatekeepers and toll collectors, offering access while charging for convenience, security, and mistakes. Their language is euphemistic—"maintenance fee," "processing charge," "overdraft protection"—concealing a quietly extractive relationship. Many only discover this after losing money to hidden fees, accumulating compounding credit card debt, or having an account frozen over a missed verification. Yet these pitfalls are avoidable, not by rejecting banks, but by approaching them with clarity and strategy—tools most first-time users never receive.

It begins with the right question: what is a bank truly for? Not what it advertises itself to be, but its fundamental role in your life. At its core, a bank provides three functions: safekeeping (holding your money securely), facilitation (enabling transactions and payments), and credit (lending options). Every other product, from loyalty programmes to "convenience features," is layered atop these essentials—often monetised. The challenge for new customers is distinguishing structural utility from commercial allure. The account with the flashiest app or the most generous rewards may not be the one you can navigate confidently.

Consider debit versus credit. Both involve a card swipe, yet they represent different contracts. Debit spends your existing funds; credit temporarily borrows someone else's. Used wisely, credit builds trust in your financial reliability and opens doors to favourable loans and mortgages. Used carelessly, it fosters late fees, interest charges, and dependency. The danger is rarely credit itself—it is ignorance. Young users are often encouraged to adopt credit before understanding repayment cycles, compounding interest, or utilisation ratios.

This theme recurs throughout banking: systems are presented before explanation. Overdraft protection is sold without clear disclosure that it is a pre-authorised, fee-bearing loan. Accounts may advertise "no monthly fees" only to reinstate charges if minimum balances aren't maintained. These are not anomalies but standardised design features. Not illegal, yet opaque. Your lack of awareness is part of the business model.

The remedy is fluency, not fear. Learn to read terms as a lawyer would. Understand the lifecycle of transactions: when payments clear, what "pending" means, how direct debits operate, and the consequences of failure. Grasp the differences between current accounts, savings accounts, money market funds, and cash ISAs—not just in name but in structure, access, yield, and risk. Banks employ compliance lawyers and analysts to optimise for margin; passivity leaves you navigating a game whose rules were designed against you.

Automation is a powerful early strategy—not in a flashy tech sense, but in disciplined routine. Setting money to move automatically towards your goals transforms intention into habit. Routing a portion of every paycheck into savings, contributing automatically to investments, or scheduling recurring bill payments reduces reliance on motivation or memory. The difference between manual transfers and automated systems is the difference between hope and structural certainty.

Ironically, banks profit most from users who behave erratically, yet the same institutions provide tools to avoid these pitfalls: alerts for low balances, temporary card locks, scheduled transfers. Many fail to use them because they are hidden under jargon or poorly explained. The tools exist; the manual does not. This chapter seeks to provide that manual.

We will examine what makes a bank trustworthy—not marketing claims, but practical measures: transparent fees, responsive customer service, integration with your financial tools, and real control over account settings. We'll unpack the hidden costs of "free" accounts, distinguish between ATMs, and reveal how banks profit even when they appear to be giving you favours. Evaluating accounts requires looking beyond the immediate offer to the long-term cost.

You will also learn to wield credit strategically: how scores are calculated, which behaviours strengthen or erode them, and how banks subtly nudge users toward debt through promotional interest rates or buy-now-pay-later schemes. Understanding these nudges allows you to navigate your bank on your terms rather than reacting passively.

This chapter does not demonise banks. It encourages moving from passive user to informed participant, cultivating a clear-eyed, strategic relationship. The goal is not to avoid every fee, but to comprehend what each transaction entails. When you understand banks as revenue-driven entities rather than benevolent institutions, your decisions serve you, not them. That awareness is financial adulthood—and it begins here.

Banking for Beginners

A bank account is often the first formal relationship a person has with the financial system, yet for most beginners, opening one feels more like ticking a box than crossing a threshold. The language is opaque, the choices seem indistinct, and the consequences of those choices remain invisible until something goes wrong—an overdraft fee, a declined payment, a locked card. Despite their central role in modern life, banks do little to educate first-time users, and much to obscure the true nature of their operations. What's sold as a convenience is, in practice, a complex web of contracts, permissions, and profit mechanisms. The beginner's challenge is not just to open an account, but to understand what that account does, how it functions, and how to choose one that aligns with their actual financial behaviour—not just their hopes or intentions.

To begin, it's crucial to strip away the branding and reduce a bank to its elemental functions. At its core, a bank performs three tasks: it holds your money, moves your money, and lends your money. Everything else—apps, cashback schemes, round-up savings features, overdraft "protections," and rewards programmes—are layers added to monetise these core functions. A current account allows you to deposit and withdraw funds, typically with a debit card and online access. A savings account offers a slightly higher interest rate in exchange for reduced liquidity or access limitations. A credit product—whether a credit card, loan, or overdraft facility—allows you to spend money you don't yet have, at a cost determined by interest and fees. Once you grasp these distinctions, the process of choosing a bank becomes an exercise in evaluating trade-offs, not gimmicks.

For first-time account holders, especially younger ones, the primary trap is misalignment between their real-world financial needs and the account's structure. Consider a student who signs up for a current account offering a £50 sign-up bonus and free music streaming, only to discover that if their balance drops below £200, they incur a £12 monthly fee. That student is not being rewarded—they're being baited. *Banks know that younger users are less likely to read fee schedules and more likely to value perks over structure. This asymmetry is not accidental; it's exploited commercially.* What matters more than temporary perks is understanding how the account treats low balances, how quickly transactions are processed, and what protections are in place if something goes wrong.

One of the most misunderstood features of a bank account is the concept of the "available balance." Most people assume that the number displayed in their app is the money they have. In reality, it's a provisional figure. Transactions often take time to clear, especially over weekends or holidays. Authorised payments may appear instantly, but the actual funds may not leave your account for days. This delay matters. If you make a series of purchases close to your account limit, you can easily trigger an overdraft without realising it. Worse, some banks intentionally reorder transactions to maximise fees—processing the largest charges first to increase the likelihood that smaller ones will bounce and incur penalties. *You are not just using a bank; you are being used by its systems if you do not understand how they're structured.*

To protect yourself, the first step is selecting a bank with transparent, accessible account information. Transparency is not a virtue often advertised, but it is a proxy for trust. Choose a bank whose terms are readable, whose customer service is responsive, and whose mobile app allows you to see pending transactions and fees in real time. Avoid banks that use euphemistic language—"arranged overdraft buffer," "maintenance coverage," or "courtesy alerts"—without clearly defining what those mean in practice. The more abstract the language, the more likely it is hiding a cost. *If you cannot explain to someone else how your account works in practical terms, you do not yet understand it well enough to use it safely.*

Another essential principle is recognising that not all accounts serve the same purpose. You should not treat your current account, savings account, and credit facility as interchangeable. Your current account is for daily use, ideally with no minimum balance and no monthly fee. Your savings account should not be an afterthought—it should be separate, slightly harder to access, and interest-bearing, however modestly. The psychological barrier of logging into a different app or waiting one business day for a transfer is often enough to deter impulsive spending. As for credit, it should be approached with intentionality. A beginner who starts with a secured credit card—where a deposit limits the amount borrowed—can build credit safely without risking serious debt. But credit used without understanding is not leverage; it's liability.

Crucially, many beginners are unaware of how banks make money, and this ignorance is not benign. Banks earn in four main ways: net interest margin (the spread between what they pay savers and charge borrowers), transaction fees, account fees, and penalties. Every swipe, bounce, or delay is a potential revenue event. What's marketed as "overdraft protection" is often just pre-authorised lending at punishing rates. What's labelled as "free banking" is often contingent on conditions unlikely to be met consistently by a new user. *The beginner's mindset should not be "What can I get for free?" but rather "Where are the traps buried, and how can I structure my financial behaviour to avoid them entirely?"*

The best way to avoid these traps is to anchor your banking strategy in your actual cash flow patterns. If your income is irregular—say, freelance gigs or part-time work—then a bank that penalises low balances is inherently unsuitable. If you make international transactions, choose a provider that offers fair FX rates and doesn't charge extortionate foreign transaction fees. If your spending skews digital and contactless, look for banks that offer real-time notifications, merchant details, and spending insights. Many digital-first "challenger banks" now offer these features natively and without cost. But even here, caution is warranted. Some of these platforms are not full banks; they may lack deposit insurance, lending services, or regulatory oversight. *The sleekest app is not always the safest vault.*

Another overlooked element is *data*. When you bank digitally, you are not just transacting—you are producing data. Banks track your spending patterns, income flows, and behavioural cues. This data is used to score you for creditworthiness, to target you with offers, and sometimes, to partner with third-party services. A beginner who links their account to dozens of fintech apps may unintentionally expose themselves to data-sharing practices they don't understand. Read permissions carefully. Deny access where it's not essential. And above all, treat your transaction history as part of your digital identity—it is not just private; it is economically valuable.

Finally, recognise that banking is not a one-time setup but a dynamic relationship. Review your accounts periodically. As your financial life evolves—whether through full-time work, travel, or moving to another country—your banking needs will shift. The account that was optimal at sixteen may be inadequate by twenty. Some banks allow seamless account upgrades; others require closing and reopening. Either way, your financial system should reflect your real life, not just the version imagined when you opened your first account.

To bank well as a beginner is not to master every technical term or chase every incentive. It is to ask smart questions, recognise structural incentives, and choose tools that align with your goals and habits—not the ones that promise the most perks. The earlier you develop this discernment, the more fluently you'll navigate the financial systems that govern adulthood. And once you understand how banks really work, you'll never look at an overdraft, a rewards scheme, or a "courtesy fee" the same way again.

Credit vs. Debit vs. Disaster

The difference between a debit card and a credit card seems deceptively simple—one pulls from money you already have; the other lets you spend money you don't. Yet that surface distinction conceals a set of deeply consequential financial dynamics that shape how you're viewed by lenders, how you're treated by institutions, and how vulnerable you are to spiralling debt or costly error. For most new users, especially those encountering banking systems for the first time, the terms "credit" and "debit" are mistakenly treated as interchangeable payment options at checkout. What they actually represent are distinct psychological contracts with entirely different incentives, protections, and consequences. To treat them as equivalents is to invite financial confusion. To understand their strategic use is to gain quiet leverage in a system that often punishes ignorance.

A debit card is direct. It draws funds from your current account instantly, which means you can only spend what you already possess—at least in theory. In practice, overdraft features, pending authorisations, and delayed transaction clearances can blur this clarity. Still, with a debit card, the risk is typically contained to your available balance. There's little danger of accumulating long-term debt, but there's also little opportunity to build a credit profile or establish financial trustworthiness in the eyes of institutions. Debit is transactional. It's practical. But in a credit-oriented economy, it's also invisible.

Credit, by contrast, is reputational. Every use of a credit card, every repayment, every delay, and every minimum payment you make (or fail to) is recorded in a sprawling system of credit reporting. This system does not care whether you meant to pay late, or whether your bank app glitched. It measures reliability through consistency and penalises mistakes impersonally. Used wisely, a credit card is not just a payment tool—it's a signalling mechanism. It says to lenders:

I can borrow responsibly. Used poorly, it says: *I'm risky. I cost more to trust.* And that assessment has material consequences—higher interest rates, stricter loan terms, or even outright denial of mortgages, student loans, or rental applications.

This makes the psychological dimension of credit use particularly dangerous. Credit cards offer the illusion of liquidity—an extension of your spending power that feels both accessible and painless. That psychological distance between transaction and consequence is not accidental. The human brain is less likely to register a credit card purchase as a loss, compared to handing over cash or seeing an immediate bank deduction. This leads to what behavioural economists call *spending decoupling*, where people spend more when using credit because the pain of payment is deferred or dulled. *The danger is not that people are financially irrational—it's that they're predictably irrational, and credit systems are designed to exploit that.*

To prevent disaster, the most important mindset shift is this: a credit card is not money. It is *a timed contract with consequences*. If you don't pay your full balance within the billing cycle, you're not just extending repayment—you're buying money at an interest rate that can exceed 20–30% annually. Consider what that means. If you spend £100 on credit and only pay the minimum monthly amount—say, £10—you could end up repaying over £140 across 18 months, depending on the rate and fee structure. That latte, that ride-share, that online purchase you barely remember? It's still costing you interest a year and a half later. *Credit cards do not forgive forgetfulness—they monetise it.*

This doesn't mean credit is inherently bad. In fact, when managed with discipline, it can be a powerful tool. Responsible credit use—paying off full balances on time, staying below 30% of your available limit, avoiding unnecessary inquiries—helps build a positive credit history.

That history can unlock better loan rates, easier access to housing, and lower insurance premiums. But that usefulness depends entirely on the assumption that the user treats the card not as money, but as *a tool for building trust.*

The trouble begins when users blur that boundary—when the credit card becomes a lifeline instead of a strategy. This is especially tempting during times of income instability or emergency spending, where credit seems like the only option. But relying on credit to plug short-term gaps can snowball quickly into compound debt. Interest doesn't just add cost; it adds *momentum* to your financial problem. The more you owe, the more you pay to owe. And unlike most other obligations, credit card debt is often the most expensive and least forgiving.

Even worse is the trap of minimum payments—a mechanism that appears helpful but is structurally predatory. Making a minimum payment avoids late fees and protects your credit score in the short term, but it ensures that the principal debt persists for as long as possible. Credit issuers know that many customers will fall into this cycle. In fact, their profitability often depends on it. They offer low introductory rates, generous limits, and cash rewards not as a favour, but as bait. *Credit cards are not designed for convenience—they are designed for extraction.* The longer you carry a balance, the more valuable you are to them.

So, what's the antidote? The first is *intentionality*. Use credit with a clear repayment plan. If you cannot pay off a purchase within the billing cycle, reconsider whether it's worth charging at all. This is not puritanical—it's strategic. Every transaction should have a built-in repayment timeline, not just an abstract promise to "catch up later." The second is *automation*. Set up alerts and auto-payments for the full statement amount. Avoid minimum payments unless there's no other option, and if you must carry a balance, prioritise repayment as aggressively as you would rent or tuition.

Third, understand the invisible calculations behind your creditworthiness. Your credit utilisation ratio—the percentage of your limit you're using—matters more than many realise. Keeping this below 30%, ideally below 10%, signals financial restraint. Paying early, even before the statement is due, can further reduce reported utilisation. Multiple small payments throughout the month are often more effective than a single lump sum at the deadline. These details may seem tedious, but they compound into serious advantages over time.

There's also the social aspect of credit culture that deserves scrutiny. In many peer groups, particularly among students or early-career professionals, there is a performative aspect to spending. Designer brands, frequent travel, or premium gadgets become status markers, often justified by "I'll just put it on my card." This isn't merely a budgeting problem—it's a signalling problem. *When identity is tied to visible consumption, credit becomes a form of social camouflage—an unsustainable costume worn at interest.* Learning to separate self-worth from spending power is as much a psychological skill as it is a financial one.

And while debit cards avoid many of these traps, they are not inherently superior. Debit lacks many of the fraud protections that credit offers. If your debit card is compromised, your actual funds may be frozen or stolen, and reimbursement can take days or weeks. Credit cards, by contrast, offer stronger consumer protections and less direct risk. For this reason, some financially savvy individuals use credit for all transactions, simply for the safeguards—*but they treat the credit limit as a hard ceiling, not a suggestion.*

Ultimately, the line between credit and debit is not just about money—it's about *philosophy*. Debit aligns with a cash-based, "pay as you go" mindset: limited risk, limited leverage. Credit aligns with a trust-based, "pay later" model: high risk, high potential. The danger lies in misunderstanding which context you're in. Used reflexively, credit becomes a trap. Used strategically, it becomes a credential.

But there is no safety net built into the system. The credit industry profits from overextension, confusion, and delay. Your best protection is clarity—about what you can afford, about what the terms really mean, and about what you're willing to sacrifice for flexibility. Because in the end, it's not the card in your wallet that defines your financial stability—it's the awareness in your decisions. And that awareness, once developed, will serve you longer than any reward point or cashback scheme ever could.

Avoiding the Hidden Fees Minefield

The financial industry does not rely solely on interest rates or investment margins for profit. A quieter but equally powerful revenue stream lies buried in the fine print: fees. These seemingly minor charges—often presented as a few pounds here or a few pence there—accumulate silently, frequently unnoticed until statements are scanned in detail or overdrafts trigger alerts. The system is not designed to make these charges visible; it's designed to make them forgettable. That is the first clue to their significance. *When a bank or financial product deliberately obscures a charge, the most rational question is not "What is this for?" but "Why was it hidden?"*

Modern financial services—particularly digital-first banks, mobile apps, and fintech platforms—have transformed how people interact with money. Convenience has become the selling point, not transparency. In a world where signing up takes thirty seconds and cancellation takes thirty emails, behavioural friction is not accidental. From account maintenance fees to transaction charges and international currency conversion levies, the reality is that a significant percentage of retail banking profits stem not from serving customers well, but from betting on the likelihood that customers won't read—or understand—the terms of service.

This is not incompetence. It is commercial strategy disguised as user experience.

Consider a common example: the "free" current account. Marketed as a zero-cost option, it comes with no monthly maintenance fee. That sounds benign, even generous. But scan deeper and the true picture emerges—penalties for bounced direct debits, unarranged overdrafts, out-of-network ATM usage, paper statements, dormant account status, and more. *Free to open, expensive to ignore.* The fine print is a paradox: necessary to read, yet written in a manner designed to discourage reading. Most people are not lazy. They are simply overloaded. Banks understand this.

Some fees are structural, grounded in operational costs or regulatory compliance. Others are opportunistic, emerging from the statistical predictability of user error. The £1.50 charge for a balance inquiry at a non-affiliated ATM? It costs the bank fractions of a penny. The £25 overdraft fee triggered by a transaction of £2.10 that posts two hours before your salary? It is less about compensating for risk and more about maximising the mismatch between banking schedules and customer expectations. The real product being sold isn't the account—it's the consequences of using it incorrectly.

Technology has only amplified this problem. Digital banking apps have normalised hyper-convenience while simultaneously making it easier to dissociate behaviour from consequence. Subscription renewals for premium account services may be automatically enrolled without clear opt-in. Payment processors charge international transaction fees despite operating on global platforms. Instant cash transfers between accounts sometimes incur fees arbitrarily, as if speed were a luxury rather than a baseline. Each instance reveals a deeper truth: *the system monetises opacity.*

Even supposedly forward-thinking institutions are not exempt. Fintech start-ups often begin by "disrupting" traditional banking with no-fee models and consumer-first rhetoric. But as user acquisition plateaus and monetisation becomes a priority, fee structures creep back in—this time disguised as features. Priority support, early access to salary, cryptocurrency wallet transfers, and account insights are quietly paywalled. The irony is sharp: the institutions claiming to "democratise finance" often become indistinguishable from the legacy banks they set out to replace.

Recognising and avoiding hidden fees is not about paranoia; it is about precision. The task requires both scepticism and literacy. Start by reading the fee schedule—not skimming it, but studying it with the rigour of a legal contract. Look for patterns in your statements. Are you being charged for ATM withdrawals despite having a debit card? Are recurring charges appearing under vague descriptors like "monthly service fee" or "maintenance charge"? Financial awareness is not intuitive; it is learned.

Some protections are embedded in regulation. In the UK, for instance, banks are required to disclose representative APRs, and they must provide at least two months' notice before increasing most types of fees. Yet the spirit of transparency often fails in practice. Notices are sent via app notifications buried under marketing messages, or posted online under sections labelled "updates to our service." The information is disclosed—but the design ensures it is rarely seen. *Transparency without accessibility is not transparency; it is theatre.*

Avoiding this minefield involves more than awareness. It involves active counter-strategy. Automate transaction alerts for all activity above a minimal threshold—£1, for instance. Categorise your monthly spending by account fees, service charges, and ATM usage. Use banks or fintech platforms that offer "fee previews" before initiating transactions. Opt out of paper statements if there's a charge; opt in if there's a discount. Set calendar reminders for annual renewals and grace periods. Most importantly, treat any "free trial" of financial services as paid unless explicitly proven otherwise.

Crucially, do not assume that loyalty will spare you from fees. Legacy banks in particular often penalise long-standing customers through inertia. Introductory offers disappear, tiered rates reset, and incentives are retracted without warning. Inertia costs money. Switching banks may feel inconvenient, but staying loyal to an inefficient institution costs more in the long term. Use comparison platforms to audit your accounts annually—not just for interest rates, but for total annualised fees. Hidden costs are rarely included in headline comparisons, but they are where the true economics of personal banking reside.

Fees are not inherently unethical. But their concealment is. A fee that compensates for real operational expense is fair; one designed to capitalise on consumer confusion is not. The distinction matters. When evaluating a bank, don't just ask what you're being offered. Ask what's being assumed. Is the product assuming you'll never make a transfer at night, go abroad, or forget a payment date? If so, it's not a financial service—it's a behavioural trap wrapped in legal disclaimers.

Some of the most egregious fee models are explicitly predatory, targeting younger users with limited financial experience. Student accounts often come with enticing perks—railcards, overdrafts, cashback. But the conditions attached to these perks can be restrictive, triggering long-term costs once the initial grace period ends. It is not uncommon for overdraft fees to skyrocket the moment a student graduates, often without a clear notification. If an incentive requires more footnotes than benefits, it is a liability masquerading as a reward.

This dynamic is compounded in the digital age. Finfluencers and pseudo-experts often promote branded debit cards or e-wallets with "zero fees," neglecting to mention currency conversion charges, merchant surcharges, and inactivity penalties. The platforms themselves may gamify spending to encourage more frequent transactions—round-ups, rewards, boost multipliers—while subtly integrating fee-based tiers. The psychology is clever. The economics are not.

Ultimately, navigating the hidden fee minefield is an act of self-respect. It means rejecting the passive role of consumer in favour of active participation in one's financial life. It means acknowledging that modern banking is not neutral ground—it is terrain designed to reward those who scrutinise and penalise those who assume good faith. To master money is to master the systems that govern it. And no system is more fundamental—or more obfuscated—than the fees charged by the institutions entrusted with our cash.

In a culture where every pound matters and attention is finite, clarity becomes power. The banks won't give it freely. But with vigilance, discipline, and critical inquiry, you can take it for yourself. That is the essence of financial literacy: not merely understanding what your money does, but understanding what others do to your money when you're not paying attention. The hidden fee, then, is not just a financial detail—it's a signal. A signal that you're being watched not as a customer, but as a margin opportunity. And the moment you see it, you can choose to step out of the trap.

Setting Up Autopilot Habits

Most people don't fail at money because of one bad decision. They fail because of thousands of tiny inactions—missed savings, unpaid bills, forgotten investments—each quietly compounding over time. Modern finance doesn't punish recklessness as much as it punishes inconsistency. And for the digital-native generation, inconsistency is an ever-present risk in a world designed to overwhelm. This is precisely why automation isn't a luxury or a fintech gimmick—it is *a foundational discipline of modern personal finance.*

To understand the value of automation, begin by recognising the limitations of willpower and memory. Human beings are notoriously poor at repetitive self-regulation. Decision fatigue erodes our best intentions, distractions chip away at our attention, and mood-driven choices sabotage consistency. Automating key financial behaviours—saving, bill payments, investing—is not about outsourcing responsibility. It is about *designing reliability into your system*, making your financial success less vulnerable to momentary forgetfulness or emotional volatility.

The most powerful aspect of automation is that it transforms good habits into defaults. Behavioural economists have long demonstrated that people tend to stick with defaults. In countries where citizens are automatically enrolled in retirement plans, participation rates skyrocket. In personal finance, the equivalent principle applies: when saving or investing is made the automatic baseline rather than a manual task, participation becomes the rule, not the exception.

Take savings. When money is deposited into your account, the typical path is to spend first and save what remains. Automation inverts that logic. By setting up an automatic transfer to a high-interest savings account or ISA (Individual Savings Account) on payday, you force the habit of *saving first, spending later.* It might be as modest as £10 or £50 a month at first, but the cumulative impact of such frictionless, regular deposits is transformative. Over months and years, the sums build silently—without requiring you to make a conscious monthly choice. *You remove the decision point entirely, and therefore remove the risk of procrastination.*

Bill automation offers another indispensable benefit: protection against penalties. Late fees on credit cards, utilities, or rent can be financially corrosive. Worse, they may damage your credit file, triggering longer-term consequences. With direct debits and scheduled payments, you eliminate timing errors and dramatically reduce the administrative burden of financial life. Crucially, however, automation must be accompanied by vigilance. A forgotten direct debit linked to an empty account can result in overdraft fees or service disruptions. Thus, automation works best when paired with periodic oversight—say, a ten-minute financial review once a week.

When it comes to investing, automation becomes not only a safeguard but a strategy. The concept of pound-cost averaging—a disciplined, regular investment into the same funds or stocks regardless of market price—is grounded in the recognition that timing the market is nearly impossible, even for experts. By automating a fixed monthly contribution into an index fund or diversified portfolio, you *smooth out volatility* and ensure long-term exposure to asset growth without requiring expert forecasting skills. It is one of the few investment strategies supported by decades of empirical research, and it fits elegantly with an automated framework.

There is a psychological advantage, too. The act of automating an investment, no matter how small, redefines identity. It transforms the individual from a passive saver to an active investor. Even £25 a month invested consistently sends a powerful message: *I participate in long-term wealth creation.* This quiet shift in self-perception lays the groundwork for increasingly sophisticated financial decisions later in life.

But automation, like any system, is only as strong as its design. There are risks of over-automating or automating without reflection. Setting up direct debits for subscriptions you no longer use, or auto-investing into high-fee funds without scrutiny, can be counterproductive. The goal isn't to eliminate human oversight—it's to conserve it for strategic thinking, not repetitive execution. Think of automation not as abdication, but *as delegation to a reliable assistant*—one that executes your best decisions on your behalf, without requiring your constant presence.

Another overlooked benefit of autopilot systems is their role in reducing financial stress. Decision fatigue—the anxiety that stems from frequent, low-stakes decisions—is a silent tax on cognitive bandwidth. Financial automation reduces the mental noise that can come from constantly asking, "Did I pay that bill?" or "Should I invest this month?" By systematising these answers in advance, you reclaim mental space for more meaningful planning and problem-solving.

Implementing automation effectively doesn't require expensive software or expert-level knowledge. Most modern banks and investment platforms offer standing orders, automatic transfers, and recurring investment options as standard features. Mobile apps such as Plum, Moneybox, or Monzo's "Pots" function allow users to ringfence funds automatically, track habits, and receive insights without daily manual input. These tools aren't magic. But they are powerful enablers—especially when combined with clarity of purpose.

That purpose should be defined early. Before setting up any automated system, the underlying goals must be honest and specific. Are you saving for a six-month emergency fund? Are you investing for long-term growth? Are you simply trying to avoid missed payments and credit damage? Automation supports purpose—but it cannot supply it. An unclear goal paired with an automatic action can quietly mislead for years. A clear goal, in contrast, makes automation razor-sharp.

There is a deeper philosophical shift embedded here. Automation replaces a fragile model of money management—one that depends on momentary motivation—with a resilient one built on structure. In a culture saturated with content about financial "grind" and effort, this approach is refreshingly unromantic. It says: *You don't need to hustle every day—you need to set the system once and keep it clean.* The real effort lies in the initial set-up, the thoughtful calibration of flows, and the periodic maintenance. But once these elements are in place, your money begins to work not just for you, but *around you*—persistently, quietly, efficiently.

Critics might argue that automation creates financial detachment, a sense of outsourcing that leads to ignorance. And indeed, it is possible to automate blindly. But the answer to that risk is not to abandon automation. It is to pair it with intentional review. A monthly check-in, a quarterly audit of investment allocations, or a semi-annual subscription purge can ensure that systems remain aligned with evolving priorities. In this way, automation does not replace engagement—it *focuses it*, allowing the user to zoom in on strategy, not chores.

For young people especially, setting up autopilot habits early creates a compound advantage. Not just compound interest—but compound discipline, compound clarity, compound emotional detachment from impulse. As income rises, these systems scale naturally. Savings percentages can increase. Investments can diversify. Automation doesn't cap your ambition—it *accelerates your trajectory*, ensuring that foundational behaviours are already in motion while you tackle more complex financial goals.

Ultimately, autopilot is not about removing yourself from your finances. It's about building a system that supports your best financial instincts without constant negotiation. The real mark of financial maturity is not how much effort you put into managing money—but how little effort is *required* to keep it growing responsibly. In that light, automation is not a shortcut. It is a structure for longevity. A quiet scaffold for wealth. A signal that your finances are not reactive—but *designed*.

Chapter 10
Money and Your People

The most challenging conversations about money seldom occur in boardrooms or budgeting apps. They surface instead in quiet frictions at dinner tables, in the uneasy pauses between friends, or in the heavy silence that follows an unpaid favour. For all our talk of earning, saving, and investing, personal finance proves most intricate—and most human—when it intersects with relationships. Money, though it masquerades as purely mathematical, is deeply emotional. It shapes power dynamics, signals values, and tests boundaries, particularly with those closest to us.

Few things unsettle financial confidence faster than interpersonal obligations. The meticulous budgeter who invests automatically may falter when a friend requests a loan. A young adult tracking every penny might feel small and uncertain when parents question their choices through the lens of outdated assumptions. The teenager quietly covering rent because their family cannot—what financial literacy course equips someone for that kind of emotional strain? Financial competence is not merely understanding compound interest; it is also about negotiating the unspoken expectations, assumptions, and dependencies tied to those around you.

Intergenerational tension is often the first battlefield. Gen Z is coming of age in a financial landscape vastly different from that of their parents. Where boomers equated success with home ownership and pension schemes, today's teens might be trading NFTs before they can legally drink. The language has shifted, the tools have evolved, and the risks have multiplied. Many parents interpret cashless lifestyles, side hustles, and crypto experiments as recklessness rather than adaptation. What seems impulsive may, in fact, be pragmatism in a different dialect. Bridging this divide demands more than a demonstration of apps or jargon—it requires patience, emotional intelligence, and a willingness to respect both lived experiences, even when decisions diverge.

Matters complicate further when children surpass their parents financially—earlier, more visibly, or through digital channels. Teen influencers earning brand deals or young coders freelancing across borders may find themselves with incomes exceeding those of their guardians. Economic authority shifting before emotional maturity can catch families off guard. Roles blur, expectations distort, and gratitude mingles uncomfortably with guilt. A teen may feel simultaneously empowered and burdened, hailed as a saviour one moment and criticised the next. Establishing financial boundaries within families is not selfish—it is a strategic choice to preserve long-term well-being.

Friendships, too, are fraught with financial nuance. Splitting a bill is straightforward; dividing assumptions, habits, and philosophies is far more delicate. Should you lend money to a friend you suspect may never repay it? Do you share costs equally when incomes differ? How does one decline without eroding trust? These dilemmas often arise in everyday contexts—shared coffees, rides, or group trips—rather than dramatic confrontations. Navigating them requires more than etiquette; it calls for clarity, honesty, and the refusal to equate generosity with imprudence.

And yet, money remains taboo. Silence dominates—even among the most open circles. Shame, confusion, or misplaced politeness prevents people from articulating their needs, setting limits, or claiming their choices. This silence is anything but harmless; it fosters misunderstanding, resentment, and the quiet erosion of financial agency. Cultivating the ability to discuss money with dignity, directness, and empathy is one of the most under-recognised financial skills one can acquire.

This chapter explores where money ceases to be abstract and becomes relational. It examines generational misalignments that hinder mutual understanding and offers frameworks for managing requests, maintaining boundaries, and preserving friendships amidst financial imbalance. It guides young people who, by necessity or choice, assume household responsibilities. Above all, it argues for dismantling financial shame—not by broadcasting every detail, but by reclaiming the right to speak clearly about what matters with those who matter.

The ultimate aim of financial education is not to produce isolated individuals hoarding wealth with precision. It is to cultivate resilient, self-aware people capable of engaging their families, friends, and communities from a place of strength rather than silence. Understanding money, then, is inseparable from understanding how it flows through relationships and how those relationships can either support or undermine long-term goals.

You can automate savings, optimise investments, and analyse spending with exacting precision. Yet, if you cannot say "no" without guilt, "yes" without regret, or "I need help" without shame, your financial strategy remains incomplete. Money is not merely arithmetic; it is language, emotion, power, and trust, all circulating through the people closest to you. Learning to navigate that current is not optional—it is foundational.

When Parents Don't Understand Your Finances

A surprising percentage of teenagers today earn money in ways that didn't exist when their parents were their age. Monetising content, reselling trainers, investing in crypto, freelancing on digital platforms, gaming economies, and even early entrepreneurship through dropshipping or digital marketing—none of these fit the traditional narrative of what a "job" or "income" looks like to an older generation raised on salaries, pensions, and printed bank statements. The result? A deep and often frustrating generational disconnect where young earners find themselves simultaneously more financially active and yet less financially understood than ever before.

The tension isn't always hostile, but it is real. A parent may scoff at a teenager's profits from a niche NFT trade while uncritically celebrating a weekend retail shift for minimum wage. Another might micromanage their child's budgeting choices without understanding that money flows in irregular bursts, not paychecks. What unfolds is not just a failure of communication—it's a breakdown in financial literacy that runs in both directions. *Young people may know how to make money in digital spaces, but not always how to frame or explain it; parents may know the old rules of personal finance, but often not the new gameboard on which it's now played.*

Bridging this generational money gap requires more than just patience—it requires fluency. Fluency in the language of respect, clarity, and shared perspective. One of the greatest myths in financial life is that we all operate from the same framework. In truth, your "income" may mean flexibility, autonomy, and passion. To a parent, it may mean predictability, benefits, and a paper trail. That difference is not a threat; it's a teaching moment. But only if both parties stop talking past each other.

Begin with clarity. Explain the mechanics of your income. Don't assume your parents will automatically grasp how Twitch revenue splits work or what affiliate marketing commissions look like. Use analogies they understand. If you generate £500 from product sales, compare it to a shift-based job they respect—"That's roughly what someone would earn after 25 hours at the café, except I did it by building a storefront." When you present new financial realities in old familiar frames, you build credibility instead of conflict.

But communication is not just about the source of money—it's about its stability and intention. Parents worry. They worry about security, legitimacy, and long-term viability. And often, their scepticism is less about control and more about uncertainty. If your income is volatile, admit it—but also show that you understand what that means. Outline how you plan to manage dry spells. Demonstrate that you're tracking expenses, saving a portion, and not letting lifestyle inflate beyond your earnings. If they see you taking your financial life seriously, they're far more likely to take *you* seriously in return.

Tensions deepen when parents feel sidelined. If they've been the gatekeepers of financial decision-making—paying bills, setting budgets, handling school expenses—it can be jarring to realise their teenager is operating with an independent wallet. They may react with control, over-correction, or dismissiveness. But this is a natural recalibration. Their job used to be making money work *for* you. Now, they're watching you make it work *on your own*. Invite them into the process—not for permission, but for perspective. Ask for feedback. Share your plans. Show the spreadsheet. When financial transparency replaces secrecy, suspicion often dissolves.

This is not about ceding authority or seeking validation. It's about acknowledging that economic maturity doesn't mean cutting your parents out of the loop; it means helping them understand the loop itself. Just as you wouldn't expect someone to support a thesis they haven't read, don't expect your parents to endorse your financial decisions without visibility. Make them partners in your financial literacy, not obstacles to it.

Sometimes, though, the divide runs deeper. Some parents may project their own financial anxiety, trauma, or limitations onto you. Perhaps they've struggled with debt, distrust new technologies, or grew up in environments where financial experimentation was dangerous. When their resistance feels disproportionate, it's often a signal of past experiences—not present facts. Approach this not with defensiveness but empathy. Ask questions: "What worries you most about this?" "What part feels unfamiliar or unsafe to you?" When you seek to understand *their* financial logic, it becomes easier to invite them into *yours.*

It's also worth noting that financial conflict can mask larger emotional dynamics. For example, a parent who's reluctant to acknowledge your earnings might not actually distrust your competence—they might fear losing relevance. They've spent years providing for you. Watching you become financially self-sufficient may feel, to them, like a loss of role or purpose. That's not your burden to carry, but it is your opportunity to show emotional intelligence. Reassure them that while your economic independence is growing, your respect for their guidance hasn't diminished.

Of course, not all conversations will go smoothly. Some parents will remain sceptical. Others may offer grudging support laced with condescension. And a few may outright dismiss your financial efforts as unserious. That doesn't mean you're wrong. It means you're early. Generational change always feels awkward in real-time. Many of today's most respected digital entrepreneurs and creators were once told by someone older that their work "wasn't real." Time proved otherwise. Let your consistency be your rebuttal.

Still, even when full understanding isn't possible, basic boundaries are. If a parent repeatedly undermines your financial decisions or uses your income to manipulate or control your choices, it's essential to set limits. Make your values and intentions clear. Use direct language. "I appreciate your concern, but I've researched this path, and I'm comfortable with the risk." Or: "I'm always open to feedback, but I need you to respect that this is my income and I'm managing it with care." Boundaries are not disrespect—they are the architecture of trust.

Lastly, understand that your goal is not to win a debate, but to grow a shared language. Money is not just currency—it's culture, belief, habit, and history. Your parents may have been shaped by recessions, bank failures, or job loss. You're growing up in a world shaped by fintech, digital marketplaces, and side hustles. The gap is real. But so is the opportunity. When two generations speak openly—not just about numbers but about meaning—financial literacy expands. Not downward, but in both directions.

Splitting, Sharing, and Lending to Friends

Few experiences test our financial maturity more subtly—and more personally—than money shared among peers. Whether it's splitting the bill after a meal, fronting a concert ticket, or lending a friend cash until payday, these moments rarely come with instruction manuals, but they shape our social lives and financial confidence in equal measure. What makes peer-to-peer financial interactions uniquely complex isn't just the numbers—it's the emotional calculus embedded within them: loyalty, embarrassment, reciprocity, expectation. And too often, it's these invisible dynamics that end up costing far more than the actual amount exchanged.

Modern youth culture is steeped in a hyper-casual ethos of shared expenses. Rideshares are co-booked, streaming accounts are family-planed with barely related friends, and apps like Venmo, Revolut and Monzo make splitting costs nearly frictionless—technically. But socially, the expectations are often murkier. Does splitting mean exactly equal, or "roughly fair"? If one friend earns more, should they pay more? If you front a cost and the other delays repayment, do you ask again or stay silent? *It's precisely the absence of norms that makes these transactions so fraught, and why early clarity is not just good etiquette—it's essential economic hygiene.*

Consider the deceptively simple act of splitting a meal. Three people order vastly different things, but agree to "split it evenly." One person ordered the cheapest option and water; another went for appetisers and dessert. The bill is paid, and the social tension lingers. Was this an act of generosity or quiet resentment? Did someone just subsidise another's lifestyle under the guise of convenience? It's a common scenario with a surprisingly consistent lesson: *fairness without discussion is rarely mutual.* One of the most useful financial habits a young adult can build is the courage to clarify expectations before money is spent, not after.

Technology, ironically, has solved the *mechanics* of splitting costs while often obscuring the *emotional transparency*. With payment apps, a request for £4.87 can be sent instantly—but it's not the ease of sending that matters; it's whether that request feels socially acceptable. Too formal? Too petty? Too assertive? These are questions rarely answered in budgeting guides. But they matter because money among friends isn't just about precision—it's about perception. If you're not careful, you can easily become "the friend who always counts pennies" or "the one who never pays back"—not because of bad intent, but because of mismatched assumptions.

This is where proactive boundary-setting enters the picture—not as a sign of stinginess, but as a demonstration of mutual respect. Before committing to group purchases or lending scenarios, it's reasonable (and smart) to ask: "Are we splitting evenly, or based on what each person had?" or "Just to confirm—do you want me to cover this and you'll send me your part later?" These aren't awkward questions—they're preventative ones. And far from damaging friendships, they signal maturity and reduce the kind of silent resentment that corrodes trust over time.

Lending money to friends, meanwhile, demands an entirely different level of caution—because once money crosses the boundary from shared cost to personal loan, the stakes shift. A loan is not a favour; it is a financial agreement. But in peer culture, it's rarely treated that way. Most peer-to-peer loans begin informally, based on urgency or guilt: "Can I borrow £50 until next week? I swear I'll pay you back." What's often missing is a mutual definition of accountability. What if they don't? What if the week stretches into months? What if your reminder is taken as an insult?

Here, the principle is simple: *Never lend money you can't afford to lose—and never lend without terms.* That doesn't mean every £10 spot needs a contract, but it does mean even modest sums benefit from verbal clarity. Will it be paid back in one lump or over time? Is there a deadline? What happens if they can't repay it? Saying this out loud is uncomfortable—but far less so than navigating a silent breach of trust when things go unspoken. Clarity, again, is the currency of respect.

Of course, the ethics of peer lending cut both ways. If *you* borrow money, repay it quickly and without prompting. Nothing strains friendships like needing to chase down a repayment. And if you can't repay on time, communicate clearly and proactively: "I expected to pay you back this Friday, but something came up. I can get you £30 now and the rest by next week. Is that okay?" Ownership of your obligations is not just financial discipline—it's a test of character.

Then there's the grey zone of gifting—when friends insist on covering each other without repayment. This often arises from uneven income levels or generosity norms. While kindness is admirable, it's essential that gifting not become a hidden expectation or coercive generosity. A wealthier friend covering a night out for someone on a tighter budget might mean well, but if it becomes habitual, it can disempower rather than uplift. Financial generosity, to be ethical, must come with consent—not assumption.

The paradox here is that money, while deeply practical, always travels with social subtext. When friends repeatedly "treat" others, they may be performing status. When someone never repays, they may be signalling disregard. And when someone always splits to the penny, they may be projecting insecurity rather than fairness. *What matters is not just the transaction—but the trust it builds or erodes.* Money doesn't ruin friendships—mismatched money expectations do.

In navigating these complexities, two rules stand above all: discuss early, and document lightly. A message confirming who's covering what is not overkill—it's smart protocol. A follow-up reminder when repayment hasn't arrived is not rudeness—it's integrity. And choosing not to engage in financial arrangements that feel uneasy is not cold-hearted—it's responsible. Your job is not to make everyone feel financially comfortable at your expense; it's to ensure that financial interactions don't damage what matters more: trust, clarity, and mutual respect.

There's also a longer arc to consider. How we handle money with friends now sets the tone for later adult life—flatmates, business partners, colleagues. Learning to say, "Let's split that based on what we each ordered," or "I'm happy to lend, but can we set a clear plan for repayment?" isn't about being difficult—it's about building financial fluency in contexts where emotion runs high. The sooner you practise, the stronger your instincts will become.

Ultimately, friendship thrives on shared experience—but that doesn't mean shared finances have to be messy. You can split generously, lend wisely, and gift thoughtfully—all while maintaining boundaries. And when you do, you're not just managing money—you're managing the deeper, more fragile currency of trust. A true friend doesn't just show up with cash when needed. They show up with respect when it counts.

When You're the Breadwinner at Home

Few realities upend the traditional script of adolescence more than becoming the primary—or only—earner in your household before you've finished school. For teens and young adults who step into this role, the transition is rarely framed as financial empowerment. More often, it's survival. You're no longer just learning about money; you're responsible for it. The stakes are immediate, the margin for error slim, and the emotional toll silently steep. While most of your peers might be budgeting for trainers, takeaways, or weekend plans, you're thinking about rent, food, transport, and how to stretch your next paycheque. And yet, this lived reality—quietly carried by so many—remains largely invisible in conventional personal finance discourse.

Being the household breadwinner before the age of twenty is not an anomaly. It's a growing demographic reality. In families hit by illness, immigration hurdles, job loss, or generational poverty, a teenager's part-time job or freelance gig can shift from pocket money to essential income. Sometimes it's gradual; other times, it happens overnight. A parent loses their job. A sibling needs medication. The heating bill doubles. And suddenly, your after-school hours are no longer elective. They are essential.

This transition forces a premature maturity, but it does not come with a guidebook. In the abstract, earning money young can seem like a badge of honour. But when the money goes not to your savings account but to keep the lights on, the narrative shifts. There's pride, yes—but often also guilt, exhaustion, and resentment. These emotions are real and valid, and they do not make you ungrateful. *They make you human in a system that often demands adult responsibilities without offering adult autonomy.*

The first tension breadwinning teens must resolve is internal: *Where does my duty end, and my boundary begin?* Family culture complicates this question. In many households, especially those shaped by immigration, collectivism, or hardship, financial contribution is not merely appreciated—it's expected. It can be wrapped in language of honour, sacrifice, or responsibility. But if not tempered with care, that expectation becomes a burden that depletes rather than dignifies. It is entirely reasonable to support your household while also setting limits. In fact, *setting boundaries is not selfish—it is strategic.* It's how you sustain your ability to support others without sacrificing your future in the process.

One of the most vital tools at your disposal is clarity—financial and emotional. This begins with understanding *exactly* what is expected of you. Are you covering fixed expenses like rent and groceries? Contributing a fixed amount weekly? Paying ad hoc bills? Are you also being expected to fund siblings' expenses, or contribute to parental debt? These distinctions matter. Too often, teens are asked to "help out" in ways that remain vague until a crisis hits. This ambiguity erodes your ability to plan, save, and negotiate. You are not a walking ATM. If you're contributing, *you deserve transparency about how your money is used.* Don't be afraid to ask.

This brings us to a second, more sensitive tension: *What happens when the adult figures in your life are not financially responsible, and you are?* For many young earners, this is the quiet tragedy—watching their hard-earned money vanish into family spending patterns that feel impulsive, opaque, or outright reckless. A parent buys a new phone while bills go unpaid. Money meant for groceries is redirected to non-essentials. And you're left wondering: do I keep contributing blindly, or do I speak up?

This is a high-stakes dilemma, because it's not just financial—it's relational. Questioning a parent's choices may feel disrespectful or even dangerous. But staying silent can feel like complicity. Here, discernment is key. If your safety allows, it is worth having direct, calm, factual conversations about household budgeting. "Can we agree on a fixed amount that I contribute weekly, and have a list of what it covers?" or "I want to help, but I also need to save for school. Can we find a balance that works for both of us?" These are not easy conversations, but they are acts of courage that honour both your role and your limits.

Meanwhile, the practical side of breadwinning cannot be neglected. If you're earning money, *you need a system.* Track every expense. Automate your savings. Create separate buckets—essentials, family contribution, personal goals. Do not let your earnings be absorbed into an amorphous "family pot" unless there is shared visibility and accountability. You must treat your income with the same professionalism as any adult supporting a household. Not because you're cold, but because you're clear.

And you must make room—no matter how small—for your own future. Saving even £10 a week towards a personal emergency fund is not selfish. It is protective. Investing £25 a month into a long-term account, even while helping your family with utilities, is not disloyal. It is smart. *Your family's needs are real, but so are yours.* The trap many young breadwinners fall into is delaying their own progress indefinitely in the name of familial duty. But when you burn out or fall behind, you reduce your ability to support anyone—including yourself.

At the heart of this conversation lies a deeper truth: *being a breadwinner does not mean forfeiting your boundaries, goals, or sense of self.* Yes, you may need to compromise. Yes, you may have to say no to things your peers take for granted. But you are still allowed to dream, plan, and build beyond the confines of your current role. You are allowed to decline extra shifts if they threaten your education. You are allowed to spend some money on yourself without guilt. You are allowed to imagine a future where you support your family not by sacrifice, but by success.

For those who find themselves in this role, seeking external support is not weakness—it is wisdom. A school counsellor, a trusted teacher, a community organisation, even a youth financial coach can offer perspective, resources, and advocacy. You should not have to navigate this complexity alone. And if support within the household is unavailable or unstable, building external networks becomes even more crucial.

Finally, it must be said that *none of this is your fault.* You did not ask to be in this role. You are stepping up not because you were trained for it, but because life demanded it. That in itself is an achievement. But strength without sustainability is short-lived. The world often praises young breadwinners for their resilience—but resilience should not be the price of basic stability. You deserve systems, support, and tools that make your strength strategic, not just stoic.

So if you're earning to support your home, start where all strong financial plans begin: with clarity. Know what you can give. Know what you must save. Know where to draw the line, and when to ask for help. Most importantly, know that your value is not measured solely by how much you give, but by how wisely you navigate what you give up. Breadwinning young may feel like being forced to grow up fast. But if done with intention, it can also be the beginning of a financial fluency most adults never reach. And that fluency—earned, not inherited—will be your edge.

Talking Money Without Shame

There are few topics more universally relevant and yet more culturally silenced than money. The irony is stark: everyone earns it, spends it, saves it—or wishes they could—but far fewer feel confident talking about it. Whether at the dinner table, in friendships, romantic relationships, or even professional settings, financial conversations are often laced with tension, embarrassment, and an undercurrent of defensiveness. This silence is not a neutral absence; it is an active cost. It costs people fair wages, financial literacy, informed choices, and in many cases, a sense of dignity. *To talk about money without shame is not merely a personal skill—it is a form of empowerment.* It is the bridge between surviving the economy and shaping your place within it.

Shame is a social emotion. It thrives in secrecy and comparison, and money—unlike almost any other domain of life—is loaded with both. From a young age, people are taught not to ask others how much they earn, not to say if they're struggling, not to admit if they don't understand interest rates or overdrafts. Financial illiteracy is treated as a personal failing, rather than a systemic omission. And because money is often seen as a proxy for success, intelligence, or responsibility, people conflate having less with *being* less. This is the origin of financial shame—not a lack of money, but a sense that having less somehow disqualifies you from full participation in the conversation.

But silence does not protect you from harm; it protects harmful systems from being questioned. Think about how many students sign up for student loans without understanding compound interest. How many employees accept salaries below market value because they don't know how to negotiate. How many young people are locked into debt cycles because they're too embarrassed to ask for help. *The less we talk about money, the more we reinforce inequity—not just economic, but informational.*

To talk about money without shame, then, requires confronting three key myths. First, that you're supposed to already know everything. Second, that financial hardship is proof of personal failure. And third, that it's rude to ask or share. Each of these ideas has cultural roots, but none of them serve a functional purpose in today's economy. In fact, dismantling them is essential to any real financial confidence.

Start with the first myth: the illusion of assumed knowledge. Schools rarely teach personal finance in depth. Families often pass down inconsistent or outdated advice. Media offers tips skewed toward those already earning disposable income. And yet, young people are expected to navigate bank accounts, credit scores, rent agreements, tax forms, and more with fluent confidence. When they don't, they blame themselves. But not knowing how overdraft fees work is not a moral flaw—it's a gap in instruction. *Financial literacy is not innate; it is learned. And you cannot learn what you're too ashamed to ask.*

This is why normalising financial questions is radical. When you ask your bank to explain their terms without pretending to understand, you reclaim power. When you ask a mentor how they negotiated their salary, you gain context. When you admit to a friend that you're budgeting tightly this month and suggest free alternatives instead of splitting a pricey bill, you build trust. These are not awkward confessions. They are acts of intelligence, self-respect, and relational honesty.

The second myth—hardship as failure—is harder to shake. Money troubles often carry deep emotional weight. If you've grown up hearing that financial success is the result of hard work, then struggling feels like an indictment of your effort, character, or choices. This logic is both cruel and incomplete. *Hard work is necessary, but it is not always sufficient.* Economic mobility is shaped by countless variables—family circumstances, location, access to education, health, and even luck. To talk honestly about money is to reclaim nuance. It is to say, "This is where I'm at, and it does not define me." Your net worth is not your moral worth. Your debt is not your destiny. And your income does not entitle or disqualify you from respect.

The third myth—politeness as silence—is particularly prevalent in British culture, but not uniquely so. It suggests that money is too personal, too transactional, or too socially volatile to be discussed openly. But what is often labelled as discretion is in practice a silencing tactic that reinforces hierarchies. Why should it be considered rude to ask how someone affords a house deposit, yet perfectly normal to speculate on their wedding or holiday spending? Why is it taboo to talk about wage disparities among colleagues, when those very disparities fuel structural inequality? *The boundaries of polite conversation often mirror the boundaries of power.* Respectful money talk doesn't mean prying or over-disclosure. It means creating space for honesty without judgement, curiosity without condescension, and vulnerability without consequence.

So how does one actually begin to talk about money without shame? The answer is not performative transparency, but strategic openness. It begins with self-awareness. What are your financial values, fears, and assumptions? What do you feel comfortable sharing, and where do you draw your lines? Who do you trust to have these conversations with, and why? These questions shape not just the content of your conversations, but their tone. Are you approaching them to impress, confess, educate, or connect? Clarifying intent helps you speak with integrity rather than defensiveness.

Consider this example: two friends planning a trip. One is on a tighter budget but feels embarrassed to say so. The other suggests expensive hotels by default. If the first friend says nothing, they might end up overcommitting or withdrawing. But if they say, "I'd love to come, but I'm budgeting for other things right now—would you be open to a cheaper option?" they don't just preserve their finances—they model financial dignity. They shift the conversation from assumption to dialogue, from obligation to collaboration.

The same applies to romantic relationships. Financial compatibility is not just about income brackets; it's about attitudes toward saving, debt, lifestyle, and future goals. Too many couples wait until there's tension before discussing money, which means those conversations happen under stress. But if you can talk about spending styles before they clash, or debt burdens before they compound, you build a foundation of mutual respect. You don't need to have identical habits—but *you do need to understand each other's realities.*

Talking about money early is not unromantic. It is responsible. And it allows love to operate in reality, not illusion.

Workplace conversations offer another frontier. While many companies discourage open discussion about pay, there is growing recognition—especially among younger workers—that wage transparency is a tool for equity. Sharing your salary with trusted peers is not about bragging. It's about benchmarking. When done respectfully, it allows underpaid employees—especially women and minorities—to advocate for fair compensation. Secrecy benefits the institution. Solidarity benefits the workers.

None of this is to say that talking about money is easy. But it is a skill, and like any skill, it improves with practice. You can start small. Reflect on your own money story. Share one financial lesson with a friend. Ask one question you've been holding back. Set one boundary around spending. The point is not to disclose everything—it is to stop defaulting to nothing. *Silence around money is not neutral. It is the soil in which shame grows. Voice is the sunlight that stops it spreading.*

There is no moral purity in wealth, and no disgrace in financial struggle. There is only complexity. And navigating that complexity requires a language we have too long denied ourselves. When you learn to talk about money without shame, you do more than improve your bank balance. You improve your sense of agency. You build the muscle of critical thinking, emotional intelligence, and strategic negotiation. And you create space—for yourself and others—to be both honest and ambitious.

Financial confidence is not just about having the right numbers. It's about having the right conversations. Not perfectly, but persistently. Not to impress, but to connect. Because when people talk honestly about money, they don't just learn—they grow. And that growth, quiet as it may be, is the real currency of freedom.

Chapter 11
Building Wealth on Your Own Terms

Wealth, as an idea, is far less complicated than it is misunderstood. The confusion comes not from its depth, but from the way it's been flattened—boiled down to figures, assets, and outward symbols of affluence. In most conversations, wealth is treated as accumulation: more money, more things, more acclaim. Yet when you strip away the noise of metrics and magazine lists, a quieter question surfaces—what is all this accumulation actually for? Without answering that, the pursuit of wealth becomes mimicry: an imitation of others' goals, a performance of borrowed values, and a race against expectations you never chose. The truth, and the provocation at the heart of this chapter, is that wealth isn't about reaching a fixed summit. It's about designing and sustaining a life that feels internally coherent—financially, emotionally, and ethically. Wealth is not a prize to possess; it is a system to be written, and you are its author.

Most young earners are inducted into money culture through systems built to keep them perpetually anxious, reactive, and externally focused. Social media parades consumption as achievement. Financial influencers preach formulas and rules that sound definitive but rarely are. Even educational content tends to glorify austerity and restraint while skipping the question of *why*. The result? A generation fluent in chasing wealth, but largely illiterate in defining it. Personal finance without personal philosophy is bookkeeping. To build meaningful wealth, you must first interrogate the language of your own desires.

Start not by asking *how much* you want, but *why*. Is it time you're chasing? Freedom of movement? The power to choose your work? Stability for your family? Influence in your community? Each answer points to an entirely different map. The freelancer who prizes mobility weighs risk differently than the parent anchored by dependents. The founder of a social enterprise will shape their system around reinvestment, while the minimalist will prize passive income and low overheads. Before you can build a plan, you must name a purpose. Otherwise, you may earn handsomely and still feel caged—by the house, the brand, or the persona you once thought you wanted.

Once that purpose is clear, wealth-building stops being imitation and becomes design. The task shifts from copying blueprints to creating alignment—a system that mirrors your values and grows as you do. This is not about instant gratification or chasing every fleeting whim. It's about engineering feedback loops that let you measure progress on your own terms. For one person, that could mean tracking net worth; for another, it might mean logging the proportion of hours spent on meaningful work. The metric matters less than the intention behind it. Measurement should sharpen awareness, not feed obsession.

Still, it's worth acknowledging a paradox. Keeping close tabs on your finances can instil a sense of control, but it can also fuel anxiety, comparison, even guilt. For perfectionists—or for those who grew up with financial instability—the instinct to monitor every penny can masquerade as discipline when it's really distrust. True financial fluency includes trust: in your earning power, your judgement, and the system you've built to hold your priorities steady. This is why automation isn't just efficient—it's liberating. When your money moves by design—towards saving, giving, investing, and living according to your principles—you buy not only time, but peace. And peace, arguably, is wealth's purest expression.

Yet no system can hold if it's built atop unexamined stories. Every one of us inherits emotional scripts about money—from family, culture, experience. Some are taught that money must be hoarded; others, that spending is identity. Some internalise that wealth corrupts; others, that it redeems. These scripts don't disappear when you open a brokerage account. They whisper beneath every decision, shaping what feels "safe" or "responsible." So the real audit is twofold: your numbers, and your narratives. Are your choices truly yours, or are you still performing someone else's fear?

Identity plays its part too. Every financial choice—where you shop, what you fund, the work you pursue—is an act of expression. Each transaction signals belief: in value, in community, in possibility. The conventional wisdom tells us to strip money of emotion, to treat it as a cold equation. But that's a fiction, and a dangerous one. A life built on numbers alone may be efficient, but it will seldom feel whole. The challenge is not to exile emotion from finance, but to weave it through with discernment. Let spending bring joy. Let investing reflect conscience. Let giving restore balance. And leave room for change, because alignment is not a fixed state—it's a rhythm.

This becomes crucial once financial growth begins to accelerate. It's one thing to talk about wealth while clawing out of debt; quite another when income expands and choices multiply. Many people lose their bearings here. They keep working from habit, spending for validation, investing for appearances. Without a guiding system—a personal financial philosophy—they drift into abundance without satisfaction. Some even build cages out of their own success. The pattern is common enough to feel like a warning: earning more does not mean living better, unless the structure holding your wealth has meaning.

A personal financial system isn't about rigid discipline; it's about clarity amid noise. It helps you weigh trade-offs consciously. Will you choose long-term investing over immediate liquidity? Cap your lifestyle growth beyond a set point? Commit to giving away a slice of every paycheque? These aren't arbitrary rules—they're anchors, quiet guardrails that steady you when distraction beckons. A well-built system doesn't suffocate spontaneity; it protects it, ensuring that your essentials are handled so your attention can roam freely.

Take the often-cited 50/30/20 budgeting rule. It's tidy, even elegant, but it assumes everyone's priorities are the same. Suppose your dream is early retirement, or a sabbatical every few years, or building a community centre. Then your ratios should look different. The aim isn't to locate the perfect template; it's to craft one that fits your contours and to adjust it as you evolve.

This chapter offers the mental scaffolding for that process. It's not about chasing higher numbers—it's about treating money as a medium, a way to translate vision into form. That vision might be minimalist or expansive, private or social, traditional or avant-garde—but it must be yours. Otherwise, you're just staging wealth for spectators who aren't even watching.

Wealth, then, is not a finish line. It's architecture—a living framework. It's the ability to sustain yourself and others with integrity. The freedom to pivot without panic. The steadiness to meet uncertainty with imagination instead of fear. And perhaps most of all, it's the feeling of coherence: that your financial life reflects who you are, not who you're pretending to be.

So, as you look ahead, resist the impulse to ask only *what* to do. Ask *what you want your money to mean.* What principles do you refuse to compromise? What risks feel worth the cost? And what kind of life are you building in exchange? Build, then, not for accumulation—but for alignment. That is the rarest, and most enduring, form of wealth.

What 'Wealth' Means to You

If you ask a thousand people what wealth is, you'll get a thousand answers that look remarkably alike—and that is precisely the problem. The default definition, echoed across media, institutions, and even well-meaning conversations, tends to collapse wealth into its most measurable form: money. But beneath that assumption lies a deeper philosophical error—*the belief that wealth is a number to reach rather than a relationship to understand.* That belief shapes everything from how people earn to how they feel about what they already have. And until it is dismantled, no amount of financial strategy will produce a sense of security or fulfilment.

It is not difficult to see how this distortion takes root. Our society elevates net worth as the ultimate scoreboard. News outlets publish lists of the richest individuals with the reverence of religious texts. Social platforms, turbocharged by algorithmic envy, showcase curated lifestyles where material affluence stands in for meaning. And financial advice, especially for the young, is often front-loaded with urgency and fear: save early, invest fast, hustle harder, or be left behind. But these directives rarely ask the more important question: *left behind by whom, and heading toward what?*

Wealth, properly understood, is not a comparative game. It is not a status contest or an insurance policy against shame. It is a form of sovereignty—the capacity to direct your life with autonomy, resilience, and coherence. For some, that may mean building multi-generational assets. For others, it might mean living with minimal obligations. It could involve property portfolios, early retirement, or funding a creative life without compromise. The shape does not matter as much as the intent behind it. *What matters is that it is yours: not inherited in narrative, only in aspiration.*

Defining wealth on your own terms begins with intellectual honesty. Strip away social pressure, familial expectation, and performative goals. What are you actually trying to build? What does financial security feel like to you? And perhaps most revealing: what would you do differently if no one were watching? These questions are not distractions from the financial conversation—they are its foundation. Until your financial choices are anchored in clearly articulated purpose, they will remain reactive. They will be responses to external cues rather than reflections of internal alignment.

Consider how often wealth is mistaken for income. High earners who spend to the edge of their means are often no wealthier, in practice, than modest earners with disciplined systems. The difference is not just arithmetic; it is psychological. *Wealth is not what you earn. It is what you retain—and how well that retention supports your values.* Similarly, ownership is often mistaken for security. Owning a home at 25 may signal success in some contexts, but if that home becomes a financial or geographic shackle, it may erode the very freedom it was supposed to represent. Again, the issue is not the decision itself but the reasoning behind it. *A wise choice poorly understood becomes a burden. A modest choice well-reasoned becomes a strength.*

This leads to an uncomfortable but liberating insight: not everyone needs the same kind of wealth. The tech founder who thrives on scale will architect a different financial life from the artist who values flexibility. The nurse who wants to retire early will build different systems from the activist who views capital as a tool for redistribution. These differences are not anomalies—they are essential. They reflect the diversity of human motivations and should be treated not as exceptions, but as case studies in intentional living.

Real-world evidence supports this multiplicity. Some of the world's most content individuals live on modest means with high intentionality. They track expenses, yes—but not out of fear. They invest—not to outpace others, but to underwrite their autonomy. They give generously—not to signal virtue, but because their definition of wealth includes *impact.* In contrast, many high-net-worth individuals—despite access to abundance—remain tethered to anxiety, comparison, or endless optimisation. The difference is rarely knowledge. It is clarity of values.

This is not to suggest that financial literacy is irrelevant. On the contrary, understanding compounding, risk, asset allocation, and tax strategy is indispensable. But without a self-defined philosophy of wealth, these tools become blunt. They serve goals that may not even belong to you. A financially literate person without self-awareness becomes merely a sophisticated mimic. An individual with both—*clarity and competence*—becomes unshakeable.

The challenge, then, is to architect a financial life that does not just succeed by conventional measures but *feels like a match for your identity.* This is not a theoretical exercise. It has immediate implications for how you budget, what you optimise for, how you negotiate work, and what you consider "enough." If your vision of wealth includes long weekends, meaningful work, and freedom from debt, then your daily decisions must reflect those priorities—even if they diverge from the crowd. *Living your definition of wealth means making trade-offs unapologetically.*

Yet many struggle to articulate those trade-offs because they fear missing out or disappointing others. This fear is not irrational—it is socialised. From an early age, we are taught that financial success is a public good, something others can approve of. But when you let external consensus dictate internal decisions, you lose agency. You begin to perform prosperity rather than experience it. You chase goals not because they matter to you, but because they are legible to others. Over time, this erodes confidence, creativity, and clarity. *You cannot build genuine wealth while outsourcing your definition of success.*

There is also a generational dimension to this conversation. For Gen Z—many of whom came of age during financial instability, climate anxiety, and digital hyper-visibility—the old scripts ring hollow. The promise that hard work leads to security is no longer reliable. Traditional careers feel brittle, institutional trust is fragile, and housing affordability is elusive. In this context, the pursuit of wealth must be reimagined not just as accumulation, but as resilience: the ability to adapt, to maintain integrity under pressure, and to sustain a life of meaning in volatile conditions. This kind of wealth is not built solely in bank accounts. It is built in *systems, relationships, skills, and vision.*

That said, no definition of wealth is complete without acknowledging privilege. To define wealth on your own terms presumes some margin of choice. Not everyone starts with the same resources, networks, or safety nets. This does not invalidate the project of intentionality—it underscores its importance. For those with constrained means, defining wealth in non-monetary terms becomes not just liberating but necessary. And for those with access, it becomes a responsibility. *The more capital you control, the more ethical clarity you need about what that capital is meant to do.*

Ultimately, defining what wealth means to you is not a luxury. It is a discipline. It requires ongoing self-reflection, courageous honesty, and a willingness to resist default narratives. But the rewards are profound. When your financial life reflects your deepest values, you no longer measure progress by comparison. You measure it by coherence. And coherence—between belief, behaviour, and balance sheet—is the surest indicator that your wealth is truly yours.

So pause. Reflect. Ask not what others expect you to earn or own or signal. Ask what kind of life you want to build—and what kind of person you must become to build it. Then let your definition of wealth emerge not from noise, but from depth. Let it be a compass, not a scoreboard. And let it evolve as you do. Because ultimately, the richest lives are not those that follow the money. *They are those in which money follows purpose.*

How to Track Net Worth Without Obsession

Few financial concepts are as simultaneously empowering and paralysing as net worth. As a metric, it offers clarity: an at-a-glance snapshot of your current financial position. Yet in practice, its psychological footprint often far exceeds its utility. Net worth has become a surrogate scoreboard for success—misunderstood, overanalysed, and weaponised by a culture increasingly obsessed with quantifying progress. But strip away the noise, and a more measured truth emerges: *net worth is not your identity, your value, or your destiny. It is simply a tool—useful only when understood in context and wielded with care.*

The proliferation of personal finance dashboards, fintech apps, and spreadsheet templates has made it easier than ever to calculate net worth. Add up your assets, subtract your liabilities, and you're left with a number. But this simplicity is deceptive. The very act of calculating one's net worth often invites a distorted comparison—either with one's past self, with aspirational peers, or with arbitrary age-based benchmarks. The result is a paradox: a number designed to provide clarity instead breeds confusion and insecurity. *Progress begins by disentangling measurement from self-worth.*

The first step is to reframe net worth as *a directional compass, not a diagnostic verdict.* At any moment, your net worth reflects a confluence of circumstances, habits, privileges, decisions, and even luck. It does not tell you whether you're good with money. It does not predict whether you'll thrive in ten years. It certainly doesn't capture your economic contribution, your resilience, or your values. What it can offer—if interpreted correctly—is a sense of orientation. Are you building assets faster than you accumulate obligations? Are your financial choices aligned with your priorities? *The number matters, but its meaning depends entirely on the questions you ask of it.*

One danger of net worth tracking is the illusion of precision. Especially among younger adults, the volatility of early career earnings, debt repayment, and lifestyle formation can produce wide swings in reported net worth. For example, a university graduate with £25,000 in student loans and £500 in savings might record a negative net worth—but this figure says little about their potential, discipline, or trajectory. Conversely, someone with a positive net worth bolstered by inherited assets may lack the habits to sustain it. *Context is not decoration—it is the difference between insight and misdirection.*

Another common trap is frequency. The digital age enables constant financial surveillance. Users can refresh their dashboards daily, watching their balances tick up or down with market movements. But this granularity invites anxiety more than wisdom. Just as weighing oneself daily can distort a healthy relationship with food and fitness, checking net worth too often can inflate short-term fluctuations and deflate long-term thinking. *The goal is awareness, not obsession.* A quarterly or even biannual check-in—anchored in reflection, not reaction—tends to produce better clarity and healthier habits.

Yet net worth does deserve to be tracked. The alternative—financial ignorance—is far more dangerous. Without visibility, it's easy to drift into lifestyle creep, to underestimate debt, or to overestimate readiness for key milestones. Net worth offers a structural view that connects disparate behaviours: saving, spending, investing, borrowing. It's the ledger that reveals whether you're building momentum or merely treading water. The key is not to abandon the tool, but to use it in a way that promotes clarity without control.

To do that, you must clarify *what* you track—and *why*. Some prefer minimalist tracking: cash, investments, debt. Others include pensions, vehicles, even items like collectibles or digital assets. The right approach depends on purpose. Are you using net worth to inform retirement planning? To monitor financial independence? To anchor monthly decision-making? *Define your goal before designing your metric.* Without this alignment, the number risks becoming either meaningless or misleading.

Tools matter too, but only in service of the goal. Some prefer manual spreadsheets for the control and intentionality they provide. Others rely on apps like YNAB, Moneyhub, or Emma that automate data aggregation and generate insights. Whatever the method, the principle is the same: *your tracking system should reduce friction, not increase fixation.* If your current setup leaves you stressed or compulsive, redesign it. Simpler is often wiser.

There is also a psychological component that must not be ignored. Many track net worth as a proxy for control—believing that if they can quantify everything, they can master uncertainty. But wealth building, especially in the modern economy, is inherently probabilistic. Investments fluctuate, careers pivot, health intervenes. Fixating on a static number in a dynamic world produces not peace, but paralysis. *A better approach is to focus on trendlines, not timestamps.* Direction matters more than position.

Equally important is knowing what net worth *doesn't* show. It doesn't reflect your liquidity—an individual with £100,000 in property equity and £1,000 in cash may have limited flexibility. It doesn't capture risk exposure, like variable mortgage rates or concentrated investments. It doesn't measure burnout, time freedom, or personal satisfaction. That's why net worth should be one lens among many, not the sole arbiter of progress. Pair it with qualitative check-ins: Are your finances supporting your goals? Are your decisions consistent with your values? Are you sleeping well at night? *Wealth is ultimately measured in outcomes, not optics.*

For some, especially those recovering from financial trauma or scarcity-driven upbringings, tracking net worth can surface old anxieties. This is not a flaw—it is a signal to proceed gently. If seeing your number triggers shame, panic, or comparison, start small. Track only the parts that feel safe. Focus on building habits—automated savings, debt reduction, mindful spending—before returning to the macro view. Financial literacy is not a race. It is a lifelong dialogue, and some chapters require more compassion than calculation.

There is also value in visualising progress without fetishising it. For example, maintaining a "net worth journal" with brief entries every few months can reveal trends without inducing fixation. Some choose to set percentage-based goals (e.g., increase net worth by 10% annually) rather than hard numbers, allowing for flexibility and resilience. Others focus on milestone markers: debt-free status, investment thresholds, or cash buffer targets. *Let your system fit your psychology, not the other way around.*

Ultimately, the healthiest relationship with net worth is one of *disciplined detachment*. You track it because it's useful, not because it defines you. You monitor it regularly, but not religiously. You interpret it critically, knowing its limitations. And you contextualise it within a broader philosophy of money—one that values meaning, not just measurement.

So yes, learn to calculate your net worth. Learn what it includes, what it omits, and how it evolves. But learn, too, to hold it lightly. Your net worth is not your character. It is not your future. It is not your worth. It is a snapshot—a mirror, not a map. And like any reflection, it becomes clearer not by staring harder, but by adjusting the light around it.

Money + Meaning: How to Align Income with Identity

Wealth, without direction, is simply accumulation. Income, without meaning, becomes a hollow metric—measurable, yes, but misaligned. In a culture obsessed with more—more money, more hustle, more output—the question that often gets ignored is *"Why?"* Why do you want to earn what you earn? Why are you working the way you are? And why does any of it matter beyond numbers on a spreadsheet? These questions are not philosophical indulgences. They are the foundation for making money decisions that not only create financial stability but reflect the integrity of who you are. When your income is decoupled from your identity, you risk drifting into a life that pays your bills but starves your soul.

This is not a manifesto against ambition or financial success. Rather, it's an argument for thoughtful alignment—for using income as a vehicle that serves your values rather than erodes them. It is entirely possible to earn well, live strategically, and still feel misaligned with yourself. That misalignment often presents subtly: burnout that feels unjustified, guilt after large purchases, a sense of detachment even when hitting income targets. These are symptoms of a larger tension—the disconnect between money and meaning.

The starting point is clarity. Not clarity around your next salary goal, but around your internal priorities. What matters most to you—independence, creativity, family, legacy, learning, or autonomy? For some, income is a tool for self-expression: funding artistic projects, entrepreneurial ventures, or travel. For others, it's a mechanism for stability: covering household needs, supporting relatives, or saving for a future family. Neither path is superior. But what causes long-term dissonance is when your income-generating activities contradict your core identity. A teen who values service but is pressured into cutthroat commission sales may succeed financially and still feel anxious every Sunday night. A university student drawn to environmental causes who finds themselves working in extractive industries may feel the conflict even if the salary impresses peers. The answer isn't to abandon the income—it's to interrogate the alignment.

One useful exercise is to reverse-engineer your financial goals. Instead of starting with how much you want to earn, ask what kind of life you want to lead. Who do you want to become? What contributions do you want to make? What freedoms do you want your money to create? These are not abstract musings. They shape every micro-decision: whether to take a second job, whether to freelance or seek employment, whether to spend aggressively on social events or invest in your own education. A person who knows they value lifelong learning might consciously channel 15% of their income into courses, books, or skill development—even if it delays purchasing a new phone. A person who places high value on community might choose a modest income in a meaningful role over a prestige job that isolates them. These decisions compound. Over time, they build a financial architecture that reflects not only economic capability but moral coherence.

Of course, alignment doesn't mean purity. There will always be trade-offs. Not every income stream will sing with purpose. You may take jobs that are boring but necessary, accept internships that pay poorly, or work in fields that aren't your endgame. That's reality, not failure. The key is knowing the difference between a strategic compromise and a permanent departure from your values. If you're detouring to fund a larger goal, there's integrity in that. But if you're drifting away from yourself without noticing, then the money—even if plentiful—starts to cost more than it gives.

Practical alignment also requires structural awareness. Your money behaviour is shaped not only by your psychology but also by the tools and systems you adopt. Consider how your budget reflects your identity. Are you tracking spending in a way that illuminates your values, or simply reacting to expenses? Are you allocating money toward what energises you, or are you defaulting to what others deem impressive? A budget that treats your time as a resource is a subtle but powerful form of value expression. If you consistently overspend on delivery apps but claim to value health and environmental responsibility, there's a values gap. If you say you prioritise learning but haven't allocated anything toward books or mentorship, the disconnect isn't moral—it's structural. Fixing it isn't about shame. It's about congruence.

For Gen Z, the pressure to perform financially is compounded by performative identity online. There's a growing impulse to showcase earnings, investments, or entrepreneurial success for social credibility. But the performative trap often leads people to confuse *perceived* alignment with actual alignment. Sharing a photo of a minimalist desk setup doesn't mean you've mastered your time. Posting stock portfolio screenshots doesn't guarantee you're investing with understanding. The performance of financial alignment is easier than the practice. But only the practice leads to peace.

This is especially relevant when considering income sources. Some side hustles pay well but feel exploitative. Some jobs look impressive but extract far more than they contribute. Asking whether the money is "worth it" is too narrow. A better question is: *"What kind of person am I becoming through this?"* The shaping effect of work is not limited to its hours. It infiltrates habits, language, posture, even self-esteem. If the way you make money requires you to constantly override your boundaries, silence your ethics, or suppress your real interests, then no hourly rate is sufficient.

The good news is that alignment isn't binary. You don't have to choose between money and meaning. You just need to hold them in constructive tension. One helpful framework is the concept of "identity budgeting"—allocating money not only based on needs and wants but based on the kind of person you're becoming. Think of it as curating your financial life the way you might curate a wardrobe: not for trend, but for truth. You want your budget, your income sources, and your saving goals to *fit you*—your ethics, your aspirations, your temperament. That doesn't mean indulgence; it means intentionality.

Another useful tool is the "values filter." Before taking on a new money commitment—be it a job, a subscription, or a new savings challenge—ask three questions: Does this move me toward or away from the person I want to be? Does it reinforce or dilute my core values? Is the energy exchange sustainable, not just financially but emotionally? These questions are deceptively simple but powerful. They turn passive money management into proactive identity design.

There's a final, often-overlooked dimension to this conversation: generosity. Aligning money with meaning includes how you give—not just how you earn or spend. Giving doesn't require wealth; it requires clarity. Some of the most values-aligned acts involve small but consistent generosity: funding a friend's project, supporting a cause, tipping extra to honour someone's effort. These choices reinforce identity because they're not transactional. They're expressive. Generosity, when rooted in values rather than guilt, transforms money from a shield into a bridge. It says: *"This is who I am, and this is how I choose to participate in the world."*

Ultimately, the alignment between money and meaning is not a static achievement. It's a lifelong calibration. You will change. Your circumstances will shift. What feels aligned at 17 may feel performative at 27. That's not inconsistency—it's growth. The goal is not to reach a final state of financial enlightenment. It's to remain honest. To earn consciously. To spend with conviction. To define wealth in a way that leaves you both secure and sincere.

Because when money becomes a mirror of your identity—not a mask, not a costume, but a reflection—you no longer chase it blindly. You move toward it deliberately. And when you reach it, you recognise yourself.

Your Financial Operating System

Systems govern far more than we often acknowledge. Behind every efficient airport, smooth-running business, or high-performing athlete lies an invisible latticework of decisions—routines, protocols, and priorities—that stabilise performance under pressure and guide action without second-guessing. Personal finance is no different. The individuals who seem most 'on top of their money'—who save without friction, invest with clarity, and make financial decisions that align with both their goals and values—are not more disciplined or more intelligent than everyone else. What they have is a functioning *financial operating system*. One that is built, not born. Designed with intention, not default.

An operating system, in this context, is not a budgeting app or a fancy spreadsheet template. It is a conceptual framework—underpinned by personal rules, automatic behaviours, contextual awareness, and ethical clarity—that allows money decisions to happen with less mental friction and more strategic precision. Without it, you risk drowning in micro-decisions: Should I buy this? Should I save now or later? Should I invest this bonus or keep it liquid? With it, those same questions become manageable, even instinctive. A financial operating system gives form to your intentions and continuity to your choices.

The architecture begins with internal logic. If you can't yet articulate your financial values, your goals, and your non-negotiables, the system will fail no matter how elegantly it is designed. Ask yourself: What do I prioritise—security, growth, autonomy, impact, or time? What trade-offs am I comfortable with? Do I need to earn more, or use what I earn more effectively? This isn't vague vision-boarding. It's an honest audit of your default behaviours and your ideal habits. If you value peace of mind but check your crypto portfolio six times a day, your system is misaligned. If you want to support your family but spend impulsively every weekend, your system isn't designed to succeed—it's designed to short-circuit itself.

Once your values are surfaced, the second layer of the system involves simplifying decisions into protocols. Think of these as standing orders—rules you create *in advance* so you don't have to re-negotiate every time a scenario arises. For instance: "I save 20% of every payment I receive, no exceptions." Or, "If I'm going to spend more than £50 on a non-essential, I'll wait 48 hours before deciding." Or, "All birthday cash goes into my emergency fund." These aren't rigid constraints. They are customised defaults that liberate you from reactive thinking. Just as professional pilots use checklists not because they lack knowledge but because they understand the limits of real-time decision-making under pressure, your financial operating system should reduce reliance on willpower.

Automation supports this principle. You automate what you want to guarantee happens. If saving is a priority, it shouldn't rely on end-of-month leftovers. If investing is part of your long-term plan, it shouldn't hinge on mood or convenience. Auto-transfer your savings on payday. Set recurring contributions to your investment platform. Enable round-up features on spending accounts that funnel change into savings or charity. The goal is not to eliminate manual review, but to embed your goals into the architecture of your money flow. This isn't laziness; it's *design*. You want to win by default, not effort.

Next, the system must include feedback mechanisms. Every effective system requires periodic review, not to invite obsession, but to ensure calibration. You might check your net worth quarterly, revisit your spending patterns monthly, or audit subscriptions bi-annually. But the spirit of the check-in matters. You are not conducting surveillance—you're assessing alignment. Are your behaviours producing your intended outcomes? Are your financial tools serving their purpose? Is your emotional relationship with money stable or showing signs of stress?

Here, emotional awareness is a critical—but often ignored—dimension of your financial operating system. If your system is technically effective but psychologically corrosive, it will break under stress. For example, saving aggressively while depriving yourself of basic pleasures may look 'disciplined' on paper but can create backlash behaviours: binge-spending, guilt cycles, burnout. Conversely, an overly flexible system with no guardrails may feel empowering until it yields chronic shortfalls. A sustainable system needs to accommodate both *structure* and *self-compassion*. It should allow for life's variability without unravelling. It should include buffers—for time, for money, for grace.

Technology can help but should not dominate. The fintech landscape is flush with apps that promise to do your thinking for you. Some are genuinely useful—offering visibility, analysis, and even nudges. But your operating system should not be outsourced entirely to an algorithm. The app doesn't know your values. It doesn't understand your guilt, your generosity, or your goals. Use digital tools to extend your system, not to replace your agency. A spreadsheet can track your goals. It cannot define them.

Social context must also be factored in. Your financial operating system doesn't exist in a vacuum. You will encounter pressure—familial expectations, peer dynamics, and cultural narratives. If your friends equate wealth with designer labels while you define it as debt freedom, tension will arise. If your parents grew up in economic scarcity and mistrust all forms of risk, your investing strategy may feel threatening to them. Your operating system must be resilient enough to withstand these forces without becoming hostile or dogmatic. That means designing communication rules too: how you talk about money with others, what you disclose, when you set boundaries, and how you handle generosity without self-neglect.

Critically, your operating system must be *adaptive*. Life will throw changes at you—new income levels, job transitions, relationships, health issues, or economic shifts. A static system becomes brittle. An adaptive one evolves without losing coherence. Maybe your savings ratio changes. Maybe your risk appetite matures. Maybe your priorities shift from wealth building to caretaking. That's not failure—it's refinement. The system isn't a cage. It's a compass.

For high-achieving teens and young adults—those already earning, investing, or supporting others—this framework is not premature. In fact, it is essential. Without it, you will likely fall into a pattern of reactive money management: chasing hacks, switching strategies, mimicking influencers. The financial operating system gives you a way to integrate everything you've learned—about budgeting, earning, saving, investing, and communicating—and translate it into a living, breathing architecture that supports your life, not someone else's.

One powerful metaphor is the idea of your system as a studio, not a factory. A factory optimises for consistency and scale, often at the expense of nuance. A studio optimises for coherence and adaptability. It holds your tools, your works-in-progress, your reference points. It has boundaries but allows exploration. Your system should not trap you in a rigid protocol. It should *equip* you to meet life's financial demands while still honouring your complexity, your capacity, and your context.

Ultimately, a financial operating system is an act of sovereignty. It says: *"I do not manage money by accident. I do so with deliberation, pattern, and self-respect."* It creates continuity in your actions, integrity in your choices, and resilience in the face of uncertainty. It does not prevent mistakes but absorbs them. It does not guarantee outcomes but ensures that your process—over time—becomes more intelligent, more tailored, and more trustworthy.

This is not a destination. It's a discipline. One that evolves with you, supports your growth, and reflects your priorities in every pound earned, spent, saved, or given. And once established, it becomes more than a system. It becomes an extension of your identity—practical, principled, and profoundly yours.

Chapter 12
Your Future Money Self

The notion of a "future you" tends to crumble under its own abstraction. Everyone insists on the virtue of long-term thinking, yet few provide a clear way of imagining what that future self—a 30-year-old you—might actually desire, fear, resist, or regret. The gulf between your present and your eventual financial life isn't merely chronological; it's philosophical. Most young adults are asked to build financial identities on paradoxes: work hard, but don't lose yourself; enjoy your youth, but avoid irreversible errors; take bold risks, but be endlessly prudent. That tension isn't a bug in the system—it *is* the system. Navigating it requires more than clever budgeting or motivational rhetoric. It calls for a reordering of how you think about who you are becoming.

Your 30-year-old self isn't some distant stranger. They will be shaped—quietly, cumulatively—by your current routines, emotions, ideas, and financial experiments, especially the messy ones. Perhaps that person will be supporting a family, travelling between cities, building a company, recovering from burnout, paying down debt, or simply living contentedly in a modest home once out of reach. The external details are secondary. What truly matters is whether that person can live *deliberately*—with choice, not compulsion. This isn't an invitation to romanticise the future; it's an argument for constructing the mental scaffolding that allows you to face it with steadiness rather than unease.

Few truths in personal finance are as neglected as this one: you will make mistakes. Not occasionally—habitually. You'll mistime an investment, overspend on something fleeting, lend unwisely, or find yourself caught off guard by an unexpected expense. None of this marks you as inept. It simply marks you as human. The real signal of maturity lies not in perfection but in resilience—in how swiftly and intelligently you recover. The earlier you accept this, the less paralysed you'll be when the inevitable happens.

Resilience, however, is not naïve cheerfulness. There's a seductive fantasy, endlessly recycled online, that if you start early, invest methodically, and tick the right boxes, financial freedom will glide towards you by your mid-thirties. The charts make it sound so neat—compound interest curves, passive income projections, early retirement promises. But starting early isn't about racing towards wealth. It's about purchasing *time*: the freedom to pivot at 27, to pause at 29, to make choices without existential panic. In essence, early action isn't a hustle; it's a quiet investment in sovereignty.

That sovereignty depends less on numbers than on vision. What kind of autonomy do you want your future self to enjoy? How wide should the gap be between what you earn and what you owe? How should money *feel*—empowering, unobtrusive, purposeful? These aren't indulgent questions for the privileged few; they're essential instruments of direction. When picturing your future, don't just imagine income streams. Imagine structure. Will your life be nimble or anchored? Your spending value-driven or performative? Will you be able to refuse the offers and obligations that drain more than they deliver?

None of this planning happens in a vacuum. The world you're preparing for is volatile—technologically, environmentally, economically. Artificial intelligence, climate instability, inflation shocks, labour disruptions—these aren't vague forecasts; they're unfolding realities. In such a landscape, adaptability isn't a soft skill. It's financial infrastructure. Building resilience means designing systems that flex, not fracture, when conditions shift. A job title may vanish, but your skills and savings remain portable. A market may tumble, yet your discipline and delay of gratification endure. Flexibility, then, is less a personality trait than a structural advantage—one you can deliberately construct.

And still, the paradox remains: the most meaningful financial choices are usually invisible. They hide in the unglamorous no's—the skipped trip, the postponed upgrade, the decision to invest in therapy instead of a gadget. They live in the quieter trade-offs: a smaller flat to fund a venture, a steady role chosen over an adrenaline-fuelled one. These choices rarely impress anyone else, but over time, they yield the kind of freedom that showier decisions never do. The "future you" who matters isn't the one with the perfect résumé or trending side hustle. It's the one who can make choices unburdened by fear or financial dependency.

This chapter resists the myth of linear progress. Life rarely moves from degree to promotion to prosperity in tidy sequence. It rewards those who recover faster, learn deeper, and choose more consciously. Here, you'll learn to reverse-engineer your goals from a version of yourself you'd respect. You'll learn to treat mistakes as information rather than failure. You'll see why "start now" is not a command but an act of mercy. And you'll come to recognise that the true dividend of early effort isn't accumulation—it's optionality.

The purpose isn't to prewrite your future script. It's to equip the future writer—you—to handle complexity, pressure, and change with composure. Wealth may or may not follow. Readiness always can.

Fast Forward: Who Are You at 30?

Most people think of turning thirty as a milestone to fear or endure—an arbitrary marker of adulthood at which one is expected to have achieved a mysterious yet definitive level of financial and personal success. But thirty is not a deadline; it is a mirror. And the reflection you see in it is not determined by external events or luck alone—it is sculpted, over time, by patterns you set long before you arrive there. The point is not to have everything figured out by thirty. The point is to be able to look back and recognise that your trajectory was shaped by intention, not inertia. That you built not a perfect life, but one that made sense to *you*.

If you've ever been told to "think long-term" with your money but found the advice vague or disembodied, you're not alone. Long-term thinking without a tangible sense of self becomes a theoretical exercise. It's like aiming for a destination without knowing what life feels like once you arrive. So let's anchor the abstraction. What do you want thirty to *feel* like? Is it about freedom of time, freedom of choice, or freedom from worry? Is it about finally stepping into a career that aligns with your strengths, or about stepping away from work to build something your own? The clearer the emotional texture of your future self, the sharper your financial decisions become today.

This is not a prescription for mapping out your thirties in obsessive detail. Life will not follow your script. But *reverse-planning* is not about prediction; it's about preparation. If you think forward with honesty and curiosity—if you allow yourself to imagine, not just wish—you give shape to your intentions. For instance, imagine you want to own your time by thirty. That might mean working aggressively now to build a buffer of savings or experience that allows for a sabbatical, a pivot, or even early semi-retirement. But if that's your goal, the foundation needs to be laid far earlier than most people assume. It requires more than income—it requires foresight, restraint, and the courage to delay gratification when others are racing ahead on shallower paths.

There is a psychological shift that occurs when you stop seeing financial decisions as isolated acts and begin to see them as votes for your future self. Each time you choose to save rather than spend, each time you invest in learning instead of lifestyle, you are reinforcing the infrastructure of the thirty-year-old who doesn't just survive but steers. And crucially, these choices aren't just financial. The career you pursue, the city you move to, the relationships you prioritise, and the habits you protect all have financial consequences—direct and indirect. Your thirty-year-old self is not just a richer version of you. They are a product of the systems you build and the trade-offs you tolerate.

To visualise this concretely, try mapping two trajectories. In one version, you follow every default setting: passive consumption, occasional saving, no investment, career chosen out of convenience or fear, lifestyle inflated to match peers. In the other, you design with purpose: regular investing from your late teens, skills built with long-term value in mind, spending aligned with your values, and a willingness to say no to what doesn't fit—even when it's popular. The divergence in outcomes at thirty may be subtle in terms of lifestyle, but profound in terms of optionality. In the second scenario, you are not necessarily wealthier, but you are freer. *That difference—freedom over net worth—is the real dividend of early design thinking.*

It's also important to reject a one-size-fits-all version of financial success at thirty. For some, it might mean owning property. For others, it could be having enough saved to travel or retrain. For someone else, it might be funding a sibling's education or starting a social enterprise. These goals are equally valid—but only if they are yours, not inherited from external pressure. This is why visioning your future self requires more than financial planning. It requires *value clarity*. What do you want your money to enable? What do you want to protect, to build, to contribute to? If you can't answer those questions, then accumulating money risks becoming performative or hollow.

One of the most common regrets shared by people in their thirties is not about having made bad financial decisions—it's about having made *unconscious* ones. They drifted. They did what was expected, or what was easiest, or what looked successful on the surface. And now they're course-correcting with urgency. But course correction is harder when you've locked yourself into financial obligations you didn't interrogate. The better alternative is not to avoid all mistakes, but to make *your own*—informed, deliberate, and value-aligned. This way, even when the path doesn't go as planned, it still makes sense in retrospect.

Reverse-planning also forces you to confront your fears. Maybe you fear being behind at thirty, being underpaid, unsupported, or directionless. But the antidote to fear is not avoidance—it's capability. It's knowing that even if your external situation at thirty doesn't match your vision, you have cultivated the mindset and muscle to adjust. This is the paradox: the more clearly you visualise your future self, the more resilient you become when reality deviates. Because you are no longer attached to an outcome—you are anchored in identity.

Consider the difference between someone who sees thirty as a fixed scoreboard and someone who sees it as a checkpoint in a self-authored life. The first person is measuring success by comparison—salary, title, lifestyle optics. The second is measuring by alignment—*Does my life reflect my values? Am I acting with intention? Do I have the freedom to choose?* The former is fragile, easily derailed by external shocks. The latter is robust, adaptive, and internally coherent.

To start building towards your thirty-year-old self, begin with questions that invite specificity and honesty. Where do you want to live—and why? What does "enough" look like for you financially? What would you do differently today if you already trusted that your future self was thriving? What do you want to be able to say no to at thirty? What do you want to be able to say yes to without hesitation? These are not abstract thought experiments. They are scaffolding for your next financial decision.

And let's be clear: the exercise of future visualisation is not a luxury for those with privilege. If anything, it is *especially essential* for those with fewer safety nets. Because when you're building your life without inherited capital, you must rely on strategic clarity. You don't have margin for trial-and-error driven by randomness. You need intentional error—the kind you learn from because you chose your risks consciously. This is how financial autonomy is forged—not through guarantees, but through strategy married to self-awareness.

Ultimately, the question isn't whether you'll arrive at thirty with more money. It's whether you'll arrive with *more agency*. And agency isn't something you stumble into. It's built through pattern, through principle, and through a willingness to ask more of your present self for the sake of your future one. So who are you at thirty? You are the person you practice becoming, today. The only thing left is to practise with care, with clarity, and with enough belief in your future self to build a life worth inhabiting.

Money Mistakes You'll Definitely Make (And How to Recover)

The most costly myth in personal finance is not that you'll never earn enough or that you'll never retire—it's that with enough knowledge, discipline, or planning, you can permanently outrun mistakes. You can't. No one can. Not the billionaire CEO, not the meticulous budgeter, not the financial advisor with three degrees. Mistakes are not aberrations in your money story. They are *chapters*. Necessary ones. Whether it's overspending, under-earning, over-leveraging, missing a market trend, ignoring taxes, or misjudging risk, the only question is not if but when. And when it happens, the quality of your recovery—not the absence of the fall—defines your financial maturity.

The modern financial environment is calibrated to test you. Algorithms are optimised for impulse. Payment systems are frictionless by design. Credit is normalised as an extension of income. Career landscapes shift with speed and opacity. Even with careful intentions, it's remarkably easy to overestimate your earning power or underestimate the cost of debt, subscription creep, lifestyle drift, or emotional spending. The first key to recovery is abandoning the illusion that intelligence alone immunises you from error. Financial acumen is not a shield—it is a toolkit for repair.

Consider the nature of most first-time money mistakes. They are rarely catastrophic in form—what makes them dangerous is repetition without reflection. You accidentally overdraw your bank account and get hit with fees. That's not a crisis. But if it happens monthly because you refuse to change your timing or tracking, it becomes a structural flaw. You sign up for a buy-now-pay-later option and miss a payment. Again, not fatal. But if the convenience leads to normalising debt-financed lifestyle consumption, the hole widens. *Recovery, then, is not about erasing the mistake. It's about metabolising the lesson so it never happens under the same conditions again.*

One of the most common early missteps is believing that income cures all financial ills. Many young earners experience a temporary income spike—through a high-paying job, side hustle, or windfall—and immediately scale up their lifestyle to match. The error isn't the spending per se—it's the implicit assumption that income growth is stable and predictable. In reality, early career earnings are volatile. Opportunities contract. Burnout interrupts. Markets shift. If your financial structure depends on a continued upward slope, any dip becomes destabilising. The recovery here is twofold: structurally, build buffers and maintain flexibility. Psychologically, cultivate satisfaction with a life that's slightly below your full spending power. That margin is your freedom.

Then there's the inverse mistake: being so afraid of financial failure that you delay action entirely. You don't invest because you're afraid of loss. You don't negotiate because you fear rejection. You hoard savings in low-yield accounts because the idea of markets feels opaque or unsafe. This is the mistake of omission—a mistake just as dangerous as misjudged action. The recovery strategy is not to suddenly become reckless. It's to build *calibrated courage*. Take small, deliberate risks that stretch your comfort zone without jeopardising your base. If you fear losing £500 in the market, start by investing £50. Learn through exposure, not paralysis.

Some mistakes are relational rather than transactional. Lending money to friends without clear terms. Entering financial commitments with a partner before trust or transparency is established. Allowing guilt or family dynamics to dictate unsustainable support. These mistakes don't just dent your finances—they compromise your boundaries. The recovery in these cases demands more than budgeting. It requires *emotional disentanglement*. You must learn to say no without guilt, to set terms without apology, to renegotiate expectations without drama. In the long run, financial health depends as much on emotional fluency as it does on numerical competence.

Another frequent—and under-discussed—form of error is misaligned ambition. You pursue a degree, job, or business model because it looks like a good financial move, only to discover it drains your energy or erodes your values. The cost here is not just tuition or opportunity cost—it's identity confusion. The recovery is not to quit at the first sign of discomfort, but to examine the feedback carefully. *Did you make this choice out of fear, imitation, or desperation? Is the goal still meaningful, or was it someone else's?* Financial clarity often follows personal clarity. Realigning your path may involve sunk cost, but that cost is compounded by inertia. Better to pivot early than to compound the drift.

Importantly, the concept of recovery assumes you are allowed to fail without shame. This is especially radical in cultures where financial success is treated as a proxy for personal worth. If you believe that money mistakes reflect your value or intelligence, you are far more likely to hide them, repeat them, or overcorrect with self-punishment. But recovery thrives on transparency. Share your setbacks with someone you trust. Examine the data without flinching. Build systems that detect early warning signs. Over time, these practices build *anti-fragility*—the ability to grow stronger because of volatility, not in spite of it.

You will also need to watch for recovery mistakes. After a setback, it's tempting to make drastic corrections: to go ultra-frugal, quit investing, or become rigidly controlling. These reactive behaviours are understandable, but often counterproductive. A useful frame is: *Is this response sustainable, or is it a trauma pattern?* True recovery is patient. It's not about revenge on your former self. It's about re-entering the system with more wisdom and less ego.

There is a deeply philosophical underpinning to financial resilience: the belief that your worth is not defined by your financial outcomes. This doesn't mean ignoring money. It means *reclaiming it as a tool, not a verdict.* Everyone you admire for their financial intelligence has failed—publicly, privately, dramatically or quietly. The difference is that they didn't stop. They recalibrated. They adapted. And often, the scars became their most instructive features. The person who has failed intelligently is often more trustworthy than the one who has never been tested.

There's also a broader cultural benefit to normalising recovery. In a society where financial perfection is performative—on social media, in career optics, in lifestyle signalling—the real revolution is transparency. Imagine a world where people shared not just their investment wins but their spending regrets. Where people admitted to the dumb risks they took and the slow lessons they learned. In that world, financial literacy would explode. Not because people suddenly became perfect, but because they stopped pretending they were.

Your mistakes, then, are not just personal—they are pedagogical. They are curriculum. They reveal your blind spots, your emotional patterns, your beliefs about risk and worth. If you study them without defensiveness, they can upgrade your financial OS. But you have to look. And you have to do so with curiosity, not contempt.

In summary, the idea that financial mastery is defined by mistake avoidance is not only false—it's damaging. The truth is richer: *real competence emerges through intelligent failure and structured recovery*. That means tracking what went wrong, naming the pattern, designing a new default, and testing that design in practice. Over time, you develop a kind of internal GPS—less reactive, more adaptive, quietly confident. That's not a fantasy. It's a capability. And like all capabilities, it's forged in practice, not in theory.

So if you're making mistakes now, you're not behind. You're right on time. What matters is what you build next. What matters is that you recover forward—not to where you were, but to somewhere better informed, better structured, and better aligned with the person you're becoming.

How to Stay Flexible in a Changing World

If you were born in the early 2000s, your economic life began in the shadow of the 2008 global financial crisis. By your teenage years, you had lived through a historic pandemic, an explosion in digital currencies, the rise of AI-generated labour, and the inflationary aftershocks of global supply chain fragility. The implicit message? *Change is not the exception—it is the baseline*. Any financial plan that assumes stability over volatility is already outdated. In this context, the most important skill for sustaining wealth and agency isn't prediction. It's adaptability.

Flexibility is often misunderstood as passive tolerance—a kind of relaxed reaction to chaos. That's not the version we're talking about here. *True financial flexibility is the proactive capacity to reposition, recalibrate, and reimagine your strategy without losing momentum or identity.* It's not about constantly reacting to noise; it's about building a structure that allows for thoughtful reconfiguration. This is what distinguishes people who merely cope with disruption from those who capitalise on it.

Start with this assumption: the job you train for today may be irrelevant—or fundamentally transformed—within a decade. That's not alarmism. It's a pattern. Career paths are increasingly non-linear. Automation isn't just replacing routine tasks—it's reclassifying what "value" means in a knowledge economy. Skills that are in high demand now—coding, data analysis, digital marketing—may be performed faster and cheaper by AI tools in five years. This doesn't mean you should stop developing them. It means your real edge lies in *meta-skills*—the capacity to learn, unlearn, and cross-apply knowledge in multiple contexts. If you can't re-skill on the fly, you are structurally fragile, regardless of your current competence.

Financial flexibility begins with cashflow design. In rigid systems, all income comes from one job, and all spending is optimised to that income's peak. This creates brittle dependency. A layoff, illness, or economic downturn turns your entire life upside down. In flexible systems, income streams are diversified—through part-time freelancing, asset ownership, licensing, content, or digital micro-enterprises. You don't need five jobs, but *you do need optionality*. If your only earning strategy is being employed full-time by someone else, you are outsourcing not just income but agency.

Likewise, spending structures should allow for contraction. A life that is just barely affordable in good times becomes oppressive in downturns. If your housing, lifestyle, and fixed commitments absorb 90% of your income, you have no room to pivot. Flexibility means preserving room to manoeuvre—

whether that's through lower fixed costs, fewer subscriptions, geographic mobility, or minimalist design. Financial resilience is not just about how much you earn or invest. It's about *how easily you can shrink or stretch your footprint without collapsing your quality of life.*

Technology will continue to shift the playing field faster than most people can anticipate. This doesn't mean you have to become a coder or start investing in every new trend. It means you need to cultivate *digital fluency*—an ongoing curiosity about tools, platforms, and ecosystems that affect how people work, earn, and interact. The platforms that seem fringe today may be the dominant marketplaces tomorrow. Think of the transition from local classifieds to global e-commerce, from 9-to-5 offices to remote-first teams, from traditional banking to fintech wallets. Being dismissive of new technology isn't a stance—it's a risk.

Even investing itself is evolving. Traditional portfolio models were built on assumptions of long-term stability and institutional control. Today's markets are faster, more fragmented, and increasingly driven by sentiment, speculation, and geopolitical triggers. This doesn't mean you abandon the basics—like dollar-cost averaging, diversification, or risk assessment. But it *does* mean you must learn to adapt your expectations. Volatility isn't an anomaly; it's a permanent condition. If you can't stay calm during downturns or adjust your risk tolerance as your life changes, you're not building wealth—you're gambling on hope.

Flexibility also means decoupling your identity from your financial methods. Many people become so attached to a certain income path or financial ideology that they resist change even when their context demands it. They stay in dying industries out of pride. They refuse to pivot careers because they once mocked others who did. Or they cling to an outdated investment style because it once worked, even as the world moves on. Rigidity of ego is often more dangerous than external shifts. *If your sense of self is so fragile that adaptation feels like defeat, you will sabotage your own evolution.*

Culturally, flexibility is often mistaken for indecision. We praise people who seem certain, who stick to their five-year plans, who never change direction. But in today's world, that kind of static vision is often a liability. Certainty is not clarity. Adaptable people don't drift aimlessly—they recalibrate with intention. They monitor inputs, update models, and adjust their trajectory while staying true to their principles. That is not indecisiveness. It's strategic agility.

One of the most powerful ways to cultivate flexibility is to build feedback loops. Most people make plans, implement them, and then ignore the results until crisis forces a rethink. In contrast, a flexible system constantly gathers signals. Is your cashflow trending in the direction you expected? Is your time investment generating the expected ROI—emotionally or financially? Are the assumptions that underpinned your last career move still valid? If not, *you don't wait for a meltdown—you adjust.* This habit of dynamic reflection doesn't require a crisis to evolve. It makes change a normal part of operations.

Geopolitical instability also demands a new layer of financial thoughtfulness. Currency fluctuations, supply shocks, war, trade restrictions, digital sovereignty laws—these are not abstract concerns for someone building a life in a globalised world. If your income is tied to cross-border commerce, or your data is stored by companies governed by foreign jurisdictions, you must think more globally. Flexibility here means not just earning in multiple contexts, but holding assets across platforms, currencies, and possibly even jurisdictions. It's not paranoia. It's pattern recognition.

At a personal level, flexibility is a mindset before it's a tactic. Do you view uncertainty as a threat, or as an invitation to expand? Can you hold competing truths—that stability is desirable, and change is inevitable—without becoming cynical or paralysed? Can you update your goals without feeling like you've failed your past self? These are not just abstract questions. They determine whether you'll be able to surf the next wave of technological and economic transition, or whether you'll drown in its undertow.

The future doesn't reward people who guess right once. It rewards people who design systems that can absorb wrong guesses, adapt quickly, and keep compounding. That means building in buffers, investing in relationships not just assets, cultivating skills instead of credentials, and choosing clarity over dogma. *It means rejecting rigidity as a virtue and embracing movement as a practice.*

In a world that changes this fast, flexibility is not a nice-to-have. It is the new foundation. What used to be a strategic advantage has become a survival necessity. The good news? Flexibility is not a fixed trait. It's a learnable discipline. It's a function of awareness, humility, and continuous design. And it may be the most reliable wealth-building asset you have in a future you cannot fully predict.

Why Starting Early Isn't About Getting Rich

It is an enduring myth that the main advantage of starting your financial life early is to get rich faster. The spreadsheets are often paraded with compound interest graphs that suggest if you invest £100 a month at age 15, you'll be sipping cocktails on a beach at 35. But that framing, seductive as it may be, fundamentally misses the point. *Starting early isn't about early retirement fantasies or beating the market.* It's about building *optionality*—the power to choose your path rather than be boxed in by necessity. Wealth, in its most functional form, is not a pile of money. It's a tool for autonomy.

This reframing matters, because the old narratives around wealth accumulation no longer serve younger generations well. For Gen Z, the financial world isn't a linear path paved by pensions, mortgages, and gold watches at retirement. It's a fluctuating terrain of gig work, remote careers, economic volatility, and rapidly evolving technologies. In such a landscape, the most valuable asset is not capital—it's control over your time, energy, and decisions. And *the earlier you begin to understand and manage money, the sooner you gain that control.*

Consider a 19-year-old who understands the basics of budgeting, saving, and low-cost investing—not as an end in itself, but as a way to create future leverage. She may still work part-time, study, and have limited income. But because she's started, she's already developed a financial reflex: knowing where her money goes, setting boundaries with spending, avoiding lifestyle traps, and resisting debt spirals. This internal muscle, not her bank balance, is what positions her differently. By her mid-twenties, she may be able to say no to exploitative jobs. She can fund a sabbatical, start a side business, move cities, or help a family member in need—not because she's "rich" but because she has space.

Financial optionality is rarely taught in traditional classrooms. Schools may touch on compound interest, but few explain the real-life implications of being financially flexible. Optionality is the ability to choose work that aligns with your values rather than simply pays your bills. It's the freedom to leave a toxic environment without financial panic. It's the confidence to invest in yourself—through education, training, or creative pursuits—without compromising your future. *It is the capacity to pause, pivot, or proceed on your own terms.*

Starting early creates compound benefits far beyond returns. Time amplifies *skills, judgement, and resilience.* A teenager who tracks her expenses for five years will learn more about her behavioural tendencies, value priorities, and risk tolerance than someone who wakes up at 28 in a financial fog. When the latter finally confronts his money patterns, he's not only late to the game—he's often entangled in commitments that limit his ability to correct course. Early starters don't just get more time; they get more room to iterate, experiment, and recover from small errors before those errors become structurally expensive.

And mistakes will happen—especially early on. You might invest in a meme stock, overspend on status items, lend to friends who never pay back, or lock into the wrong course of study because of financial pressures. These are not moral failings. They're feedback loops. The value of starting early isn't that you'll avoid mistakes—it's that you'll learn them when the stakes are lower. A £500 loss at 18 is tuition. The same mistake at 35, compounded by dependents, debt, or burnout, can be catastrophic. *The earlier you begin, the more optionality you preserve—not because you're perfect, but because you're practiced.*

This shift in narrative is especially important for those from underrepresented or lower-income backgrounds, for whom financial independence isn't just aspirational but urgent. Starting early is often framed as a privilege. But in reality, it's a necessity for anyone trying to rewrite generational cycles. If you wait for financial clarity to arrive in adulthood, you may spend your most agile years under the control of others' decisions—landlords, lenders, employers, even well-meaning parents. Early literacy and action grant you agency faster. That agency is not just economic. It's psychological.

Because here's the deeper truth: *money, once mastered, becomes quiet.* When you're not constantly worried about whether you can afford something, you begin to consider *why* you want it in the first place. Your goals sharpen. Your decisions simplify. Your creativity increases. And your sense of self solidifies. That is the real dividend of early financial mastery—not wealth, but coherence. The ability to build a life that reflects your values, not your financial emergencies.

It's also worth naming that the cultural obsession with "getting rich" distorts what early finance can offer. Wealth, if misframed, becomes a burden rather than a tool. The pressure to hit a million before 30, retire by 35, or monetise every hobby creates anxiety, comparison, and burnout. It reduces financial success to scoreboard theatre. That's not freedom. That's just a new kind of performance. *The irony is that those who build freedom often don't start with wealth as their goal.* They start with clarity: the desire to be in control of their time, their contributions, and their capacity to walk away from bad options.

You don't need to be extraordinary to benefit from starting early. You just need to be consistent. A 17-year-old who automates a modest investment monthly, checks her spending weekly, and makes deliberate money choices—even occasionally—is not just "ahead." She's building structural resilience. She may never "get rich" in the conventional sense. But by 25, she might be debt-free, professionally flexible, and able to invest in opportunities others can't even consider. She'll have space to fail, grow, change, and still remain intact. That is wealth. Quiet, portable, and powerful.

The systems you build now are not just financial. They're psychological and philosophical. When you start early, you're not just preparing for the future—you're shaping how you relate to uncertainty. You become less reactive, more strategic. Less driven by comparison, more anchored by internal metrics. You're not waiting for permission or a windfall. You're acting with agency. That mental orientation, once internalised, spills into every domain of life—relationships, learning, health, ambition.

So the next time someone tells you that the point of starting early is to be a millionaire by 30, you'll know better. That's a narrow metric in a world that's asking much broader questions. *What do you want your life to feel like? Whose terms do you want to live on? How much of your time do you want to own?* These are the real prompts behind early finance. Not flashy outcomes. Meaningful leverage.

Start early—not because you need to win some imaginary race, but because the earlier you begin, the more room you give yourself to *choose*—how you live, how you earn, how you spend, and who you become. Wealth is not a number. It is your capacity to design a life with fewer financial constraints and more personal alignment. Starting early simply gives you a longer runway to do so.

About the Author

Riley K. Morgan is a passionate advocate for youth financial clarity in a world built on digital distractions and outdated money rules. With years spent studying the emotional and behavioral roots of how young people think about money, Riley brings a rare mix of clarity, empathy, and real-world practicality to personal finance. Their mission is simple but urgent: equip teens with the tools and mindset to make confident choices long before they're expected to know how. Blending insights from culture, psychology, and tech, Riley writes for the next generation of earners who want more than money—they want freedom.

www.ingramcontent.com/pod-product-compliance
Lightning Source LLC
Chambersburg PA
CBHW031341230926
51848CB00002B/328
9789371772426